D0057068

LUCKY
LUCIANO

Also by Tim Newark

Mafia Allies

WITHDRAWN

LUCKY
LUCIANO

THE REAL AND THE FAKE
GANGSTER

Tim Newark

THOMAS DUNNE BOOKS ST. MARTIN'S PRESS NEW YORK

THOMAS DUNNE BOOKS.
An imprint of St. Martin's Press.

LUCKY LUCIANO. Copyright © 2010 by Tim Newark. All rights reserved.
Printed in the United States of America. For information, address
St. Martin's Press, 175 Fifth Avenue, New York, N.Y. 10010.

www.thomasdunnebooks.com
www.stmartins.com

Design by Meryl Sussman Levavi

Library of Congress Cataloging-in-Publication Data

Newark, Timothy.
    Lucky Luciano : the real and the fake gangster / Tim Newark. — 1st ed.
        p. cm.
    Includes bibliographical references and index.
    ISBN 978-0-312-60182-9
    1. Luciano, Lucky, 1897–1962. 2. Criminals—New York (State)—New
York—Biography. 3. Organized crime—New York (State)—New York.
4. World War, 1939–1945—Campaigns—Italy—Sicily. 5. Mafia—United
States—History—20th century. 6. Mafia—Italy—Sicily—History—20th
century. I. Title.
    HV6248.L92N49 2010
    364.1092—dc22
    [B]
                                                            2010021686

First Edition: September 2010

1   3   5   7   9   10   8   6   4   2

To Peter, my father,
who first took me to New York City

CONTENTS

Acknowledgments

For their help in the research and production of this book, I would like to thank the following:

Leonora A. Gidlund, director of the Municipal Archives, and her helpful staff at Chambers Street, New York; Mary M. Huth of the Rush Rhees Library, University of Rochester, New York; Tamar Evangelestia-Dougherty of the Herbert H. Lehman Suite and Papers, Columbia University Rare Book and Manuscript Library, New York; Eric van Slander and Timothy K. Nenninger at the National Archives and Record Administration, College Park, Maryland; David M. Hardy and David P. Sobonya of FBI Records Management Division; Richard L. Baker of the U.S. Army Military History Institute, Carlisle, Pennsylvania; Michael E. Gonzales of the 45th Infantry Division Museum; Edward Dojutrek and Carl Q. Topie of the 3rd Infantry Division Society; Charles T. Pinck of the OSS Society; Charles Radcliffe Haffenden Jr.; in London, the staff of the National Archives,

Kew, and the British Library; in Sicily, Giada Platania, Salvatore Cabasino, Maia Mancuso, and the staff of the Biblioteca Centrale della Regione Siciliana; Charles McCall, for IRS advice; Peter Newark, for his extensive crime archive; Lucy Wildman, for research assistance; Robert Miller, for lunch at Patsy's; Vicky Newark, for her good company on research trips; crime historians Richard Hammer, John Dickie, John Follain, James Morton, David Critchley, and Robert A. Rockaway, for their advice and help; and my excellent editor, Peter Joseph, and my first-class agent, Andrew Lownie.

Introduction

For the first twenty-five years of his criminal career, Charles "Lucky" Luciano was a vicious mobster who rose to become the multimillionaire king of the New York underworld. For the next twenty-five years of his life, Luciano was a legend—but a fake master criminal without real power, his evil reputation manipulated and maintained by the government agents who put him behind bars.

Drawing on once-secret government documents from archives in America and Europe, I have sought to tell the true story of the legendary gangster from his early days as a top hit man for the Mob to his exploits running sex and narcotics empires. I reveal for the first time Luciano's transatlantic trip to Weimar Germany to set up a drug-importing racket. When Luciano went to jail, his reputation was only enhanced when rumors emerged about him helping the Allies to win World War II. By cross-referencing military reports in America with personal accounts in Sicily, I have exposed the truth about what Luciano really did to assist the Allies in the war.

With his expulsion from the United States, Luciano returned to Italy where he became the arch villain for international law enforcement agencies. He was reputed to head a massive trans-atlantic narcotics network, but, in truth, Luciano was being used by government agents to justify their own bloated law enforce-ment budgets. It was a complex conspiracy in which Luciano—the fake master criminal—became the victim of far bigger powers around him. There is even some evidence that, at one time, he was working as a Cold War agent, helping the U.S. gov-ernment fight Communism in Sicily. It is an extraordinary story that has never been told fully before, but first one must deal with the issue of the most notorious book written about the gangster.

♠

Richard Hammer was a slim, fit eighty-year-old when I met him for lunch at the Atlantic Grill on Third Avenue on New York City's Upper East Side. He used to run every day, but now he just cycles. Hammer is the coauthor of the controversial best-seller *The Last Testament of Lucky Luciano*, first published in 1975. It is a dramatic account of the mobster's life told suppos-edly through his own words as he looked back over a life of crime. An exciting page-turner, it has been constantly dogged with criticism from those who believe it is bogus. Journalist Tony Scaduto unleashed a scathing twelve-page attack on it in his 1976 biography of Luciano, calling it "fraudulent" and "a complete fantasy," picking it apart error by error. So, how do you get to the truth behind the book? How do you ask an author whether he made it all up?

After speaking to Hammer on the phone and talking to pub-lishers who had chatted with him, I got the feeling that he was understandably rather irritated by the decades-old fuss about the book. It is just one of more than twenty books he has written and it is certainly not the one he is most proud of. A literature major, he wrote an award-nominated account of the My Lai Massacre in Vietnam and was a brilliant young writer for the *New York Times* before he was asked to take on the Luciano project.

Self-styled film producer Martin Gosch had met Luciano while he was in exile in Italy in 1961. He had helped the mobster write a screenplay based on his life. Luciano was fed up with all the lies written about him and wanted to tell it as he wanted it told. But just as they were looking forward to casting the actor to play Luciano, they got word from New York that his Mafia associates were not happy with the idea of a movie about them. His longtime criminal partner Meyer Lansky was behind the threats and Luciano took them very seriously. He told Gosch that the movie was off—otherwise they'd both be dead.

Instead, Luciano asked Gosch to take down his life story. He wanted the truth to get out somehow, but only on the condition that it would be published ten years after he died so as not to upset any of his gangster friends. Over the next few months, Gosch took down the memories of the mafioso. Just ten months later, Luciano was dead, struck down by a heart attack as he waited for Gosch at Naples Airport. There is no doubting that Gosch knew Luciano and heard many stories from his lips, but how true is the account that eventually appeared as *The Last Testament* more than a decade later? No one could check with Gosch because he died in 1973, fifteen months before the book was published.

"We had arguments about the book all the time," recalled Hammer, then in his mid-forties. "He thought he was a great writer."

At one stage, it was believed that the memoirs were dictated to a tape recorder.

"There were never any tapes," says Hammer. "It was the early sixties and tape recorders were big things. Martin talked to Luciano and took lots of notes. It was this pile of notes that he handed to me and I would check things over with him."

Through the course of his professional writing, Hammer has dealt with many gangsters, but as he transcribed the notes, he developed a certain respect for the chief mobster.

"Most gangsters are stupid—Luciano was a great business-man. He was the most significant organized crime figure of his period—along with Lansky."

Luciano was, however, a relentless liar. On trial in 1936, he lied from the beginning to the end of his testimony, most outrageously saying he was born in New York when most everyone knew he came from Sicily. There are many occasions in *The Last Testament* when what is supposedly the truth coming from Luciano is clearly not true and is contradicted by recorded facts and other accounts. One of the most glaring errors is his story of when he was kidnapped in 1929 in Manhattan and then dumped in a field in Staten Island after having been beaten severely. In the book, he describes being strung up by the wrists from a wooden beam and tortured by henchmen of Salvatore Maranzano, who wanted to force him to kill another Mafia boss. It is like a scene out of a gangster B-movie and may well have come from the original screenplay. It certainly has nothing to do with what really happened as recalled by Luciano in more reliable accounts.

"What people don't understand," says Hammer, "is that I told my publisher that the book should be footnoted to make the point that some of what Luciano said didn't match with the truth, but they said no. It wasn't that kind of book. The book tells the story of his life as he wanted it told. It's his slant."

And that includes all the lies he chose to tell to serve his own ends. Hammer says as much in the introduction to *The Last Testament*: "Parts of it may seem self-serving, and they may well be."

It seems highly unlikely that Gosch's original handwritten notes covered all the topics detailed in the book. It is a long book, and Hammer was hired because of his knowledge of organized crime (he had written a twelve-part series on the history of the Mafia for *Playboy*) and his research skills as a reporter. He had to add material to tell the full story. As he processed the notes, he also had to give a creative coherence to it—to evoke the character of the man himself. The voice of Luciano is highly convincing.

"Yeah, I worked hard at that," says Hammer.

For all its faults—some no doubt intended as misinformation by Luciano—the book has some value to the criminal historian. Among the numerous anecdotes are surprising nuggets that are not heard anywhere else, such as Murder, Inc. hit man Albert Anastasia torching the *Normandie* ocean liner. That is a truly sensational piece of evidence unique to the book.

"That had a ring of truth about it," agrees Hammer.

We will never be able to check the notes used by Hammer to write the book, as the widow of Martin Gosch burned them shortly after he died.

So, my approach to utilizing *The Last Testament* in this work is not to quote directly from it, as it is mired in too much controversy for this to be acceptable to the critical reader, but if a story does appear in its pages and has some interest, I have noted its origin and mentioned it. At some stage, Gosch did talk to Luciano and no doubt got some elements of truth out of him that have some value. Other interviews with Luciano in Italy in the 1950s are regarded as valid, so why not include this among them as long as we take it with a grain of salt?

It is also interesting to note that some accounts that are highly regarded by historians who have poured scorn on *The Last Testament* are closely based on the book. For example, Meyer Lansky's memoirs, as recorded in the 1979 book by Dennis Eisenberg and others, *Mogul of the Mob*, formed part of the material used by Robert Lacey in his excellent biography *Little Man*. In his source notes, Lacey condemns "the purported memoirs of Lucky

Luciano," saying "My own research has more than confirmed the doubts cast on their veracity by critics." But many of Lansky's recollections placed in quotation marks in *Mogul of the Mob* merely paraphrase discredited stories in *The Last Testament*. If you disregard one, then you should disregard the other.

Wherever possible, I have based my account of Lucky Luciano on unpublished primary documents found in archives in New York, Washington, D.C., London, and Palermo, some of which have never been fully considered before. These are mainly police and government papers, but they are often based on direct interviews with gangsters. I have uncovered several stories that shed new light on the criminal career of Charles Luciano and so I hope that this title is worthy of adding to the canon of fine works written on the history of organized crime and finally sets the record straight.

LUCKY
LUCIANO

LUCKY IN NAZI GERMANY

Jack Diamond, thirty-four years old, successful owner of the Hotsy Totsy Club on Broadway in New York City, rested comfortably in the plush surroundings of a first-class passenger car on the Ostend-Vienna Express on the evening of September 1, 1930. He'd had a wine-fueled dinner and was chatting away to four other gentlemen attired in elegant suits. The next day they would be in Germany, but at midnight the express shuddered to a halt on the frontier at Aix-la-Chapelle. German police—armed with Luger nine-millimeter Parabellum pistols—clattered through the coaches and asked the Irish-American Diamond to accompany them. As he stepped onto the platform, Diamond glanced up at a poster—it showed a man in uniform with a Charlie Chaplin–style mustache and a swastika in the background.

The German police had little interest in Diamond's companions—at least three of who were Italian-Americans—and let them continue on their journey to Cologne. They took the New York club owner to the local police station and questioned him. They asked him why he was in Germany. He explained that he was on holiday with his companions and because he suffered from stomach ailments he was going to visit one of their famous German spa towns. They asked him if he was the same Jack "Legs" Diamond, the notorious New York gangster. He said no. They then presented him with a set of fingerprints obtained from Berlin police headquarters belonging to the mobster. Even though they matched, Diamond insisted it was all a case of mistaken identity. The police checked his passport and saw that it was in order, including a stamped visa for entry to Germany.

Having arrested an American citizen, the German police were then unsure what to do next. The American embassy in Berlin said they had merely informed the German authorities of Diamond's presence on their territory but did not request his arrest or return to their country. Sensing the German police had little on him, Diamond began to get ratty and demanded to see the American consul in Cologne. After a second police interview, a local journalist was allowed to talk to him.

"It's all lies," he snarled at the reporter, clutching his abdomen. "The New York police pester me all the time. They arrested me twenty-two times in the last few years and always had to let me go for lack of evidence. I came to Europe to seek quiet. I want to go to Vichy and Wiesbaden to take the cure. My stomach is bothering me."

Unable to charge him or pass him on to another country because his visa was for Germany only, the police handed over the matter to their alien division. Doctors checked Diamond for any symptoms that required treatment at a German spa but could find nothing genuinely wrong with him. Deemed an undesirable by the Prussian minister of the interior, Diamond was accompanied by two detectives and put in a second-class compartment on a night express to Hamburg in northern Germany.

On September 6, Diamond was escorted onto the freighter *Hannover*. As a crowd of two hundred gathered on the dockside to see off the steamer, one man asked him how he liked Germany.

"I hate it," he growled. The ship had no passenger cabins, but one of the officers gave up his room for him. He would eat at the captain's mess. At the last moment, a German lawyer from Hamburg rushed on board. Calling himself Dr. Stork, he said he had been sent by Diamond's friends in the United States, but Diamond ignored him until he pronounced a special code word cabled to Diamond by his New York lawyer. Stork told him to go a particular hotel in Philadelphia when the ship docked and there he would find messages for him. Diamond instructed Stork to start an official complaint against the Prussian minister of the interior. As Diamond settled down to his sixteen-day voyage, he discovered he was to be accompanied by a cargo of several thousand canaries. The irony was not lost on him. Someone had certainly squawked about his mission to Germany.

When Diamond walked down the gangplank in Philadelphia, he was served with a warrant charging him with being a suspicious character. He was photographed and fingerprinted. "I wanted to go to Germany for my health," he insisted. "I've got a very bad stomach. But what happens? The newspapers up and hint I'm going to Europe to kill somebody." He wasn't concerned about facing the police but feared the reaction of his wife to a story printed in a German newspaper linking him to a blond German singer. He told customs officials that a Hamburg café had offered him $1,800 a month to perform in a cabaret for them. "It wasn't enough," he said.

So, if Diamond wasn't really going to Germany for his health or a cabaret job, what was he doing there in September 1930? An answer came just a month later. By then, Diamond had been shot while staying at the Hotel Monticello. He was relaxing in a luxury suite with his mistress, showgirl Kiki Roberts, when two gunmen burst in and shot him four times. Miraculously, he survived the assault, but in the following police investigation, an associate of Diamond, a bookmaker called Robert V. Miller, known as "Count Duval," admitted he had been sent by Diamond to Germany on a mission for him.

Miller was supposed to buy a consignment of rye whiskey for Diamond's nightclub and was to get 5 percent on the deal. Given traveling expenses of $500, he sailed on a separate ship than Diamond and when he heard his boss had been arrested in Germany, he aborted the trip. In Paris, he received a telegram from Diamond telling him to collect money owed him in London. Prohibition was still in force in New York and illicit liquor was at a premium, but it seemed a long way to go for a few crates of whiskey.

♠

A stronger clue to the true purpose behind Diamond's ill-fated journey to Weimar Germany comes in the identity of his fellow travelers. Before the New York mobster had reached continental Europe, his White Star liner *Baltic* had docked at Queenstown harbor in Ireland. An enterprising local reporter checked the list of passengers on board and found that Diamond was accompanied by four friends. One was Charles Green, formerly known as Entratta; the other three were called Treager, Aricidiaco, and Lucania. That fourth man was Charles Lucania—a rising gangster who, just a few years later, would become infamous as Charles "Lucky" Luciano, boss of bosses of New York's underworld. Confirmation of Luciano's presence on this voyage came five years later when an FBI memorandum referred to "Charles Luciana" accompanying Jack Diamond to "Europe in the summer of 1930." The arrest of Diamond and the resulting publicity subsequently disrupted their plans, said the report—or did it?

In December 1931, an Italian-American drug dealer called August Del Grazio was arrested by German police in Hamburg. In his possession was an invoice for a shipment of 1,430 pounds of narcotics, but when they raced to the pier to wrench open the suspicious crates, they found nothing inside. The frustrated police feared the drugs were already on a ship bound for New York. The raid came as a result of their investigation into a drug smuggler called "Afghan Moses." When the police searched Afghan Moses's home, they found receipts that led them to locate 550 pounds of narcotics hidden on a ship from Turkey. Del Grazio had been arrested as soon as he stepped off the Simplon Express from Venice via Cologne and southern Germany. When he was searched, papers linked him to Afghan Moses and an international narcotics smuggling ring.

When German detectives spoke to their colleagues in New York, they discovered that Del Grazio was from Manhattan's Lower East Side, where he was known as "Little Augie the Wop." He had been under observation ever since three tons of narcotics had been seized at Pier 84 at West Fifty-fourth Street, disguised in a shipment of woolen clothing.

Del Grazio was a longtime criminal who knew Lucky Luciano well enough to offer him help nineteen years later when the mobster was in prison. Federal narcotics agent George White testified to the Kefauver Committee inquiry that Del Grazio approached him on behalf of gangster mastermind Frank Costello with a deal to get Luciano out of jail.

In 1931, it seems likely that Del Grazio was completing a narcotics deal that had been set up by Luciano in Germany a year earlier. The Bureau of Narcotics report, quoted by the FBI, said "a conspiracy existed to smuggle narcotics from Europe into the United States" and had subsequently failed because of Diamond's arrest, but this was only partly right. Diamond's arrest had thrown his own personal part of the deal into disarray, but Luciano must have completed the deal in the shadows. Otherwise, why would Del Grazio—known well to Luciano and his associates—still be there a year later?

It seems remarkable that Charles "Lucky" Luciano should be walking the streets of Weimar Germany in 1930. At the same time, Adolf Hitler and his Nazi party were campaigning hard to win national elections, and on September 14 they won over six million votes, making them the second-largest political party in the country.

Luciano would have seen their election posters and anti-Semitic slogans everywhere. He might even have seen Nazi Brownshirts bullying Jewish citizens. He had grown up in a heavily Jewish populated district of New York and many of his closest friends and business partners were Jewish. Seeing German Nazis at close quarters gave him a bitter dislike for Hitler and his racist cause that would endure into World War II.

It is important to note that Luciano's business trip to Nazi-infested Germany has not been mentioned before in any of the studies of the mobster and his career. It is not mentioned at all in *The Last Testament of Lucky Luciano*, the book that controversially claimed to be based on the firsthand recollections of his life. Even when Meyer Lansky, his closest lifelong criminal associate, related his memoirs to an Israeli journalist, he failed to mention Diamond and Luciano's journey to Germany. The reason for this is not altogether surprising. In later life, Luciano and Lansky were happy to talk about their profiteering during Prohibition and their shoot-outs with other gangsters, but they were certainly not going to admit to being at the heart of an international drug-smuggling network.

♠

In 1930, dealing in illicit drugs was a relatively new criminal business. Heroin—the most infamous of narcotic drugs derived from morphine—was first manufactured in Germany in 1898 by Bayer Pharmaceutical as a cough medicine. Early users said it made them feel "heroic," and from that was born its commercial name. By the first decade of the twentieth century, heroin was marketed widely in the United States and attracted its first recreational users from the middle classes, but the habit soon spread to the less affluent, who became increasingly desperate to fund their next fix.

Tales of these "junkies"—so called because they sold anything, including junk metal, to raise money for heroin—stirred the government into action and they banned its use without prescription in 1914. "The most harmful form of opiate with which we have to deal is heroin," declared Dr. Charles B. Towns in 1915, an early campaigner against it. "Heroin is three times as strong as morphine in its action. It shows more quickly a deleterious effect upon the human system, the mental, moral and physical deterioration of its takers being more marked than in the case of any other form of opiate." In 1917, the *New York Times* ran a headline claiming there were three hundred thousand drug addicts in New York City—the majority of them from the prosperous middle classes. Two years later, doctors were banned from prescribing heroin altogether, but by then an underworld market in illegal drugs had already been established.

Charles Luciano's first and only prison sentence, until the mid-1930s, came about because of his involvement in dealing heroin in the Lower East Side in 1916, when he was just eighteen years old. In April 1924, a bill prohibiting the importation of crude opium for the purpose of manufacturing heroin was put before the House of Representatives in Washington, D.C. Sidney W. Brewster was the deputy warden of Hart Island prison in New York City, and he gave chilling testimony at the bill hearings.

"In 1910 or 1911 and up to four or five years ago in the underworld the drug chiefly used was morphine and cocaine, morphine being termed a necessary drug and cocaine a luxury," explained Brewster. In the last four or five years heroin has gradually succeeded morphine and to quite some extent cocaine. The reason for this is that heroin is approximately three times as powerful as morphine, and further, the addict in taking heroin gets some of the effects which he ordinarily would get from cocaine."

Brewster said that a cocktail of drugs was used by a variety of addicts from actors to gangsters to "jazz up" their lives, but he said there was a worrying trend for drugs being used during criminal acts.

"At the present time, in one of the most recent crimes of

violence," said Brewster, "the Diamond case, in New York, which involved the robbing and murder of two bank messengers in broad daylight, two of the actual perpetrators of the crime were under the influence of heroin. In many cases the leaders of the various gangs of gunmen do not use narcotics themselves but when they send out members of the gang on a crime to commit murder or robbery they see that they are well charged before they go."

The jazzed-up robbers who killed the two bank employees in November 1923 were Barlow Morris Diamond and Joseph G. Diamond. They were no relations of Jack Diamond, but the crime made the headlines. Clearly, drug use among psychopathic criminals only enhanced their level of violence. In his testimony, Brewster quoted New York police records for 1923, saying there were approximately six thousand arrests in the city in connection with illegal drugs.

"The man who uses heroin is a potential murderer," said Brewster. "He loses all consciousness of moral responsibility, also fear of consequences."

Did Luciano use drugs himself? In later life, he admitted that as a teenager he smoked opium. "I used to hit the pipe joints in Chinatown when I was a kid, we all did," he recalled. An unlicensed dentist gave him his first smoke. "I liked it, the stuff did funny things to my head. But I'd never let it suck me under." He saw it more as a business opportunity.

In 1923, European government medical experts met in Paris to discuss the abuse of heroin. For them, it seemed to be largely an American problem. "If heroin is abused in America," said a British Ministry of Health report, "let Americans who like prohibition forbid it, but why should countries where heroin is not abused be put to all the trouble for the benefit of the United States." This narrow-minded view would be blown apart a few years later.

By the time Diamond and Luciano took their voyage to Germany, smuggling heroin and other narcotics had expanded into an international business with enormous profits to be made. On March 17, 1930, one hundred U.S. customs agents boarded an ocean liner that had arrived from France. They had been tipped off that two thousand pounds of narcotics manufactured in Germany were on board. Shortly beforehand, a trunk-load of narcotics valued at $200,000 was seized on a New York pier after the arrival of the White Star liner *Majestic*. Later, before a grand jury, an English passenger explained that he had not recognized one of his heavy leather trunks deposited on the pier, despite it bearing his name. He left the trunk behind and customs agents became suspicious when another man claimed it.

The international network stretched from America to Germany to Turkey. Major-General T. W. Russell Pasha was commandant of the Cairo police and he was very well placed to observe the flow of the narcotics market. He reported back his findings to a League of Nations committee set up to investigate the global trade. Although countries suffering from the traffic tended to "think in grammes and kilogrammes" he explained, "the unit of calculation in the central European manufacturing countries when talking of narcotics is the metric ton."

Russell Pasha identified one illegal factory in Alsace in 1928 that had produced 4,349 kilograms of heroin—more than two and half times the legitimate requirement of the world population—and that was just one factory. Recently, his Central Narcotics Intelligence Bureau had broken up a gang of Polish smugglers operating out of Vienna who sourced narcotics from Austria, Switzerland, and France. These were then passed on through ports in Italy, Greece, and Turkey to end up in the drug dens of Alexandria, Egypt, servicing the needs of an estimated five hundred thousand addicts. One of the arrested dealers was an outwardly respectable doctor who claimed he was simply "engaged in making and selling something for which there was a world-wide demand. No visions of demented, tortured victims of his poison came ever to disturb him." The raw materials for this trade —opium—came mostly from Turkey, although factories in Istanbul were also responsible for shipping thousands of kilograms of heroin and morphine.

The United States established its own Federal Narcotics Control Board and Narcotics Division as a result of the Harrison Narcotic Act in 1914. In June 1930, these were combined to form the Federal Bureau of Narcotics (FBN), part of the U.S. treasury department. It was this agency that pointed the finger at Luciano and Diamond setting up a drug-smuggling network in Germany. They passed their information on to the FBI, who made the connection between Italian gangsters in New York and the drug business. Early on, they claimed that narcotics were arriving hidden in barrels of olive oil. Much of this came to the Lower East Side of Manhattan—the heart of the Italian immigrant community. This was the place where Charles Luciano began his criminal career as a teenage peddler of heroin.

How to Become a Gangster

Salvatore Lucania sat at the back of a classroom in Roman Catholic Public School 19. He was nine years old with thick black hair and a sunburned complexion. He couldn't understand a word the teacher was saying. The other kids in the class were much younger than he, but they all spoke English. He knew nothing but his native Sicilian. He was embarrassed and stubbornly refused to enter into the lesson. He stared out the window at the decrepit tenement blocks of the Lower East Side. Outside on the streets of New York, he vowed to make himself understood and respected—and feared. By the time he reached his goal, he would have a brand-new name to go with his brand-new American character—Charles "Lucky" Luciano.

Salvatore was born in Sicily on November 11, 1897. In the spring of 1907, he left the Mediterranean island with his family to emigrate to America. Their point of entry was the Lower East Side in New York City. In just one day in May 1907, twenty thousand immigrants arrived there, breaking all previous records by five thousand. It was a human flood of economic refugees that included Italians, Irish, Portuguese, and Jews. Salvatore Lucania and his family arrived by transatlantic steamship from Palermo on the northern coast of Sicily. In the previous year, a total of 273,000 Italian immigrants had come to America. They were just one more family added to an army of poor people looking to earn a better living.

Salvatore's family numbered his mother, Rosalie, and father, Antonio, older brother, Giuseppe, and his older sister, Francesca. A younger brother, Bartolo, was born later in the United States When the family finally stepped ashore and wandered through the teeming streets of southern Manhattan, jostled by thousands of other immigrants, they took a deep intake of breath. The smell of poverty was different in America. Back home in Lercara Friddi, a little village in the dusty heart of sun-blasted Sicily, it had been the reek of sulfur dug out from the mine where Antonio labored. Here it was a pungent multitude of odors: rotting fish, decaying garbage, stale alcohol—the smell of the big city. It would only get worse.

The Lower East Side was paralyzed by a series of strikes in the summer of 1907. One of these was led by Italian street cleaners. Garbage piled up on the streets outside tenement blocks. In the heat, clouds of flies buzzed around and the city's health commissioner feared an outbreak of disease. His men poured chloride of lime and bromide solution over the rotting piles, but his biggest concern was for immigrant children. "They play freely all over them," he said, "and rummage among them to find playthings. They smear themselves with the refuse and then eat with unwashed hands. Therein lies the real risk; the smell is only unpleasant."

The Italian street sweepers wanted to raise their $720 a year income to $800, the same as the drivers of garbage carts, and were violently supported by their wives and friends, who threw bricks and fireworks at the police escorting strikebreakers. Later, in the summer, Teamster union members who packed meat for big wholesalers went on strike. Jewish kosher butchers had to pick up the meat themselves, but when the prices went up, they refused to buy. No meat was bought for the Jewish Sabbath and all the Lower East Side went without, Italian butchers included. Mounted police had to guard wagons of meat driven by strikebreakers from the city abattoirs. Conflict was in the air as poor immigrants fought to get their fair share of American riches. Sometimes they turned to gangsters to help them out.

Dopey Benny was a renowned thug hired by Italian union officials to attack strikebreakers. "I got my men together," he later admitted to a district attorney, "divided them up into squads and saw that they were armed with pieces of gas pipe and with clubs, but this time not with pistols, and when the workmen came up from work the men I had got set on them and beat them up." It was one of the earliest lessons Lucania learned about the way things worked in New York City.

♠

Among the main immigrant communities of the Lower East Side, the Irish were the oldest and most senior, with many of their members in the police force. The Italians included Sicilians, Neapolitans, and Calabrians, while the Jews came from Eastern Europe and Russia. Sharing the Catholic faith, the Irish and Italians tolerated each other and looked down on the more alien-looking Jews, but each community hung tightly together and viewed other nationalities with suspicion. The Lucania family first lived in a tenement block on First Avenue, between East Thirteenth and Fourteenth streets. This was on the northern boundary of the Lower East Side in an area now called the East Village. To the south were Little Italy and Chinatown.

"Home came equipped with a fire escape for summer sleeping," is how one Jewish immigrant remembered the cramped living conditions. "Every floor had four railroad flats. On our floor, the one toilet in the hall served the four families—two Jewish, one Russian, and one Polish. There was a yard in the back and a house in the rear, two stories high. Here lived the poorer of the poor—in back, unable to see what went on in the tumbling, fierce activity and continuous gabble of the streets."

A typical tenement apartment from this period had just three rooms for a family to live in. Only one outside window illuminated the interior, so a second window was built into the wall of the living room to allow light to pass through into the kitchen; the interior bedroom was in complete darkness. At different stages of the day, the front room served as work space, dining room, and a second bedroom. The majority of immigrants worked in the clothing industry. The head of the family set up his sewing machine by the outside window while the rest of his family busied themselves in the gloomy, stuffy interior, finishing off dresses and suits destined for swanky shops in uptown Manhattan. Aside from working and sleeping, most life in the tenement blocks was lived out on the streets.

Antonio Lucania had been a sulfur miner in Sicily and carried on with his law-abiding but humble existence as a laborer in New York. Whenever his son Salvatore got into trouble he would beat him, but in the overcrowded tenement blocks, it was easy for boys to get into gangs and compete with each other to establish their reputation. Salvatore Lucania was no different from any of them and gravitated to the street corner and the network of kids involved in petty crime.

"There are thousands of New York boys attending organized schools for crime," wrote one reporter in 1908. "Their operations during the day, conducted out of school hours, also provide much more than a comfortable income for the masters of these schools for pickpockets, thieves, and gamblers. The problems that beset the Principals of the schools of the Lower East Side, with its predominating un-American population, are more perplexing and multifold than in any other metropolis in the world."

The reporter compared the situation to Charles Dickens's tale of *Oliver Twist* with young men—teenage "Fagins"—training teams of kids to act as thieves for them, knowing they would not face harsh punishment if caught. In the Lower East Side, many of these boys, as young as six, were involved in illegal crap shooting games, in which they tried to hustle other kids out of their money. They were also taught how to pick pockets on the rear end of trolley cars, subway trains, or ferry terminals, wherever a crowd of well-off commuters could be found. The money was brought back to their adolescent Fagins who would first reward them with sweets but then bully them if they failed to bring in enough revenue.

Salvatore Lucania absorbed early lessons in crime when he ran with these child gangs. They broke into neighboring apartments and mugged people in the streets. A tough and fearless kid, Lucania organized his own protection racket, offering to shield Jewish boys on their way home from school from being attacked by other Italians or Irish. On one occasion, he offered his services to a puny-looking schoolboy. "If you wanna keep alive, Jew boy," he said, "you gotta pay us five cents a week protection money." The little Jew fixed him with a stare and told him—"Go fuck yourself." The defiant kid was Meyer Lansky, who would later become one of Lucania's leading crime associates.

As Lucania caused mayhem on the streets of his neighborhood he also skipped more school. Finally, in 1911, he was punished for his persistent truancy by being sent to a secure school in Brooklyn. Full of similar rough-minded kids like him, all he learned was how to perfect his criminal skills. When he emerged four months later, his reputation was enhanced on the streets and he never went back to school.

He was fourteen years old and got his first job as a shipping clerk for the Goodman Hat Company on Greene Street. He was paid $5 a week and this rose to $7. He must have got on well at the hat factory because he stayed there for four years, but all the time he was watching who had the real money in his community—who wore the flash clothes and drove the smartest cars. He was observing the world of organized crime and wanted part of it.

♠

Over the previous decade, the Lower East Side underworld had been dominated by several well-known criminal characters. There was "Humpty" Jackson, whose gang worked out of East Fourteenth Street. He got his name from his physical deformity—a hunchback—and he wore a pistol in his derby hat. Then there was "Nigger Mike" Salter, who ran a bar in Chinatown and got his name from his very dark Mediterranean coloring. His gang killed "Eat-'em-up" Jack MacManus, who had been lording it over his rivals by wearing an elegant suit and overcoat and carrying a silver-headed cane. MacManus was found dead one night in Houston Street with his head crushed in by an iron bar. He had been a lieutenant to Paul Kelly, chief of the long-established Five Points Gang, who was not in fact Irish but Italian.

Many of these gangs gained their prestige from their connection with corrupt Democrat politicians from Tammany Hall who paid them handsomely on election days for delivering votes for their party. When these gangs demonstrated their power openly in 1903 by taking over sections of the Lower East Side and raiding saloons, the police moved in strongly and ever after kept them in the shadows with frequent raids on their headquarters.

A more insidious criminal organization was the Black Hand. They were an early form of the Italian Mafia and were notorious for bombings and kidnappings. At first, they had preyed largely on their own countrymen, but by 1911, as their confidence in moving among the English-speaking community increased, they widened their zone of activity to include rich Jewish businessmen. Their mode of action was to send threatening letters to their wealthy victims—when they refused to pay up, mobsters would kidnap their children or blow up their properties.

In 1911, there were seventy bombings in New York City credited to the Black Hand gangsters. Sometimes the victims fought back.

On August 14, 1911, the whole Italian community of the Lower East Side was celebrating the feast day of Saint Rocco. Four Black Hand assassins threaded their way through the crowds on East Eleventh Street to enter the grocery store belonging to the Calandro brothers—they had persistently refused their letters of blackmail and were now going to pay the price. But Sylvestro and Antonio Calandro recognized the gangsters through the shopwindow and pulled out pistols as soon they entered the store. Shots rang out and the four mobsters ran out into the street, causing panic as bullets flew everywhere. One gangster fell mortally wounded just outside the grocery store. A crowd gathered around him and called for a priest, but as soon they recognized him as a Black Hander, the mood changed. "Beware of *La Mano Nera!*" one shouted, and the crowd disappeared, leaving the man to die alone on the sidewalk. The Calandros were tried and acquitted for his murder.

Two years later, Black Hand mobsters turned to poisoning the horses needed for delivering goods. When Jewish blacksmith Louis Blumenthal still refused to pay up, gangsters drove a car that cost them $3,400—all raised from frightened local businessmen—to his street, where they shot him dead. His murder roused all the other traders to get together and work with the police to run down the murderers. They succeeded, but they faced another major problem. "The immunity of the gangster from arrest has been due to the fear of the victims to appear against him," said Eighth District Assemblyman Solomon Sufrin. "The only way to prevent the development of gangs in future will be found in giving more attention to the growing boy in the streets."

One of these growing boys was Salvatore Lucania, and he keenly followed the news of all the latest gang outrages. At the age of fourteen, he acquired his first gun. As he was showing it proudly to a friend, it went off and the bullet grazed his left leg.

It gave him a scar he would bear for the rest of his life—the only time he would ever be shot. When his father found the gun, Antonio pointed it at his son and said he should shoot him for bringing disgrace on their family.

"So I stopped coming home, when he was around," Lucania later recalled. "I'd sleep in empty apartments in the neighborhood, or in pool halls. I'd only go home in the daytime, to get a hot meal from my mother. But I stayed away from my old man as much as I could."

His friends out on the street were his family, and it was them—not his brothers or his parents—who would help him get on in the world. When he got some money, he shared a furnished flat on East Fourteenth Street with two other men, one of them another wannabe gangster called Joe Biondo.

Working as a delivery boy for the Jewish hatmaker Goodman helped shield Lucania's criminal activities, but all the time he was building up his name as a gang leader with a following of violent kids who would do anything for money. Lucania and his mates would steal old-fashioned pocket watches and gold chains from wealthier Italian immigrants. He said he averaged a haul of three items a day. Early on, he was aware of the market in illicit drugs—especially heroin and cocaine—and started running errands for a local drug dealer. One day he delivered a vial of heroin to a prostitute in a bar who turned out to be a police informer, and he got caught. On June 27, 1916, at the age of eighteen, Salvatore Lucania was sentenced to eight months in prison at New Hampton Farms Reformatory.

A later probation report declared that he had already acquired a "definite criminalistic pattern of conduct" by this age. "His freedom from conscience springs from his admitted philosophy: 'I never was a crumb, and if I have to be a crumb I'd rather be dead.' He explains this by stating that a crumb is a person who works and saves and lays his money aside; who indulges in no extravagance. His description of a crumb would fit the average man."

When he came out on parole after six months, Lucania was acclaimed as a "stand-up guy" by his criminal associates. He'd taken his punishment like a man and hadn't squealed. He also had a new name. He didn't like the fact that Salvatore could be shortened to Sal or Sally. It invited sexual advances from convicts. Besides, he was an American gangster now and he wanted an American name, so he took up "Charlie" and became Charles Lucania. That was the name that would feature on his police reports over the next decade.

Lucania went back briefly to his shipping clerk job, but finally quit when he won $244—nearly a year's wages—in a floating craps game. For him, crime paid, and that was an end to his honest living.

♠

Just as the teenage Charlie Lucania was forging his reputation, so other notorious gangsters were also on the rise. "Terrible" Johnny Torrio was in his teens when he first came to prominence in the Lower East Side. He was a short, tough Italian, whose ruthless skill with his fists and knives got him a job as a bouncer at Nigger Mike's bar. He became a lieutenant to the Five Points Gang leader, Paul Kelly, the Italian with an Irish name. Hungry for his own criminal territory, he took over a bar and brothel for sailors in Brooklyn. He took a liking to an effective street fighter called Al Capone and kept him close to him. In 1915, when Torrio was thirty-three years old, his uncle, "Big Jim" Colosimo, offered him a job in Chicago, looking after his extensive vice operations. Four years later, he called on Al Capone to join him there.

Capone was two years younger than Lucania, born in Brooklyn to Neapolitan immigrant parents. At school, he beat up his teacher and quit. He joined Torrio's James Street Gang and also got to know Lucania. The two became firm friends. Capone got his nickname "Scarface" after a fight in a bar over a girl when he got his left check slashed open. By 1919, he was a professional murderer and was happy to escape police interest in New York to join the older Torrio in Chicago.

On January 16, 1920, came Prohibition—the biggest break for organized crime in the United States. Campaigners against the evils of alcohol had succeeded in getting the government to introduce a ban on the sale of liquor. Almost immediately, illicit drinking bars called speakeasies sprang up in major cities and these had to be supplied with bootleg booze. The gangs stepped in to ensure this supply and made a fortune over the next thirteen years. Some of the money was used to bribe police and the legal system, as many of those entrusted with upholding the ban were happy to turn a blind eye to it, especially if it lined their pockets. It introduced a level of corruption into public affairs that enabled criminal gangs to get a firm grip on the American metropolis.

In Chicago, Big Jim Colosimo did not see the golden opportunity straightaway and clashed with Johnny Torrio over supplying illicit booze because he didn't need the extra cash and the risks that came with it. With Capone at his side, Torrio organized the assassination of Big Jim. The way was now clear for them to take over the bootleg business and make themselves immensely rich. While Capone organized the strong-arm stuff, Torrio took on more of a management role and realized that the old way of street gangs fighting each other for a piece of the action was a waste of everyone's effort, especially when there was so much money to be made from Prohibition. He called together many of the Chicago gangs, regardless of their ethnic background— Italians, Irish, and Poles—and divided the city up so that each gang had its own territory, secure in knowing that no one else would mess with them. That way, they could concentrate on shaking off the police and bringing in the cash.

Of course, not everyone went along with Torrio's business model. The Irish North Siders led by Dion O'Banion double-crossed Torrio, and others cheated him. But the main proposition was not a request— it was a threat. Join up with this plan or face annihilation. Most of the time Torrio got his way, but in 1925 his luck ran out and he was ambushed in his limousine, nearly killed by a shotgun blast and four pistol bullets. Out of the hospital, he told Capone he was retiring and left Chicago to Scarface.

Back in New York, other powerful criminal characters were emerging out of the underworld. The Lower East Side was rich in Jewish gangsters such as Meyer Lansky. He was born Maier Suchowljansky in 1902 in Grodno, Poland. His parents fled pogroms there and Lansky fought anyone who tried to intimidate him in America. His family had had a bellyful of that. As he formed his own teenage Jewish gang, the small-statured Lansky got together with a tall, good-looking boy called Benny Siegel, who was three years younger. Quick to anger, Siegel had a formidable reputation as a street fighter and was happy to use a gun from an early age. Lansky saw this both as strength and weakness.

"His big problem was that he was always ready to rush in first and shoot, to act without thinking," said Lansky. "That always got him into trouble. I explained patiently to him again and again that if you're going to succeed, it's better to work from behind the scenes." It was advice that Lansky would take himself, but Siegel was too much of a hothead to stay out of trouble for long. According to Lansky, his best friend got his moniker "Bugsy" because he was "crazy as a bedbug." A later FBI report said he "acquired his title of Bugsy because many of the associates in the old days considered him as 'going bugs' when he got excited in that he acted in an irrational manner."

Lansky and Siegel turned their teenage gang into muscle for hire and made a fortune in the early years of Prohibition. They offered protection to bootleggers or hijacked their shipment if they failed to come through with the cash. In their gang were other hoodlums who made names for themselves, including Abner "Longy" Zwillman, Louis "Lepke" Buchalter, and Arthur

Flegenheimer—who became famous as Dutch Schultz. Ever since they'd met as kids in the Lower East Side, Lansky and Charlie Lucania had kept up their friendship, but the time was not yet right for them to come together as a powerful criminal alliance.

In 1920, the king of the New York underworld was a stocky, five-foot-two Sicilian called Giuseppe Masseria, known as "Joe the Boss." Fleeing a murder charge in his homeland, Masseria had joined the Morello gang, an early Mafia crime family based in East Harlem. When their top killer, Ignazio Lupo "the Wolf," was jailed, Masseria had taken over the gang and his influence extended throughout Manhattan and into Brooklyn. When Lucania's and Lansky's gangs clashed with his soldiers in the Lower East Side, Masseria recruited the up-and-coming Sicilian as a gunman, but told him to ditch his friendship with Lansky. As an old-style Italian Catholic, he hated Jews.

On August 8, 1922, Masseria was at home on the Lower East Side in his three-story brownstone house on Second Avenue near East Fifth Street. Just after midday, a blue Hudson touring car stopped outside a kosher butcher's shop nearby. Two men stepped out of the car and walked into a restaurant across the road from Masseria's house. One of the men was thirty-four-year-old Umberto Valenti, a veteran hit man and associate of Peter Morello, who resented Masseria taking over his gang. Two months earlier, Joe the Boss had knocked off Mob rival Silvio Tagliapanna, and Valenti was looking to equalize things.

For an hour, Valenti and his accomplice toyed with cups of coffee and slices of cake, keeping a sharp eye on Masseria's house. At just after 2:00 P.M., the tubby Italian Mob boss sauntered down the steps of his brownstone. He was wearing a light summer suit and straw hat. He turned north to stroll along Second Avenue. Valenti and his friend bolted out of the café and strode after Masseria. As Joe the Boss spotted them, Valenti pulled his weapon. Unarmed, Masseria tried to dodge inside a hat shop but was caught outside a women's clothes store.

"The man with the revolver came close to the other fellow

and aimed," said one of the shop owners. "Just as he fired the man jumped to one side. The bullet smashed into the window of my store. Then the man fired again and this time the man being shot at ducked his head forward. Again the man fired and again his target ducked his head down. The third shot made a second hole in the window."

How Valenti, a professional gunman, could miss three times at point-blank range is a mystery, but it gave Masseria the nickname "the Man Who Could Dodge Bullets." Joe the Boss didn't hang around to wonder why and sprinted off toward his home. Seeing witnesses gathering, Valenti and his accomplice ran back to their parked car. As their Hudson careered down the road, they were confronted by a crowd of striking garment workers pouring out of a hall near the Bowery.

"The gunmen realized that an attempt to ram their way through the throng would take time and might prove unsuccessful," said a newspaper report. "They resorted to more desperate measures. Two of them got on the running board and fired point-blank into the crowd."

Some twenty shots were fired. Eight of them hit home, wounding the striking men—one died later. Panic spread down the street, especially when some of the garment workers fled into a nearby nursery school. A policeman commandeered a car and chased the gunmen north, but at East Thirty-second Street, the Hudson cut ahead of other vehicles in the dense traffic and escaped.

In the meantime, Masseria was sitting on the edge of his bed at home, poking a finger through the two bullet holes in his straw hat. A few hours later, he sent out a message to call a meeting with Valenti and his cronies to make things right. But he had no intention of turning up to face his incompetent assassin. He ordered three of his young gunmen to make the meeting. One of them was most likely the twenty-four-year-old Charles Lucania—ambitious to do some high-profile business for his boss.

Three days later, around midday, Masseria's men met with Valenti and his gunmen on the corner of East Twelfth Street and Second Avenue, not far from where Lucania's family first lived when they came to America. It was a heavily Jewish populated area and witnesses were shocked at the sudden explosion of violence as the group of mobsters broke apart and started firing at each other. An eight-year-old girl playing outside her grandfather's store was hit in the chest in the crossfire. A road sweeper fell into a gutter seriously injured. Almost everyone else ducked for cover as Valenti ran out into the road and jumped on the running board of a taxicab. But one gunman stayed calm and stood rooted in the middle of the road, aiming carefully, firing methodically after the fleeing mobster.

"It was the coolest thing I ever saw," said a teenager. "People were shrieking and running in all directions, and this fellow calmly fired shot after shot. He did not move until he had emptied his weapon."

The ice-cool gunman was determined to complete his job. When Valenti pulled out his Colt to fire back, he was struck in the chest. He collapsed from the side of the taxicab, mortally wounded, blood pouring through his shirt. As police rushed to the scene, a passerby indicated the hallway of a tenement block into which the assassin had disappeared. The police ventured into the dimly lit building, but the gunman had climbed a ladder at the rear to escape into a yard—he knew his way too well around the neighborhood. A witness later described him as young, short, dark, and neatly dressed. It had likely been Charlie Lucania. Emerging out of the shadows, he was fast becoming one of the deadliest mobsters on the street.

As an expert gunman, Lucania had bought a country cabin near Nyack, on the banks of the Hudson, north of New York City. There, he and his mobster friends practiced their shooting skills while hunting and blasting off rounds from machine guns.

Lucania thrived under Joe the Boss and made a small fortune out of Prohibition, but he was only a low-level gangster. To earn

serious money and gain the power he hungered for, he had to
make friends with another legendary villain, Arnold Rothstein—
known variously as "Mr. Big," "the Big Bankroll," and "the Brain."
The lessons Lucania learned from Rothstein would put him on
the road to becoming king of the New York underworld.

UPTOWN GAMBLER

To rise above the level of an ordinary hoodlum, Charles Lucania had to make a connection with a patron of crime—an enormously rich and influential underworld potentate who could link the Lower East Side with uptown Manhattan. None came bigger or more powerful than Arnold Rothstein—the original Mr. Big. This man has been credited with founding organized crime in New York City. Small-time gangsters had paid off local policemen to turn a blind eye to their activities. Rothstein took graft to a whole new level by dealing directly with politicians, paying them to alter the legal procedure. During Prohibition, he intervened with well-placed payments to get thousands of court cases dismissed.

Rothstein directly invested in the enterprises of leading bootleggers such as Jack "Legs" Diamond, Dutch Schultz, and "Waxey" Gordon and made sure they were protected from prosecution. He established good relations with European distilleries to bring in high-quality liquor and when he foresaw that

Prohibition would come to an end, he promoted international networks importing narcotics. Any up-and-coming mobster sought his favors and this included Johnny Torrio in Chicago and Lower East Side newcomers Charlie Lucania, Meyer Lansky, and Frank Costello. Above all, Rothstein liked to keep out of the limelight and that was the very best advice he could give to any aspiring crime boss.

Although he moved in rarefied circles in the 1920s, Rothstein came from the Lower East Side like so many other mobsters on the make. Born in 1882 to a native New Yorker, it was his father, Abraham, himself the son of a Bessarabian Jewish immigrant, who had made the leap from poverty to wealth—but he had done it the law-abiding way, through sheer hard work and business enterprise. So Arnold had a comfortable middle-class upbringing. At school, he excelled at numbers but when he should have been going to Hebrew studies he was out on the streets winning pennies from other kids.

"I always gambled," said Rothstein in a rare newspaper interview in 1921. "I can't remember when I didn't. Maybe I gambled just to show my father he couldn't tell me what to do, but I don't think so. I think I gambled because I loved the excitement. When I gambled, nothing else mattered. I could play for hours and not know how much time had passed."

When his father tried to get him into the family textile business, Arnold just played pool with his father's employees. He preferred studying people to studying books and believed he could analyze the motives of other men at a glance and get the best of them. He got odd jobs in poolrooms, so named because they were places where lottery tickets were sold and the prize money paid out of the "pool." Billiards tables were installed to keep lottery customers occupied and the game was adapted for quicker play, resulting in what is now known as "pool." Rothstein had a talent for the new game and represented the house, sharing the profits with the poolroom owner who always bet on him. As a teenage gambler, he also played dice and poker, using his winnings to buy friendships with bigger, tougher boys. He had a slim build, was no hard man, and sought out muscle for protection.

As Rothstein's bankroll grew bigger, he peeled off bills to lend to other gamblers. When they didn't pay up, he employed Monk Eastman, a street-brawling gang leader, to collect for him. Eastman also delivered votes for the Democrats at Tammany Hall at election time. Thus, Rothstein learned the connection between crime and politics—a relationship he would develop to an extraordinary degree.

Rothstein generated more money by organizing places to gamble. When regular gambling houses were shut down, Rothstein invented the "floating game" that moved from secret location to location. His bankroll just kept on growing. Flashing his hundred-dollar bills earned him respect in what were called "sporting circles," in which gamblers bet on all kinds of sports from prizefights to baseball and horse racing.

As his personal wealth grew, he moved among more sophisticated New Yorkers and had the conversational skills to match. He was articulate and well informed. The only flashy thing about him was his ever-present bankroll; otherwise he dressed expensively but quietly. He never wore jewelry. He rarely drank, never smoked, didn't play around with women. "Rothstein rarely exhibited anger," said a contemporary report. "He might burn with indignation, but he never let it show. The heavy lids of his eyes might narrow a trifle, his pale, heavy face flush ever so slightly, but he kept his tongue under control. He shunned quarrels and if a disagreement arose he would depend on his ability to talk himself out of a tight corner"—or his ability to hire a mobster to do the dirty work for him.

In 1919, Rothstein broke his cardinal rule of criminal discretion when he hit newspaper headlines for the first time. In January of that year, two New York detectives broke into an apartment on West Fifty-seventh Street where Rothstein was playing a high-rolling game with some associates. They'd knocked on the door but the gamblers refused to open up. Suspecting they were holdup gunmen, the gamblers drew their pistols and fired through the door. The detectives were wounded in the hail of fire and Rothstein was charged with assault. He was released on $5,000 bail—a sum he paid out of the bankroll he carried on him—and a judge later dismissed the case, saying that it was a waste of time and public money with not a word of evidence produced to show that Rothstein had committed an assault on anyone. It set the pattern for Rothstein's future relations with the law.

The next year, Rothstein made far bigger headlines—as the man who tried to fix the 1919 World Series. The Chicago White Sox was one of the great baseball teams in America at the time. They looked like easy favorites to win the World Series. With millions of baseball fans betting on them, the odds were stacking up against the Cincinnati Reds, but a group of sporting gamblers saw an opportunity. If they could raise $100,000, they could pay off ten Chicago team players to throw the game. Ex-featherweight boxing champion Abe Attell acted as a go-between and approached the Big Bankroll for the money. Did he finance the deal or not? The White Sox threw the end-of-series game and when rumors of the fix got out, a grand jury trial was called in September 1920. There was little evidence to prove that Rothstein was involved. He testified against the leading conspirators and the jury exonerated him of any involvement in the scandalous action of the "Black Sox" intentionally losing the game. What probably did happen was that once Rothstein heard of the conspiracy, he made sure not to be involved, but that didn't stop him from placing $60,000 on Cincinnati and winning $270,000. That was clever and typical of Rothstein's ingenuity. For him, intelligence could be as effective as criminal action.

♠

Even though Rothstein was cleared of any wrongdoing, his brilliance in making money out of the notorious baseball fix added to his aura of invincibility and attracted young criminal acolytes. "Rothstein had the most remarkable brain," said Meyer Lansky. "He understood business instinctively and I'm sure if he had been a legitimate financier he would have been just as rich as he became with his gambling and the other rackets he ran. He could go right to the heart of any financial problem and resolve it unerringly. I tried to keep up with Rothstein in reducing every business or financial operation to its basics—I asked his advice, asked questions."

Charlie Lucania was equally impressed by his discretion. "You gotta stay out of the papers," he later said, "you gotta pay people good to stick their necks out while you stay in the background. Arnold did that, Frank [Costello] did that, Johnny Torrio did, all the smart ones stayed out of the papers. Even Joe the Boss moved into a place on Central Park West and called himself an importer—and he was a greasy old *cafoni* [peasant]." In accordance with this lesson, Lucania disliked socializing with the more flamboyant gangsters, such as Al Capone, whenever he came to New York in his armor-plated Cadillac. He drew too much attention.

Lucania even aped the Big Bankroll's personal style. Rothstein gave him advice on how to dress with conservative good taste, how to behave in sophisticated restaurants, and how to act around a lady—"If Arnold had lived a little longer, he could've made me pretty elegant," he joked. It was supposedly Rothstein who gave him a taste for silk shirts, ties, and pajamas purchased from France.

Embarrassed by being forced into the spotlight by the World Series scandal, Rothstein announced his retirement as "Gambling King" in September 1921. "It is not pleasant to be, what some call, a 'social outcast,'" he told the New York *Mail*. "For the sake of my family and friends, I am glad that chapter of my life is over." Having made a fortune estimated between $3 and $4 million, he explained that he intended to devote his future life to his real estate business and his racing stables. In reality, he concentrated on extending his control over New York's underworld.

Rothstein got into the business of Prohibition-busting through his criminal friends. When they got arrested for supplying illicit liquor, he posted bail for them. From that, he took a little piece of all their enterprises. His massive bankroll enabled him to fund bootleggers and rumrunners. Jack Diamond started out as his bodyguard. When Rothstein acquired the trucks to shift the booze, Diamond took over this business for him. So widespread were his contacts that Rothstein could take care of every aspect of the bootleg business, and that included bribing the necessary politicians and police—even the Coast Guard.

Irving Wexler, known as "Waxey" Gordon, wanted to borrow $175,000 for Rothstein to increase his importation of whiskey from Canada. Rothstein countered by investing more money into the venture by extending the business to importing high-quality liquor directly from Europe. Rothstein was, in effect, merchant banker to the underworld. It was a small step to extending his reach to include the smuggling of narcotics and diamonds into the country.

It was through Jack Diamond that Rothstein exerted his grip over the gangs of New York. In 1919, at the age of twenty-three, Diamond started working for Rothstein as a thug hired to settle labor disputes. Strikes had blighted the Lower East Side ever since Lucania and his family first arrived there. To combat the strikebreakers hired by employers, the unions turned to gangsters to help them out—for a fee—and as a result mobsters became closely involved with union officials, eventually putting themselves forward for fixed elections as union leaders.

When the garment district was rocked by a major series of strikes, Rothstein stepped in and many of his key henchmen, including Diamond, got involved in the street battles. At a September 1920 meeting of New York Central Trades and Labor delegates at the Central Opera House on East Sixty-seventh Street, a riot broke out between strikers. "Men ran about, punching each other in the face indiscriminately," said a reporter. "In the rear of the hall there appeared to be in progress a free-for-all fight. Several delegates rushed up and declared that one man already had been killed and others were being unmercifully beaten."

By the mid-1920s Louis "Lepke" Buchalter had usurped the chief union racketeering role from Rothstein. When garment-making factories hit hard times and took loans from the Mob, gangsters ended up becoming employers and derived an income from that, too.

From hired thug, Jack Diamond graduated to becoming Rothstein's personal bodyguard, paid $1,000 a week to protect him from sore losers and ensure that losing "sports" paid up. On the side, Diamond, with his brother Eddie, established their own bootlegging business, often hijacking consignments that had not paid "insurance" to Rothstein. Diamond was a psychopathically violent man who thrived on the adrenaline rush of an armed robbery. One of the top recruits to his gang was Charlie Lucania.

Lucania had already proved himself as an ice-cool hit man for Joe "the Boss" Masseria and been rewarded by promotion within his Mafia organization. He ran Masseria's downtown gambling rackets as well as continuing his involvement in nar-cotics dealing and neighborhood protection. On December 15, 1921, he was arrested in Jersey City, New Jersey, for carrying a concealed weapon, but the charge was dropped.

Like most mobsters, Lucania exploited the gold rush pro-vided by Prohibition. He did this in several ways. One was to provide the means by which local residents could brew their own liquor. Nick Gentile was an influential Sicilian-born ma-fioso, and he recalls how this worked for him. He started by opening a wholesale grocery store.

"The commodities that I sold most were sugar, tin cans and yeast which the bootleggers needed for the distillation of alco-hol," he said. "In a few months, I succeeded in bringing 75% of the bootleggers to my store. In this manner, I succeeded in earning about $2000 a month."

Lucania and his associates were alert to this and quick to provide similar supplies. Joe Biondo, Lucania's old friend from the days when they shared an apartment in East Fourteenth Street, devised a method of mixing a liquid with denatured spirits—not prohibited by law—that once distilled became pure spirits. Another scam was to obtain the pure alcohol used in the manufacturing of perfumes. Showcase bottles of perfume were kept by barbers, but the rest of the alcohol they bought from federal storehouses was sold to bootleggers at $15 per gallon, rather than the usual $5 per gallon. Lucania worked alongside Willie Moretti and others to open their own distilleries throughout New York State.

Sometimes this work could be dangerous. Joe Bonanno started off his career as a mobster with a basement distillery that he ran with his cousins. One of them, Giovanni Romano, was working through the night distilling whiskey when the building was rocked by an explosion.

"Giovanni had apparently dozed off," said Bonanno. "Alcohol spilled on the floor and flowed under the burner, igniting the still. A screaming Giovanni ran into the street. His clothes, flesh, and hair were on fire." Passersby slapped him with their jackets to put out the flames, but Giovanni didn't survive the night.

A more lucrative—and safer—line of business was providing the muscle to protect bootleggers and their illicit breweries—or rip them off. The Diamond brothers were successful at this. Connected to the Big Bankroll, they attracted some of the most vicious hoodlums in the city. Lucania had been handpicked by the Diamonds for his reputation—along with another rising gangster, Dutch Schultz.

The Diamonds liked Schultz because he was a firebrand, a man whose hair-trigger temper spread fear among other mobsters. He was the complete antithesis of Lucania and insulted the Sicilian's taste for fine clothes. "Only queers wear silk shirts," he told a reporter. "I never bought one in my life. A guy's a sucker to spend $15 or $20 on a shirt. Hell, a guy can get a good one for two bucks."

In return, Lucania derided Schultz's meanness. "The guy had a couple of million bucks and dressed like a pig." With such dissonant characters in the Diamond gang, it was bound to end badly—but in the short term they made themselves rich.

Inevitably, Diamond's freelance hijacking provoked the wrath of other mobsters. By 1924, "Big Bill" Dwyer had become the biggest importer of whiskey into the United States and was fed up with his consignments being ripped off by Diamond. So, even though Diamond was Rothstein's chosen bodyguard, Rothstein gave permission to Dwyer to deal with him.

In October 1924, as Diamond was cruising in his limousine along Fifth Avenue, a car drew up alongside and gunmen blasted him with shotguns. Pellets slammed into him but he put his foot on the accelerator and drove himself to hospital. "I don't have an enemy in the world," he told the police, but the fact that Rothstein had allowed this to happen sent out a message to the underworld that Diamond's gang of all-star mobsters was at an end. From then on, it was open season on Diamond. He miraculously survived several further attempts on his life. Despite all that—and probably against the good advice of his quieter associates—Lucania kept a close relationship with Diamond, who frequently stayed at his home when the heat was on.

♠

That Lucania still had a considerable interest in narcotics dealing was proved by an incident in June 1923. In a poolroom on East Fourteenth Street, he met a regular client he'd been supplying for a few months called John Lyons. On June 2, Lucania sold him two ounces of morphine, then two days later an ounce of heroin. On the fifth, Lucania sold him another two ounces of morphine and Lyons pulled a badge and a gun on him. A second armed figure stepped out from a nearby booth. They were undercover narcotics agents and Lucania was under arrest. This was a considerable blow to the gangster. A second arrest for drug ped-dling meant he faced ten years in jail.

Lucania had to think quickly. Under interrogation, he was asked to inform on his supplier. He broke the Mafia code of *omerta* and coughed up an address where the agents could find a considerable amount of narcotics. But the address he gave at 163 Mulberry Street directed them to his own stash of drugs with a street value of $150,000. As a result of delivering this impressive haul, the case against Lucania was dropped. So, when he was later asked if he'd become a stool pigeon for the police, he could answer "no," because technically he was not informing on anyone but himself, simply giving up his goods to stay out of a jail—a sensible deal. But the smell of "informer" clung to him after this incident and others claimed that dealers were arrested because Lucania gave names to the police. Cer-tainly, it revealed that Lucania was willing to negotiate with the authorities. This knowledge would encourage future secret deals with the government.

It seems extraordinary that Lucania should expose himself to imprisonment for a handful of dollars. One of his earliest close associates, Frank Costello, was equally surprised. "Dope is for suckers," he told Lucania. "Dope isn't like booze and gambling. The best people want to drink. The best people want to place a bet. They'll thank you for helping them drink and gamble." The implication was that dope was for lowlifes, but Lucania knew better than that. Narcotics appealed across the social landscape and he knew that Rothstein was okay with it and was not afraid to make links with top dealers. So Lucania nodded his apprecia-tion for the softly spoken advice of Costello, but carried on with business as usual—only paying more attention to whom he dealt with.

By the mid-1920s, the international traffic in smuggled nar-cotics was well organized and stretched all the way to Europe. A secret report compiled by the commanding officer of the Royal Canadian Mounted Police in Montreal, Quebec, in January 1924, revealed one avenue of drugs into New York. It focused on the activities of a notorious drug smuggler named George Howe who spoke to an undercover agent called "Dufresne."

"Howe has told Dufresne," said the report, "that one Rosenblatt a heavy narcotic dealer of New York City who has recently visited Montreal, has given Howe some $2000 with which to purchase narcotics in Europe."

Howe was born in Belgium but traveled on a British passport issued in Ottawa. In 1920, he oversaw the shipment of a number of statuettes purchased in Brussels, Belgium. Nine of the statuettes contained $51\frac{1}{8}$ ounces of morphine sulphate and two others $5\frac{1}{2}$ ounces of cocaine hydrochloride. They were destined for a millinery store in Quebec, but the deal went bad when the recipient—a "Madam Howe"—was arrested.

Howe was also closely connected with Laurent Deleglise, who headed a major smuggling network bringing drugs from Europe into Canada. One of his favorite methods of trafficking narcotics was described in another Canadian police report of September 1923.

> The shipper of the drugs would load up one or two trunks full of drugs and send them aboard the ship, taking tickets, he would then miss the boat and the baggage would be held unclaimed. The shipper would then arrive by another route or boat and go to some small town and wire or write for his trunks, omitting to send the keys. The Baggage man would explain the difficulty of opening the trunk to the Customs Officer who would not bother his head and pass it out, or possibly the Customs man was squared, this is not known. It is known that he was either crooked or too lax to open the trunks.

This was just one way in which narcotics flowed into Canada and on to New York in the 1920s. When Deleglise forwarded narcotics to the United States, he had them sent by express to a

Japanese store in New York—his distribution center for the city. This may well have been the source for Lucania's narcotics during this period. By the end of the decade, the market had grown enormously and it was this that attracted Lucania, Jack Diamond, and their associates to set up their own narcotics importing business based in Germany in 1930.

♠

Frank Costello was learning, like Rothstein, that life in the shadows was much more profitable than headline-making gangster antics. A Calabrian by birth, he and his family came to East Harlem and he earned an early reputation as a teenage tough guy. But as his own gang grew and developed their interests in bootlegging, he could see the real power lay in organization and fostering links with the establishment, leaving the rough stuff to the mad-eyed hoodlums. A few years older than Lucania, he would become an important elder statesman in the New York Mafia.

Other key figures also started to coalesce around Lucania and Lansky. There was Louis "Lepke" Buchalter, who worked for Rothstein first as a union enforcer and then graduated to running major labor racketeering as well as dealing in narcotics with Lucania. Then there was Vito Genovese, a coldhearted assassin who operated under Masseria's wing but recognized Lucania's potential. Willie Moretti carved out gambling and bootleg interests in Brooklyn and New Jersey, recruiting a small army of some sixty gunmen. Among the up-and-coming young killers were Joe Adonis and Albert Anastasia.

By the mid-1920s, this association of top liquor racketeers was known as the "Big Six" and was said to include Lucania, Lansky, Siegel, Lepke, Longy Zwillman, and Jacob "Gurrah" Shapiro. A later FBI report doubted whether they were ever known at the time as the Big Six, quoting a criminal informant who said that "the term 'Big Six' probably referred to the better known men controlling bootlegging in the East who had allotted territories in which they operated." This informant also stated that the groups maintained liquor headquarters at many of the leading hotels in New York City. This was true. Sometime in 1924, Charlie Lucania and Meyer Lansky leased a suite in the Claridge Hotel. That was their base, but their business stretched everywhere.

Even though he wasn't part of the Diamond gang, Lansky had impressed Lucania with his business skills and they forged their own alliance. Lansky had met Rothstein and the Big Bank-roll gave him his blessing as a trusted associate. But the mobsters who didn't like each other were the old Sicilian gangsters—led by Joe "the Boss" Masseria—and the Jews. Whenever they could, they beat up on each other. According to Lansky, an opportunity arose with the arrival of a consignment of Scotch whisky in Atlantic City. It was destined for an associate of Rothstein—Waxey Gordon—in Philadelphia and he had arranged for Joe Masseria's heavies to guard the convoy of booze.

Bugsy Siegel, Meyer's violent sidekick, got word of the deal and their gang grabbed their weapons and, wearing masks like old-time outlaws, prepared an ambush for the Italians. A tree was cut down to block the road. At 3:30 A.M., the four trucks loaded with bottles shuddered to a halt and ten of Masseria's gunmen climbed out to pull away the tree trunk. A fusillade of bullets tore into them. The mobsters that survived the gunfire quickly surrendered but were savagely beaten by the vengeful Jews, who hated the way they looked down on them.

The problem for Lansky was that one of the surviving Sicilians recognized him and reported the hijack back to Masseria. Joe the Boss wanted Lansky and Siegel dead but knew he couldn't move against them because they were close to Lucania and he valued their business alliance. Word was passed on to Waxey Gordon, who also wanted revenge for this humiliation, particularly as he owed Rothstein his slice of the business, but Gordon held his tongue, too, because Rothstein hated Masseria and didn't want Masseria knowing that he'd subcontracted his business to the Sicilians. In that way, Lansky and Siegel got away with the ambush, but it was not forgotten, and it exacerbated the vendetta between the Sicilian and Jewish mobsters.

Sometimes Lucania got caught up in the frequent ambushing of liquor deliveries. On February 9, 1927, truck driver Joseph Corbo reported to the police that he had been held up in Brooklyn by three men armed with revolvers. Their truck was loaded with sacks of grain and denatured alcohol. Corbo and his assistant were ordered into a Flint sedan and taken to Seventh Avenue and Twenty-second Street in Manhattan, where they were told to walk away. The sedan was licensed to Anthony Scalise, who was arrested for the robbery, along with Carmine Napoletano, Charles Paradiso, and John Manfredi. Lucania was associated with the Scalise family and he was arrested as a material witness. He was promptly dismissed from the case, but Scalise and the others were convicted of the armed robbery and received hefty prison sentences.

It was in 1927 that Lucania moved into the plush Barbizon-Plaza Hotel, where he rented a suite. To shield his real identity, he registered at the hotel under the Anglo-Saxon name of Charles Lane. The anonymity of hotel life suited Lucania and he stayed there on and off for several years. Sometimes hotel living provided other opportunities.

Joe Bendix was a thief who preyed on hotel guests, stealing jewelry from them. In the summer of 1928, he stole an emerald necklace and some bracelets, rings, and brooches worth a total of $50,000 from an out-of-towner at the Ritz-Carlton Hotel. Thinking of how to dispose of it, he approached Lucania. They rode around Central Park in a taxi as Lucania examined the jewelry. From there, they went down to the Jewelers Exchange on the Bowery near Canal Street, where Lucania had the stolen property appraised. A week later, he met Bendix at the Chesterfield Hotel.

"I went into one of the pay toilets there," said Bendix on oath at a later trial, "and he looked it over, looked over the things to see if they were the same things; checked up on them and turned over the money to me. He had the money in a little brown paper portfolio." Bendix claimed Lucania paid him $24,000 for the stolen emerald necklace and other pieces. Perhaps it was intended as an impressive present for one of his uptown lady friends.

♠

After the breakup of Diamond's bootleg gang, Lucania went back to working with the Sicilians as well as developing his own business with Lansky. At the same time, Rothstein was stepping away from bootlegging. Instead, he preferred to fund speakeasies and make a mockery of the law by subverting thousands of illicit liquor court cases. As Rothstein let slip his control of the underworld, Joe the Boss stepped up the activities of his Mafia family with Lucania firmly back in the crew. But even though liquor no longer linked Rothstein to Lucania, narcotics did. This business suited Rothstein's links with Europe and he invested his money in importing heroin and opium. He opened up links with Asian sources in China and British Hong Kong. The drug shipments were hidden in a string of art galleries and antique shops set up by Rothstein in Manhattan.

With the money still pouring in, Rothstein continued to gamble heavily. It was his first passion and he couldn't give it up. It cost him his longtime marriage to his wife, who eventually decided she was finished with long nights spent alone. In September 1928, he joined a high-rolling game in a friend's apartment in midtown Manhattan. Eight men sat around the table. They started first with dice, moved to stud poker, then, wanting to "speed" the gambling, went for cutting the deck with the highest spade winning. Rothstein's good luck—and gambling skill—deserted him and by the time the game ended, he was out $340,000. He threw down a bankroll of $37,000 and everyone knew he was good for the rest. But two months later, he still hadn't paid up.

On the evening of November 4, he was sipping coffee at Lindy's delicatessen and restaurant at Fiftieth Street and Broadway when at 10:45 P.M., a telephone call came through for him. He got up from his usual booth, slipped on his overcoat, and told the headwaiter, "McManus wants me over at the Park Central." McManus was one of the players he owed, and Rothstein dispatched his chauffeur waiting outside Lindy's to get some cash from his apartment.

Twenty minutes later, Rothstein was found staggering toward the service entrance of Park Central Hotel. A bellboy thought he was drunk and called the house detective. By then, Rothstein was leaning against a wall and asked them to call for a doctor. Rothstein had been shot in the groin and was rushed to the hospital for an emergency operation. Two days later, he was dead. He told no one who shot him—and in the end no one was convicted for his murder.

In the meantime, Rothstein's attorney, William Hyman, realized there were some highly incriminating financial records sitting in his deceased client's apartment. Every deal he ever made, every politician and lawman he ever paid off, every aspect of the New York underworld was carefully annotated in the pile of ledgers he kept meticulously throughout his career. "If these papers are ever made public," said Hyman, "there are going to be a lot of suicides in high places."

It was now a race between the district attorney and the Mob to see who could lay their hands on the most sensitive of these records. Charles Lucania was one of the first mobsters through the doors of Rothstein's apartment, and he grabbed the papers he wanted. It indicated the degree to which he had become involved in Rothstein's empire. He had himself to protect, as well as gathering information on his rivals. Alongside Lansky, he was ambitious to position himself as the new Rothstein, but so were many other mobsters.

Thirteen days after Rothstein's killing, Lucania was arrested alongside George Uffner, a narcotics associate of Rothstein, and

James "Fats" Walsh, his bodyguard. Bizarrely, they were accused of a payroll robbery near Central Park on October 5, 1928, in which two men got away with $8,374. In truth, it was just a way for the police to question the three men informally about what they knew of the Rothstein murder. When witnesses to the robbery failed to identify the prisoners, they were discharged.

The ripples caused by Rothstein's death spread out like an earthquake. Documents from his desk were leaked to shame the ruling political and police administrations. In the following years, a thorough investigation was carried out into the magistrates courts of New York, and new lawmen were brought in to sweep away the old corrupted system. Among them was a young special prosecutor called Thomas E. Dewey, who would in due course become nemesis to Charles Lucania.

Rothstein's death left a gap in the New York underworld that the Sicilian Mafia rushed to fill. In truth, Rothstein's decline in real power had already allowed them in, but his removal certainly left the question open as to who could replace him—an uncertainty that would provoke rival gang leaders into outright warfare. The outcome of this vicious conflict would determine whether Lucania had the cunning and the brutality to become the new boss of bosses.

SURVIVING THE RIDE

In 1925, an elegantly dressed man stepped off a ship arriving in New York from Palermo in Sicily. Tall for a Sicilian at five feet nine inches, Salvatore Maranzano was powerfully built. At thirty-nine years old, he was in the prime of his life. Well educated, he spoke Latin and liked to use elaborate and poetic vocabulary. He had trained to be a priest. One young hoodlum, himself recently arrived in America, was very impressed by him. "He dressed like a conservative businessman," recalled Joseph Bonanno, "preferring gray or blue suits, soft pinstripes on the blues. He didn't wear any jewellery other than a watch and his wedding band." Bonanno was twenty-one years old and ready to be led by such a man. "His voice had an entrancing echolike quality. When Maranzano used his voice assertively, to give a command, he was the bellknocker and you were the bell."

He was the direct antithesis of Joe "the Boss" Masseria—even those who worked closely with him regarded him as a peasant, a pig, in his manners. Within three years, Maranzano and Masseria would be at war with each other—and Charles Lucania would gain most from their bitter struggle.

There were several reasons why Maranzano arrived in New York in the mid-twenties. In Sicily, the Fascists were in power and Benito Mussolini had vowed to eradicate the Mafia. The Italians could not have two masters, he declared, and the criminal families had to be brought to heel. His chief prosecutor, Cesare Mori, jailed hundreds of mafiosi and hounded them remorselessly. As well as Maranzano, Joseph Bonanno fled the island after he refused to don their black shirt and join the Fascist party.

But there was another stronger reason why Maranzano came to America—the smell of money. Stories of the fortunes to be made from Prohibition had flowed back to the old country and Maranzano was an accomplished operator. He came with the blessing of Don Vito Cascio Ferro—the boss of bosses in Palermo who had mercilessly shot down an American detective in a park when he came to investigate the links between American and Sicilian organized crime.

Maranzano was respected and had close links already with several established mobsters in the United States. They all came from the seaside town of Castellammare del Golfo, a few miles to the west of Palermo. A little fishing port dominated by the remains of a castle, it was the birthplace of Stefano Magaddino, Gaspar Milazzo, Joe Aiello, and Joseph Bonanno. "The Castellammarese tended to stick together," said Bonanno. "We had our own distinct neighborhoods, not only in Brooklyn and Manhattan, but also in Detroit, Buffalo and Endicott, New York. Not only did we all know each other, but were often related to one another." It was a ready-formed Mafia family.

Using his natural authority and charm, Maranzano carved a niche for himself in the bootlegging business, seeking slowly but surely to attract key mobsters away from Joe the Boss. He approached Lucania, but even though the Lower East

Sider recognized his sophistication, he resented his old country manners. He didn't want to bend the knee and kiss the ring on the don's finger. Also, like Masseria, Maranzano hated the Jewish gangsters who formed an essential part of his crew. Lansky warned Lucania against getting too close to either of the Sicilians.

"Once you accept such an offer," he told him, "you'll find yourself under their total control. Neither will hesitate to kill you the minute he thinks you've stepped out of line. Each of these guys wants to maintain his own empires and squeeze the life out of the other. You're the pawn in their game. Only it isn't a game. Our lives are at stake."

Lansky's strong-arm man, Bugsy Siegel, wanted to take on the Sicilians and wipe them out, but Lucania and Lansky decided to play the long game. Taking their cue from the master— Arnold Rothstein—they wanted to assert their power by making money and buying influence. "Shooting and killing was an inefficient way of doing business," said Lansky. But no one told that to the Sicilian bosses. Was Lucania, in fact, an early victim of the conflict between Maranzano and Masseria?

♠

Underworld legend has it that on October 17, 1929, Charles Lucania was found stumbling along Hylan Boulevard in Staten Island at 1:00 A.M., his face a bloody mess, his eyes so swollen he could barely see out of them, his neck and throat slashed. He'd been taken on a one-way ride in the back of a car, thoroughly beaten, and left for dead in a wooded field. When he regained consciousness—he couldn't believe he was still alive—he just wanted to get back to Manhattan. The first person he saw, he barked at to get him a taxi. The man was a patrolman and took him to the 123rd Precinct station, where a surgeon from the Richmond Memorial Hospital treated his wounds.

Realizing they had a top mobster in their custody, the police swarmed around him, asking him questions. Lucania said he had been abducted by several men he didn't know as he stood at Fiftieth Street and Third Avenue. They had put handcuffs on him, dragged him into a car, and when they finished with him threw him into a field. He said he believed it had all happened in New Jersey—he didn't know it was Staten Island. Beyond that, he wouldn't give any more information and told Detective Gustave Schley to "forget about it." He didn't want the police to take any further action—he would take care of it himself.

But the police weren't buying it and believed the whole situation was too suspicious to leave alone. Lucania was charged with grand larceny of an automobile pursuant to a police alarm on October 16. He was arraigned on October 17 and released on bail of $25,000 two days later. In the meantime, he was taken to Richmond Memorial Hospital for further treatment.

Detectives visited the location where he had been found—eight hundred feet from the Terra Marine Inn—and when they searched the ground about ten feet from the road, they found small pieces of adhesive tape and a bandage saturated with blood. Witnesses who had been on the corner of Fiftieth and Third at the time of the abduction were questioned, but no one knew anything. Lucania had $300 in cash on him and a watch and chain worth $400, neither of which was stolen from him—so it was not a simple mugging.

Twelve days after the ride, Lucania appeared before a grand jury at Richmond County Court House, St. George, on Staten Island. As he stood up in court to give his testimony, he gave his name as Charles Lucciano—two "c"s noted in the court transcript—possibly the first official record of his now familiar name.

For the last four years, he said, he had lived at a house in Ardonia, Ulster County, the northernmost county of the New York metropolitan area. He was not married and lived alone. When he was not living in Ulster County, he said he stayed with his parents at 265 East Tenth Street. His main business was a restaurant he owned at 232 West Fifty-second Street, but he had sold that eight months previously and was living on the money. He was currently occupied as a private chauffeur and owned a Lincoln 1928 model automobile, but he had no taxi license and could not give the names of anyone he had driven. Richmond County District Attorney Albert Fach then noted the scars on the mobster's neck.

"How did you receive those?"

"I really don't know how I received them," said Luciano, "because the time I was picked up by the men in the car I was knocked out and that's all I remember until I woke up in the woods on Staten Island."

Four men picked him up at 6:30 P.M., while he was waiting to meet a date he called Jennie. They claimed they were police officers. One put handcuffs on him and pulled him into their car. Once inside, they started kicking and punching him.

"One of the men then put a handkerchief over me and hit me and that's all I know," said Luciano.

At some stage, they stuck adhesive tape over his face. Beyond that, Luciano could give no further information. DA Fach then tried to paint a picture of Luciano's criminal life.

"Have you ever been known by any other name?"

"Lucky."

"Anything else?"

"That's all."

"Was that the family name or a combination of the Charles and your last name?"

"Charles Lucky," said the mobster, not quite answering the question.

Fach then listed some of Luciano's previous criminal charges, including felonious assault. Luciano denied everything.

"You realize you are under oath?" said the DA.

"I suppose you have the record of arrests I was under and I couldn't tell you if I remembered them all."

Exasperated, Fach tried to relate some of Luciano's past activities to the abduction and beating.

"You have enemies?"

"Not that I know of."

"Make any in the drug business?"

"None at all."

"Engage in liquor traffic?"

"No."

"Sure about that?"

"Yes."

"Never been charged with violation of the Prohibition Act?"

"No."

Getting nowhere fast, Fach returned to the central mystery
of the attack on the gangster.

"What is it all about?"

"I don't know," Luciano said, shrugging. "I haven't the least
idea. If I did, I wouldn't have been in that car or found in the
woods."

"Did you ever have such an experience before?"

"Never."

Luciano denied ever saying he would take care of the perpetrators of the assault and with that, he was dismissed and
released from custody. Shortly afterward, Ulster County authorities sought to revoke a pistol permit they had issued to him, but
he denied ever having a permit and had no revolver. Ever helpful, Luciano promised to check in with the authorities when he
next went home upstate.

Rumors ran wild that Luciano was the victim of a gang war,
and when the so-called confessions of *The Last Testament of
Lucky Luciano* came out forty-five years later, it seemed to con-
firm this. In that account, Vito Genovese is supposed to have
picked him up on the Manhattan street corner on the seven-
teenth and driven him to Staten Island, where he was met by
Maranzano. The Castellammarese boss told Luciano that he

wanted him to kill Masseria. Luciano refused and the next thing he knew he was hanging up by his wrists from a beam. Men masked with handkerchiefs used their fists, clubs, and belts to beat him, burning him with cigarette stubs. Meyer Lansky, in his recollections, *Mogul of the Mob*, backs up this version and also links it to the Castellammarese feud with Masseria. He reasoned that Maranzano wanted to threaten Luciano into doing his dirty work for him because he was so close to Masseria and could get around his security.

When Lansky visited the battered Luciano, it was the opportunity to dub him with his famous nickname. "From now on we're going to call you 'Lucky,'" said Lansky, "because you ought to be dead."

In the light of seeing the actual court transcript of Luciano's statement just two weeks after the ride, this all now seems nonsense. Luciano was already known as Lucky and was happy to use the name, unlike other accounts, which claimed that no one dared used it in his presence. In fact, a *New York Times* article described him as "Charles (Lucky) Luciania" in their report just the day after the event.

The more fanciful story of torture by Maranzano also unravels as other mobsters who knew Luciano closely told a different tale in later years. First, there is the obvious flaw that a beating delivered by Maranzano's men to a mobster with a reputation like Luciano would achieve the very opposite of what they wanted—it would turn Luciano into Maranzano's undying enemy. In which case, once the humiliation had been inflicted, it would have been better to finish him off, as the Sicilian would get his revenge one way or another—and Maranzano, being of the old school, would have known that very well.

It was Luciano's longtime associate Frank Costello who gave the most convincing inside account of that night to his attorney. He said that Luciano was picked up by several men in the back of a car and driven to Staten Island. They were not mobsters but cops. Costello said they wanted Luciano to tell them where Jack "Legs" Diamond was because he had disappeared after committing a murder in his Hotsy Totsy Club.

Luciano wouldn't tell the police and he was punished with a beating that consisted of his head being stomped on and boots ground into his face. According to Costello, there was no knife slashing or use of ice picks or hanging from rafters. It was a police interrogation with force. The irony of the situation was not lost on Costello, who said that Luciano "almost got himself killed on Staten Island just to protect a jerk he didn't even like." That isn't exactly true, as Luciano liked Diamond enough to let him stay at his house in the country, often when he was on the run.

Costello's version is backed up by Sal Vizzini, an undercover narcotics agent who talked to Luciano about the incident in 1960. Fifteen years before Luciano's so-called memoirs appeared, Vizzini said that Luciano told him that he was picked up outside his house by plainclothes police. He was pushed down on the backseat of the car and tape was stuck over his eyes and mouth. Luciano believed he was on a car ferry to New Jersey and kicked out the side windows of the car to attract attention, but no one responded, except one of the cops in the car who worked him over.

"One of them was pounding me in the face," recalled Luciano. "He must have had on a big ring or something because he busted my lip under the tape and cut my chin open and ripped my throat. I could feel blood all over me and I kinda passed out."

That was how he got his scars. After the ferry trip, the car stopped and Luciano was pushed out onto some rough ground. The police ripped the tape off his mouth and one of them held a gun against his head.

"The guy who did all the talkin' says I better tell now where they can find Legs [Diamond] or they're gonna blow my damned brains out. I tell him he'd better get to it then because I got no goddamned idea where he is."

Knowing the men weren't mobsters, Luciano gambled they weren't going to kill him. He said nothing and the police tired of the beating, leaving him in the muddy field. As he staggered away from the field, he was picked up by the local police and ended up in hospital surrounded by reporters. "The upshot is that the papers had all the garbage about how lucky I was to get away," Luciano told Vizzini. "I guess that's how it got to be Lucky Luciano. I still don't like it."

In the wake of Luciano's 1929 testimony at Richmond County Court, this last statement is unconvincing—as he volunteered the name "Charles Lucky"—but the rest of the story seems the best account there is of the incident. The beating was nothing to do with the Castellammarese at all, but the encounter did leave Luciano with the scars that made him look like a gangster.

It also brought him into the public eye—and that was a big mistake as far he was concerned. As soon as he entered the public arena, he became an irritant to the authorities and that meant they'd never give up on him until he was behind bars.

Curiously, it may have been Luciano's own fault that he was grabbed by the police searching for Diamond. Just seven months before the ride, he was in Ardonia on Good Friday enjoying some hunting with friends. They were shooting pheasants, but it was closed season for the birds and he was in violation of the local conservation laws. When state game protector Ed Nolan came to arrest Luciano at his upstate home, he was accompanied by the state trooper in charge of the district, who noted that Jack Diamond was staying at the house with Luciano.

That Diamond regularly stayed with him in the country was indicated by a story later told by Luciano in which Diamond tested out a machine gun on one his prized fig trees, shooting it to pieces. Luciano was furious with the trigger-happy mobster and told him to practice shooting at the brick wall behind the house. That the police would come calling on Luciano while hunting down the murderer Diamond was not exactly surprising.

Luciano, incidentally, was fined $50 on March 31, 1929, for shooting a pheasant out of season—the only killing he was ever successfully prosecuted for.

War of the Sicilian Bosses

The Castellammarese War began at a low level with rival Sicilian gangsters hijacking each other's convoys of illicit booze. Castellammarese gunmen shot it out with Joe "the Boss" Masseria's soldiers. "We carried pistols, shotguns, machine guns and enough ammunition to fight the Battle of Bull Run all over again," said Bonanno.

Sicilian-born New York mafioso Nick Gentile blamed the war on "Joe the Boss." "The actions of the administration of Masseria were imposed in dictatorial and exasperating commands which did not allow reply," said Gentile in his typically elaborate Italian. "They used to govern through fear."

Masseria had links with Al Capone in Chicago and encouraged him to make a move against Joe Aiello, one of the leading Castellammaresi in that city. Elsewhere, Masseria tried to split away Detroit gang leader Gaspare Milazzo, another key Castellammarese figure. The plan was to drain Maranzano of his network of support throughout the United States and isolate him so Masseria could finish him off on the streets of New York. In May 1930, this culminated in Milazzo being shot dead in a Detroit fish market. In response, Maranzano called a war council of his followers in Brooklyn.

"It's a dirty spot on the honor of Castellammare," he told the assembled mobsters. "It was as if he were sounding our battle cry," said Bonanno. Maranzano dominated the meeting and even though other senior members of the crime family wanted to quiet down the affair so they could carry on with their business, the well-groomed Sicilian took them to war against Masseria in New York. Even Stefano Magaddino in Buffalo, the elder statesman of the clan, granted him permission to become their warlord.

Maranzano had two Cadillacs fitted with armor plating and bulletproof windows and these formed the core of his convoy as he patrolled his fiefdom. "Maranzano would sit in the back seat of his car with a machine gun mounted on a swivel between his legs," said Bonanno. "He also packed a Luger and a Colt, as well as his omnipresent dagger behind his back."

On August 15, 1930, Maranzano struck back at the very top of Masseria's organization. Peter "the Clutch" Morello was so called because of his maimed right hand, on which only the little finger remained. Born in Corleone, his brothers had grown rich out of muscling in on legitimate immigrant businesses. His half brother Ciro was known as the "Artichoke King," because of his domination of the vegetable racket, and Peter controlled the Bronx building racket. With his droopy mustache, he was a classic old-style Sicilian, dubbed a "Mustache Pete," and had become a valued adviser to Joe the Boss. At 3:50 P.M. on the fifteenth, the sixty-year-old Morello was sitting in a sparsely decorated office on the second floor above the Sassone Realty Company on East 116th Street. Across a table from him was twenty-six-year-old Joseph Perrano, who was looking forward to going back to Italy the next day, and a third associate called Gaspar Pollaro.

There was a loud rap on the office door, and Morello opened it a crack to see who it was. Two men armed with pistols pushed their way into the room. They aimed point-blank at the Clutch and nailed him with five bullets, one through the forehead. The other two men sat motionless before they realized the gunmen could not leave any witnesses and the gunmen turned on them. Two shots hit Perrano as he jumped through the second-floor window, crashing to his death on the sidewalk below. Pollaro was shot once and seriously wounded.

Twenty minutes later, farther along the same street in a building housing the Harlem Casino, there was another hit. Benjamin Prince, a gambler and narcotics dealer, was just about to enter a Hungarian restaurant when he was called to the telephone in the barbershop on the floor below. As he turned around, an assassin hidden in the corridor washroom stepped out and executed him with a shot to the forehead. It looked like a day for clearing up unfinished business.

As a crowd gathered outside the Morello headquarters, the police asked for witnesses, and a little boy handed them a black book he had picked up off the street. The book contained more than fifty names with large sums of money written next to each one. It seem likely that one of the two assassins had taken it from Morello but dropped it as he ran to the getaway car waiting for them.

The Morello killing was a very high-profile blow against Joe the Boss, and several rival mobsters later claimed responsibility for it. Bonanno says Maranzano was behind it, while the government informer Joseph Valachi, a minor Maranzano gang member at the time, says it was a fresh-faced gunman hired from Chicago known only as Buster. Buster had supposedly told Valachi the detail that Morello just wouldn't go down when he shot him and he had to chase him around the office with four more shots before he finished the job. It has since been suggested that Valachi made up the killer "Buster from Chicago" to cover his own role in murders ascribed to him, although other sources have identified Buster as the professional killer Sebastiano Domingo.

In *The Last Testament of Lucky Luciano*, it is claimed that Luciano ordered the killing of Morello and it was his gunmen, Albert Anastasia and Frank Scalise, who shot him. This contradicts Valachi's testimony and doesn't make sense. Why would Luciano bother doing this when the Castellammaresi were on a war footing anyway? In *Mogul of the Mob*, Lansky also claims it was Anastasia and Scalise, but this clashes with his own stated intention of letting the Sicilians shoot themselves to pieces without getting involved. Yet again, this casts doubt on certain aspects of *Mogul of the Mob*, first published in 1979, which tries too hard to accord with the *Last Testament*, which appeared four years earlier

Regardless of who was behind it, Masseria was furious and blamed Maranzano. He put word through to Al Capone to shoot Joe Aiello, his major Castellammarese rival in Chicago. In October, Aiello was struck by fifty-nine slugs from two Thompson machine guns and a sawed-off shotgun. As the bodies stacked up on both sides, Luciano and Lansky stayed out of the war until the end of the conflict approached. In fact, Luciano was so keen to stay out of the firing line that it was in late August 1930 that he accompanied Jack Diamond on the transatlantic trip to Weimar Germany to set up their drug-importing business.

The high-profile deaths of gangsters and innocent citizens caught in the crossfire were attracting too much attention from the authorities and those not directly involved wanted an end to it. Nick Gentile, in his chronicle of the Castellammarese War, says he was visited by a lieutenant of Al Capone who asked him to exert his influence on Maranzano. Otherwise the Chicago Mob would wage their own war against him. "We will employ even airplanes!" he was warned.

Gentile took the suggestion and later had a meeting with the Castellammarese leader. "We were brought in the presence of Maranzano who appeared in all his majesty: with two pistols stuck in his waist and encircled by about ninety boys, who were also armed to the teeth. I had the impression that I found myself in the presence of 'Pancho Villa.'"

Maranzano talked at length to Gentile and tried to convince him that Masseria was at fault. "Masseria has always been our enemy," argued one of Gentile's associates, "to end this war it is necessary that Mangano should kill Masseria being that he has unlimited trust in him." He was referring to Vincent Mangano, who was part of the Brooklyn Al Mineo crime family, closely linked with Masseria, and including a young Albert Anastasia. Other members of Masseria's army had to be convinced, however, and that included Luciano.

♠

On February 2, 1931, Charles Luciano was arrested for felonious assault. Police file photographs were taken of him and on the reverse of one of them his name was given as Charles Lucania "Lucky," with another Anglo-Saxon alias of "Charles Reed." He gave his address as 265 East Tenth Street. His height was recorded as 5 feet 9¾ inches, his build Mediterranean, his eyes brown, his complexion dark, his hair "blond," but presumably this is a mistake or some form of police humor, as his hair was clearly black. His occupation was logged as chauffeur. Shortly after he was released, Maranzano approached Luciano with an offer too good to ignore.

The Castellammarese War was bad for business and Maranzano let it be known that the best way to end the fighting was for someone to knock off Masseria. Once that had been completed, he vowed, he would not take vengeance on any of Masseria's gang. It was a tempting solution and Luciano visited him in March 1931 to discuss it further. Joseph Bonanno was at the meeting and said it was his first opportunity to see the man he had heard so much about.

"He was a thin man with a full head of black hair and a scarred and pockmarked face," he recalled. "He walked obliquely, lurching slightly to the side. His Sicilian was scant, but what words he knew he spoke well. He usually expressed himself in American street slang. But he was not a big talker; he liked to get to the point without any flourishes."

They met at a private house in Brooklyn and Luciano was accompanied by Vito Genovese. The two chief mobsters spoke briefly and without naming Masseria.

"Do you know why you are here?" asked Maranzano.

Luciano nodded.

"Then I don't have to tell you what has to be done."

Luciano said he would organize it over the next two weeks and would personally take charge of it.

"Good," said Maranzano, "I'm looking forward to a peaceful Easter."

In bright midday sunshine on April 15, 1931, Joe the Boss drove his steel-armored sedan with inch-thick bulletproof windows to Coney Island for lunch with Charlie Luciano and two associates known to both of them. They were meeting at Nuovo Villa Tammaro, a newly built two-story restaurant at 2715 West Fifteenth Street, where the owner's mother-in-law, Anna Tammaro, cooked excellent Italian seafood. Masseria liked his food and was anticipating a friendly chat about business. He arrived shortly after 1:00 P.M. and ordered spaghetti with red clam sauce and lobster, all washed down with some Tuscan red wine. Luciano picked at his food and marveled at Masseria's huge appetite; he touched little of the wine. After the meal, Luciano suggested all four men play some cards, but first he had to go to the restroom.

"At 2 o'clock the quiet of the little street near the bay was broken by the roar of gunfire," said a newspaper report. "Two or three men walked out of the restaurant to an automobile parked at the curb and drove away. When the police got there they found Mrs. Tammaro bending over the body of Joe the Boss. He lay on his back. In his left hand was clutched a brand new ace of diamonds."

The card was an invented embellishment, based on the fact that a deck of cards was scattered over the floor of the restaurant. On the table were several banknotes and a small amount of silver—about $35 in all. An autopsy showed that Masseria was shot three times in the back and twice in the neck and face, just above the eye, as he turned around to see his killers.

Legend has it that Luciano remained at the scene when the police arrived, looking bewildered. He'd gone for a "long leak" and the next thing he knew his lunch guest was sprawled across the floor dead. He'd seen nothing and neither had the restaurant owner who'd gone out for a long walk. Anna Tammaro had been in the kitchen and not surprisingly the dining room was empty of customers. In truth, none of the contemporary news reports mention Luciano being there, so most likely he left with the assassins.

Four hours later, the getaway car was found abandoned at West First Street in Brooklyn. Three pistols were recovered from the backseat, one fully loaded. Two more pistols were found in the alley alongside the restaurant. In total, four guns had been used. Three abandoned hats and coats were found in the restaurant, presumably belonging to the killers. They all came from Brooklyn shops.

The whole lunch had been a setup. When Luciano glanced at his watch and left the table—more likely 3:30 P.M. than the 2:00 P.M. reported—that was the signal for the gunmen parked across the road. Two of Luciano's top hit men walked into the restaurant and let loose a storm of shots alongside two other mobsters already inside. The assassins are said to have been Bugsy Siegel, Vito Genovese, Albert Anastasia, and Joe Adonis. Five bullets entered Masseria's body as he dragged the tablecloth with him to the ground. That four key gangsters had been chosen for this job meant that no one gunman could be hunted down. If any of Masseria's crew wanted vengeance they'd have to come after all of them. It was a clear signal from Luciano to the underworld—this was an end to the fighting.

Luciano was happy to take personal responsibility for the killing of Joe the Boss because he was not merely carrying out a task for Maranzano. Nick Gentile was at Luciano's home when he heard him make this declaration to a fellow mafioso.

"Tell your *compare*, Maranzano, we have killed Masseria, not to serve him but for our own personal reasons. Tell him besides that if he should touch even a hair of even a personal enemy of ours, we will wage war to the end."

It was a straight challenge to the wily old Sicilian, but for the moment he chose to ignore it and there were celebrations among the Castellammaresi. They had won the war. Maranzano marked his victory by calling a meeting of all his Mafia family henchmen—some five hundred in all—in a big hall in the Bronx. Such a public display violated everything Luciano had learned from Rothstein about keeping in the shadows and did not bode well for the reign of the Castellammarese clan. But Maranzano wanted everyone to know about his victory, and he strutted before his gangster minions like a politician. The room was hung with Christian icons and a massive crucifix hung over the end of the hall where Maranzano sat. If any unwelcome visitor entered, they were supposed to think it was a religious meeting.

Maranzano had a grand vision for organized crime in New York and he wanted to lay it out so everyone knew where they stood. Joseph Valachi was witness to it.

"I didn't know until later that he was a nut about Julius Caesar," said Valachi, "and even had a room in his house full of nothing but books about him. That's where he got the idea of the new organization."

Maranzano addressed the hall in Italian and declared himself *Capo di tutti Capi*—"Boss of all Bosses." From now on, every one of New York's major Sicilian gangs would be organized into five families. Each family or *borgata* would be headed by a boss with an underboss. They would be advised by a *consigliere*. Beneath them were ranked lieutenants and they would command the ordinary gunmen known as "soldiers."

The bosses of the five recognized families were Charlie Luciano, taking over from Masseria, Joseph Bonanno, Joseph Profaci, Tom Gagliano, and Vincent Mangano. Vito Genovese was named as Luciano's underboss.

"Whatever happened in the past is over," said Maranzano. "There is to be no more ill feeling among us. If you lost someone in the past war of ours, you must forgive and forget. If your own brother was killed, don't try to find out who did it to get even. If you do, you pay with your life."

Maranzano's rules stated that no member of a family could touch a member of another family without first clearing it at a meeting of the heads of the families. Senior members of the Cosa Nostra—"our thing"—were untouchable.

A separate celebration was organized by Maranzano on August 1, 1931, at the same Coney Island restaurant where Masseria was killed. It turned into a three-day banquet to which all the top mafiosi from around the country were invited.

"On a costly and sumptuously decorated immense table towered a majestic tray," recalled Nick Gentile, "in which, those who came, placed handfuls of dollars. A group of high-spirited boys provided to receive guests greeted them with 'Long live our Capo' and conducted the guests to the tray, watching the offering. Many of them, trying to look like noblemen, did not make offerings of less than $500. On that night, Maranzano picked up $100,000."

Gentile was careful to listen to Marazano's conversation to a fellow Mob chief. "This victory has intoxicated me," said Maranzano. "I feel like I am in a ball of fire. I wish I were going to Germany to be more secure."

It was an odd statement to make—only fully explained by later revelations. Gentile interpreted it as a sign of weakness from someone positioning himself as capo over everyone else. At the end of the feast, the donated sum of $100,000 was supposed to have been distributed to relatives of victims of the gang war, but Maranzano pocketed it all.

As far as Luciano was concerned, the assassination of Masseria had been very good for him. It placed him among the top six gangsters in New York, but having risen so high in organized crime, he was very tempted to press on and eliminate Maranzano to become boss of bosses. The momentum that had begun with the killing of Masseria was hard to stop. Maranzano might be good at speeches, but it was Luciano's gunmen who ended Masseria's rule. The setup was too attractive—just one more slaying and Luciano would be top of the pile.

On a personal level, Luciano had never liked the posturing Maranzano. He was too imperious and had brought old-world manners to New York City. Among these was a Sicilian prejudice against Jews. Lansky had warned Luciano of this attitude, and when Maranzano invited Luciano to accompany him on a trip to visit Al Capone in Chicago to explain the new regime, Luciano asked him if Lansky could come along, too.

"All right," said Maranzano, "but he can't be in the room with us when we meet."

This profoundly irritated Luciano. Not only was Lansky an old friend from the Lower East Side, but he was also a much valued criminal ally and financial partner. There was no room for this nonsense in Luciano's modern world of crime.

This personal animosity was not lost on Maranzano, who revealed his own anxiety to Valachi.

"I can't get along with those guys," he said of Luciano and Genovese. "We got to get rid of them before we can control anything."

He also added Frank Costello, Willie Moretti, Joe Adonis, Dutch Schultz, even Al Capone, to his list of undesirables.

Word of this hit list got to Luciano, and he prepared his response with a degree of irony. If Maranzano so undervalued the importance of Jewish gangsters, then it was they who could deal with him. Luciano recruited a crew of Jewish gunmen from out of town led by Samuel "Red" Levine. An observant Jew from Toledo, Ohio, Levine saw no conflict between his faith and his job, and if he had to carry out a hit on the Sabbath he would simply wear a yarmulke under his hat.

In the meantime, says Gentile, whenever Luciano visited Maranzano he always made sure he was accompanied by five bodyguards, and if Maranzano asked him for his home address, Luciano said he did not have a permanent residence.

While Lansky oversaw the instruction of Levine and his team in the Bronx, Maranzano also went outside the Sicilian community to hire an Irish gunman—Vincent "Mad Dog" Coll. When Luciano and Genovese got the call to see Maranzano at his smart new office suite above Grand Central Station at 270 Park Avenue in September 1931, Luciano activated his own assassination plot.

Just after lunch, on September 10, four men arrived at Maranzano's office and identified themselves as Internal Revenue Service agents. Maranzano had been having trouble with his tax records, and Tommy Lucchese, an associate of both Maranzano and Luciano, had passed this information on to Luciano. Expecting a call from the IRS, Maranzano's bodyguards let in the men. The guards were unarmed because their boss had told them to leave their guns at home in case of just such a surprise audit. It was a fatal mistake.

"When I arrived at the Park Avenue office," said gang member James Alascia, "I found Maranzano and others lined up with their faces against the wall. I was told to face the wall."

Maranzano was asked to step into an office by himself, which he did, still considering the men to be IRS agents. With the door closed behind them, Levine and a second hit man pulled out knives to kill him quietly, but Maranzano was strong for his age and fought back. Alongside six stab wounds, the Jewish assassins had to shoot him four times before he fell. They then cut his throat to make sure he was dead.

A stenographer who worked for Maranzano told a slightly different story to the police. She was in the office suite at the time and said she saw three men pin him against the wall—"one of the trio slashed him with knife. Then the three backed away and fired five shots at him."

The assassins left the building with no one daring to stop them. A little later the same day, Vincent Coll arrived at the Park Avenue offices to see Maranzano but was told he was dead. He shrugged his shoulders and quickly departed, keeping the cash advance he had been given to kill Luciano. Five months later, Coll was shot dead by Bugsy Siegel in a telephone booth.

In the subsequent police investigation, it was discovered that a main source of Maranzano's wealth was not the usual business of the Mafia but the smuggling of illegal immigrants into the country on a massive scale. The majority of documents in his Park Avenue office revealed a ring of corrupt officials and human traffickers that led all the way to Germany—finally explaining his earlier statement about feeling safer in that country. Several associated gangsters were arrested there. They were responsible for easing the entry of eight thousand illegal aliens into the United States at a total price of $20,000,000. It was a staggering sum and with this money Maranzano had been able to bribe judges and immigration officials in Washington as well as provide counterfeit documents.

Alongside Luciano's transatlantic drug network, this people-trafficking business was an indication of the global stretch of organized crime in New York in the early 1930s. The pot of gold available to ambitious mobsters was growing by the day. It also put the lie to the perception that Maranzano was an old-fashioned gangster. His many rackets were a vast and sophisticated operation. In the end, it just came down to a face-off between two distinctly different criminal characters.

Even Joseph Bonanno, who had been so impressed by Maranzano when he first arrived in America, agreed that his personal attitude did not suit New York in 1931. "Maranzano represented a style that often clashed with that of the Americanized men who surrounded him," said Bonanno, who shortly after the man's death made his own peace with Luciano.

The night after Maranzano's death, according to Mafia legend, several gangsters closely associated with him were also slaughtered. This has subsequently been dubbed "The Night of the Sicilian Vespers," after a notorious massacre in medieval Sicily. Although the number of killings has been estimated at forty, just a handful of murders have been actually identified, and it appears that few underlings had to be eliminated to ensure peace. Maranzano's henchmen were more than happy to escape death and join the enterprise of their new boss, and that included gunmen like Joe Valachi.

It was Nick Gentile who claimed to have devised what should happen next to avoid any further bloodshed among the Italian Mob. Instead of conferring the title of boss of bosses on one man, "who might become inflated with importance and therefore commit unjustified atrocities," he recommended the setting up of a commission of seven top mafiosi. These included the heads of the Five Families—Luciano, Mangano, Profaci, Bonanno, and Gagliano—plus Capone in Chicago and Ciccio Milano of Cleveland.

"With the administration of the Commission," said Gentile, "a more confident air was breathed. Peace returned and everybody could peacefully perform their individual labors. Everybody remained satisfied because justice had been done. The administration or governing body, so composed, gave assurances of confidence because each person was able to turn to them without being coerced as to their own ideas and free to be able to ask for their proper rights."

It all sounded like the League of Nations, but Luciano was not that interested in such lofty ideals. He always hated the pretensions of the traditional Sicilian mafiosi and was more interested in exploiting his business connections among the wider underworld community.

The Castellammarese War and Luciano's triumph is usually portrayed as the victory of a modernizing American Mob over the Mustache Petes. Yet many of the traditional Sicilian mafiosi, such as Bonanno and Profaci, remained in charge of their families for decades afterward. Luciano had not and did not seek to remove all these old-style Sicilian mafiosi from New York. He simply wished to stop them interfering with his own criminal enterprises. In that he succeeded spectacularly. No one would mess with Luciano for the next five years. He was in his thirties and it was time for him to enjoy his success.

As for Nick Gentile, he was cut out of the new order, ending up as a narcotics smuggler.

"The men of importance of the Mafia, old foxes of New York," he lamented, "had monopolized and cornered the positions that were most profitable. These men had forgotten me, whom they had used to resolve many risky situations, and risking my life especially during the struggle against Maranzano, during which I had played an important role and for which I was threatened with death many times . . . Oh ingratitude of humanity!"

That was just the kind of flamboyant Sicilian statement that irritated Luciano.

TOP OF THE PILE

Charlie Luciano was a multimillionaire, but unlike his teenage friend Al Capone, he chose not to live in a palatial mansion protected by an army of bodyguards. He preferred the luxurious anonymity of plush hotels. In the early 1930s, Luciano lived first at the Barbizon-Plaza and then at the Waldorf Towers, part of the Waldorf-Astoria. Possibly the finest hotel in the world at that time, the new Waldorf-Astoria was the height of luxury living and was the tallest and largest hotel in the country. Replacing the old Belle Epoch building—which had been demolished to make way for the Empire State Building—the hotel opened at 301 Park Avenue in October 1931. When the Waldorf-Astoria first opened its doors, President Herbert Hoover delivered the welcome address. Its interiors included entire rooms taken from English country houses and refashioned into private clubs and dining suites. The Starlight Roof supper club had a retractable roof so you could dance under the stars, while the grand ballroom was the only four-story dance floor in the city—but it was the modernity of its Art Deco interiors that marked it as something extra special.

When Luciano stepped out from suite 39C in the Waldorf Towers, he would descend to the ground floor of the Waldorf-Astoria in a wood-paneled elevator fronted with nickel-plated doors portraying ancient Greek muses. He then strolled across a golden yellow Wheel of Life mosaic floor, past palm trees and giant silver urns, into the Park Avenue lobby adorned with French neoclassical murals portraying heroic men hunting animals and hauling in fish. It was a long way from the tenement blocks of the Lower East Side.

Sometimes, however, rich hotel living bored Luciano and he yearned for simpler pleasures, like home cooking. Peter Ross was in charge of room service at the Barbizon-Plaza between 1934 and 1935 and on one occasion noted that Luciano had ordered a table, dishes, and silverware to be sent to his room but, unusually, no food. Puzzled and wanting to ensure first-class service for his guest, Ross knocked on the door of the room. When Luciano answered, the two spoke in Italian, as Ross was a Florentine Jew. As he stepped in the room, he could see Luciano was entertaining two friends and in the middle of the table was a large dish of Italian spaghetti. Luciano explained that the pasta had been brought over by one of his guests, whose mother had cooked it in Brooklyn for them.

The anonymity of living in hotels suited Luciano very well, especially as he gave alias names when he registered with them. It protected him from rival gangsters, he said. Whenever he was arrested, he invariably gave his home address as that of his parents living at 265 East Tenth Street. Luciano claimed to have lived there after he left school at the age of fourteen, so from about 1912 onward. His parents lived there until 1933, and this address is the only one that can truly be connected with him as a family home. The five-story tenement building still stands today, painted green on street level and redbrick above. A police investigator visited it in 1935 and spoke to the superintendent of the building, who said that the Lucania family had lived there for some time prior to 1933. The superintendent had never seen Charlie Luciano but regularly saw his mother and father, Rose and Antonio, and a girl, presumably his sister. They lived in apartment five, paying from $24 to $30 a month rent.

In 1933, the Lucania family moved to a more modern apartment, 205 East Tenth Street, where Luciano's younger brother, Bartolo, signed a lease for them at $960 rent per year. The superintendent there said he saw Luciano visit his parents several times late at night. By this time, his older sister, called Fanny, had married a plumber and moved to White Plains. Bart Lucania lived in Brooklyn and was the secretary and treasurer of the Associated Master Barber's Chapter 629. In early 1935, Luciano's mother became seriously ill and left the building, dying in the hospital. His father then quit the building in September of that year, owing two months' rent, to live with his daughter in White Plains.

Generally, Luciano lived the life of a man about town, calling on a variety of girlfriends, some coming from the brothels he was connected with. He never got married and never seems to have yearned for that kind of intimacy or long-term friendship with a woman—certainly not when he was young. He never expressed the wish for a family and acknowledged no children. He loved straight sex with young women, but sometimes he was slowed down by venereal disease that reoccurred throughout his life.

For such a wealthy and powerful man, rubbing shoulders with politicians, businessmen, and show business stars, Luciano sometimes chased after high-profile women, but, generally, he didn't like to be outshone by his girlfriends. One woman closely associated with Luciano was Gay Orlova—the stage name of a twenty-year-old chorus girl in a Broadway show. Luciano, reputedly, fell head over heels for her. Born in Russia, she had left with her family during the revolution. Luciano met her in 1934 after she performed in a show at the Palm Island Casino in

Florida. He was staying with Al Capone's brother, Ralph, in his mansion. After that first meeting, they were smitten with each other and seen around town together. Lee Mortimer, a gossip columnist, asked her what she saw in Luciano.

"How can you go for that gorilla?" he said.

"I love Charlie because he *is* so sinister," she replied.

♠

For Charles Luciano, being a gangster was all about business and making money. The raw adrenaline of robbing, fighting, and killing had energized him in his teens and twenties, but by the time he hit thirty he had a more sober approach to criminality. With his like-minded associates, Lansky and Costello, he adopted the persona of a businessman. A businessman who used the ultimate persuasion of personal injury and murder to get what he wanted, but a businessman nevertheless, more interested in managing his commercial interests than in running around the streets shooting people. As Joe Profaci, head of one of the five Mafia families, was heard to say one day: "We were just interested in business, and going legit someday so our kids wouldn't have the gangster curse. We didn't really care who was boss."

Luciano was always happy to take tips on management techniques from those with more experience. Johnny Torrio, who had retired from the underworld in Chicago, handing it over to Al Capone, was living in New York and gave advice to Luciano over games of cards at the Barbizon-Plaza. It was his idea of a national convention to settle points of conflict between the leading gangs. Luciano had attended such a gathering in May 1929 in Atlantic City—one of the first of several sit-downs where criminal bosses tried to bring a more businesslike tone to their activities.

All the leading gangsters agreed to work together to ensure they didn't compete with each other and thus lower the price of illicit booze. Most important, Al Capone attended the meeting.

Calling it a "peace conference," he accepted the need to reduce his incessant killings in Chicago after his headlining St. Valentine's Day Massacre three months earlier. As a result of the meeting, Capone handed himself over to a friendly policeman so he could serve a brief ten-month period in jail for possession of a gun in order to allow other cooler heads to run his business empire more efficiently. Typically, neither Maranzano nor Masseria attended this conference because they would not sit down with Jewish gangsters on an equal footing.

With the killings of Masseria and Maranzano and the establishment of what was dubbed the Commission, Luciano had abandoned a dictatorial vision of organized crime and settled on something more discreet and collaborative. He discouraged the old Sicilian manner of greeting fellow mobsters with a kiss—a simple handshake would do—drawing less attention. Negotiation, not fighting, was the preferred way forward, but that didn't stop Luciano and his associates from using guns when necessary to settle any business problems—that's what gave them their competitive edge against regular corporations.

Aping Rothstein, Luciano made sure he developed his own political contacts and firmed up a strong relationship with New York State governor Al Smith, ensuring the appointment of several friendly politicians in his administration. In 1929, Smith was succeeded as governor by Franklin Delano Roosevelt, and there is no reason not to expect that Luciano also had links to him, as he did with all leading Democrat politicians in New York at the time. It was the historic legacy of the Lower East Side gangs and their assistance to Tammany Hall. Luciano's go-between in political matters was Albert Marinelli. During the early years of Prohibition, Governor Smith had appointed Marinelli port warden of the city, a position that allowed him to ensure the unloading of bootleg whiskey was carried out without intervention.

In July 1932, Luciano and Marinelli, along with Lansky and Costello, attended the Democratic convention in Chicago. Both

Smith and Roosevelt were the leading presidential contenders. Eventually Roosevelt was chosen, partly because he was less tainted with Tammany Hall than Smith, and the next year he became president. It was a new era for the United States.

The Wall Street Crash of 1929 had brought an end to the heady postwar boom and reduced some of the money that flowed into criminal coffers during Prohibition. With the Great Depression taking hold of the country, citizens wanted an end to the discredited period of rapacious capitalism headed by the Republicans and wanted someone to clear up the mess. That person was Roosevelt. Three weeks after becoming president, on March 23, 1933, he signed into law an amendment to the Volstead Act, which allowed the manufacture and sale of certain kinds of alcoholic beverages. By the end of the year, Prohibition was repealed and the business of bootlegging was at an end. Luciano and his fellow gangsters had known the end was coming to this lucrative trade and were already prepared for it.

In May 1933, another national convention of gangsters was arranged—perhaps by Luciano—at a Park Avenue hotel. Johnny Torrio again took center stage as the voice of wisdom. His argument for a more secretive and cohesive approach to organized crime had been proved by the jailing of Al Capone more than a year earlier. Capone's brand of shock-and-awe gangsterism had eventually pushed the authorities to nail him for income tax evasion, and this more sophisticated method of law enforcement was not lost on the gang bosses, who also took note of Capone's hefty eleven-year sentence. They had to stay out of the limelight for their own survival or face a more determined crackdown on their activities.

Luciano understood the virtue of working together, said Torrio. He had overseen the establishment of a successful monopoly over illicit liquor. Now that bootlegging was coming to an end, the same approach had to be taken with other rackets. When it was Luciano's turn to speak, he carried on the theme of criminal cooperation. He argued that the major gangs should establish a nationwide syndicate. Each city or region would belong to its leading gang and other subsidiary gangs would recognize their supremacy. It didn't matter that they were not a hundred percent Sicilian or Italian, as in the old Mafia. Any ethnic gang that had fought its way to the top had earned its title. But if those gangs started messing around in the business interests of another gang in another city, then a meeting should be called of the national syndicate to discuss the misdemeanor and sort it out before it ended in war.

If one gang wanted to carry out an enterprise within another gang's sphere of influence they had to ask permission before barging in. They should also share any of their valuable assets, such as corrupt politicians who could help out other gangsters. It all operated on a currency of favors owed and repaid. Some territories were to be considered open and gangs could come together to invest in developing criminal interests there. This would include areas such as Nevada or Cuba, where gambling casinos were built with Mob money. Luciano repeated his assertion there would be no boss of bosses—just an association of key gangsters who would work together to oversee the peaceful development of the underworld. The presence of Meyer Lansky, Louis Lepke, and Longy Zwillman reassured the large Jewish contingent that this syndicate was not a purely Italian club.

As he surveyed the underworld around him, Luciano was pleased to see how many of his teenage associates had prospered alongside him. This satisfied him, for he felt that everyone should have a slice of the pie and not lord it over the others, as Masseria and Maranzano had tried to at their cost. This really was the secret of Luciano's success. Through good fortune and the power of his personality, Luciano was at the center of a group of friends who had all established themselves in various aspects of New York crime. Their strength was their friendship and the money they channeled into their various enterprises.

It should also be emphasized that although much of the

literature about Luciano portrays him as a master criminal in New York in the early 1930s—with him presiding over gangster conferences like a chairman of the board—this is probably more legend than reality. It is partly a construct of the crime busters who later confronted him, as they needed to show him as a master criminal to justify their own expensive crusades against him. Luciano was too interested in managing his own money-making rackets—and the countless day-to-day problems with them—to devote much time at all to overseeing a national syndicate, if it ever really existed. Most Mafia enterprises were local businesses operating in specific parts of cities. They liked to emphasize the importance of their personal contacts and this gave them considerable reach throughout the country if they needed it.

In the same month as the Park Avenue conference calling for an end to gang warfare, there was a spectacular gunfight on Broadway that somewhat undermined the pacifying words of Luciano and Torrio. On the evening of May 24, as crowds were coming out of movie theaters, they came under fire from two expensive sedans racing northward along Broadway. Bullets flew everywhere and wounded three bystanders, including a forty-five-year-old nurse who was taken to the hospital in critical condition. At West Seventy-ninth Street, one car drew abreast of the other and the fedora hat–wearing passengers inside sprayed it with bullets.

"Careening wildly from side to side," said a newspaper report, "the riddled sedan sped north to the intersection of 84th Street, where its driver lost control. The car smashed into the railing surrounding the island park just north of the street crossing and was almost completely wrecked. Two men jumped out of the car and lost themselves in the street crowds. The police found that although the sedan was equipped with bullet-proof glass an inch and a half thick, at least 11 shots had penetrated the body of the sedan. In the back seat were fresh bloodstains."

The gunfight was thought to be linked to the death of two

henchmen working for chief bootlegger Waxey Gordon. No one had told them about the need for criminal coordination.

Throughout this period, Meyer Lansky remained Luciano's leading associate. He had imbibed the lessons of Rothstein and was an expert moneyman, investing the Mob's money wisely and effectively and always open to the next big opportunity. He was Luciano's number one adviser and commanded the respect of all other Jewish gangsters. He was happy to let Luciano be regarded as head of the Mob, because he was the brains behind the operation and preferred life in the shadows. He was never happier than sitting in his book-lined study at home reading about the life of another physically small but determined operator—Napoleon Bonaparte. Lansky remained close to Bugsy Siegel and would use him to open up new territories in the future, but for the moment, his childhood pal remained a feared gunman.

Louis Lepke consolidated his control over the garment district, the Amalgamated Clothing Workers, and other unions. The labor racket brought in millions of dollars and he lived the life of a playboy. He also headed a major narcotics smuggling network. Longy Zwillman, along with Willie Moretti, took care of illegal operations in New Jersey. Frank Costello was the fixer, forging close links with politicians and judges, and dispensing annually thousands of dollars to law enforcers, to protect the Mob's interests. His slice of the business was gambling, and it is claimed he used his influence on the racetrack to provide FBI supremo and gambling addict, J. Edgar Hoover, with surefire winners. It helped to keep the FBI off their backs. Costello liked to spend his fortune on dressing well and when a lawyer later asked him to wear a cheaper suit for a trial he said, "I'm sorry counsellor, I'd rather blow the goddam case."

The muscle needed to keep Luciano and his associates at the top of the pile was provided by Murder, Inc. Headed by Albert Anastasia and Joe Adonis, younger members of Luciano's original gang, this was a group of professional gunmen who were called in to execute a contract on anyone obstructing their ambitions. The idea was that orders for killings were passed down from chief mobsters through lieutenants to gunmen who knew neither their bosses nor their intended victims, so it was very difficult to link them to the murders. It was nothing personal, just business, and anyway, as Bugsy Siegel famously declared, "We only killed each other." Actually, that wasn't true. Murder, Inc., was directed to kill anyone who got in their way, including "civilians," fringe criminals, and trial witnesses.

That these top gangsters were still not immune to deadly threats from rival mobsters was revealed in a violent incident on November 9, 1932. Tony Fabrizzo was a hit man for Waxey Gordon, who had a long-term vendetta against Lansky and Siegel. Fabrizzo went to the Hard Tack Social Club at 547 Grand Avenue, New York, where Lansky and Siegel liked to meet. The Italian assassin lowered a bomb down the chimney of the building but failed to take into account that the chimney had a right-angle offset that caused the bomb to become stuck before reaching the meeting room level. The bomb went off and did not kill the intended victims, but it still did considerable damage to the building and Siegel was taken to hospital with severe head injuries caused by flying bricks. Eleven days later, Siegel tracked down Fabrizzo and shot him dead.

♠

Thomas E. Dewey was a baby-faced attorney with mighty ambitions. Eventually, he would become governor of New York and run for president of the United States. In early 1931, however, there was no sense of the illustrious career to come his way. He was just twenty-eight years old, earning a salary of $6,400 a year, and only had experience in handling civil cases related to family estates, big hotels, and banks. It was through one of these cases that he managed to impress George Z. Medalie, one of New York's most successful trial lawyers.

When Medalie gave up his lucrative private practice to assume the role of U.S. attorney for the southern district of New York State, the much older lawyer offered Dewey the position of chief assistant U.S. attorney in March 1931. It was an extraordinary post for someone so young and inexperienced in criminal law, and it came with a federal prosecuting office of sixty lawyers working for him. But Dewey grabbed the opportunity and applied himself diligently, mastering every aspect of the task before him. His appointment coincided with the national mood for political change and an end to the rotten practices of the 1920s. He came from a family of leading Michigan Republicans and was no friend of New York Democrats. Indeed, his father had told him: "Tammany Hall represents all that is evil in government." He stayed beyond the reach of Luciano, Costello, and their Democrat stooges.

At first, Dewey took on cases of fraud. He helped Medalie prosecute a Harlem lottery racketeer called Henry Miro. They used tax law to pursue him, just as it had been used to get Al Capone. The case opened Dewey's eyes to the vast sums of money being made in the New York underworld. He calculated that Miro alone was making something like a million dollars a year, and he was just one of ten or fifteen such crooks.

"If this is a fact," he later broadcast to a radio audience, "then the underworld takes ten to 15 million dollars a year out of the numbers game alone to finance its depredations against legitimate business and the lives of the people of New York. With such a war chest, organized crime has abundant means for corrupting public officials and buying immunity from punishment."

As Dewey delved deeper, he came across the activities of the erratic and dangerous Dutch Schultz. Schultz was one of the other great criminal associates of Luciano—never one of the Big Six because of the independent character of his business, but certainly in alliance with them as part of a New York syndicate. Another protégé of Rothstein, he took over the numbers racket in Harlem and ran bootleg beer in the Bronx. In 1931,

Dewey discovered that Schultz had deposited $856,000 in various bank accounts and doubted very much that he had paid a penny in tax on it. Later in the same year, Dewey took on Jack Diamond and successfully prosecuted him for operating a still, for which he received a fine of $11,000 and a four-year prison sentence. In a subsequent trial, Diamond was acquitted, but by the end of the year he had been shot dead.

Over the next two years, Dewey set his investigators onto Dutch Schultz and Waxey Gordon. By early 1933, they had enough evidence to proceed against both mobsters on the basis of tax evasion. Schultz had already got word of the investigation and disappeared. Gordon tried to escape but was captured and went on trial. Before he confronted the multimillionaire bootlegger in court, Dewey and his team had questioned more than a thousand witnesses and investigated the records of some two hundred bank accounts. It was an indication of the thoroughness with which Dewey prepared his cases and served as a model for his later assaults on gangsters.

"Good law enforcement," said Dewey, "will be procured when competent and trained investigators work, with modern technique and approach to their task, together with competent, vigorous lawyers who are willing to devote long, quiet effort to the investigation and prosecution of crime."

It was the paper trail and the accumulation of witness testimony that would prove to be his most potent weapons. Waxey Gordon and two of his associates were indicted for tax evasion on an income of $1,618,690 over two years. Presented with such a tight case built on the statements of witnesses who had worked inside Gordon's business, it took the jury just fifty-one minutes to find him guilty on all counts. Waxey Gordon was fined $80,000 and given a sentence of ten years incarceration. In retrospect it probably saved him from being rubbed out by his fellow gangsters.

Luciano had already been moving in on Gordon's business earlier that year. A newspaper report described a gun battle in

May in which three passersby were hit in the crossfire at Broadway and Eighty-first Street. "According to the police," said the report, "the machine-gun battle was between rival gangs headed by Waxey Gordon on one side and by Charles (Lucky) Luciano and Louis Buckhalter, alias Lipke [*sic*], on the other." In all, the police said more than a dozen men had been killed in the gang warfare. It has even been suggested that it was Meyer Lansky who fed information about Gordon's tax affairs to the Internal Revenue Service in the first place.

By the end of 1933, Dewey's boss, Medalie, decide to retire and recommended Dewey for his post. Despite the newly empowered Democrats eyeing the position, the Republican Dewey was unanimously elected—at thirty-one years old, the youngest ever U.S. attorney of New York. One headline called him the "Baby Prosecutor." It was bad news for New York mobsters and everyone knew it—including Luciano. But the Democrats persisted and Dewey was replaced after just a month in the role. As Dewey prepared to make some money in private practice, the Mob dared to hope that their operations would be safer with a more malleable Democrat in the job. But public uproar at the corrupt nature of the Democratic legal regime encouraged the governor of New York to intervene and appoint Dewey as special prosecutor. He was subsequently given free hand as deputy assistant district attorney to pursue his own campaign against organized crime. The heat was back on the Mob.

Dewey moved his operation into the fourteenth floor of the Woolworth Building. A twenty-four-hour police guard was put on the Gothic skyscraper. Special measures were taken to protect witnesses giving testimony: frosted glass installed in partitions in interview rooms; venetian blinds placed on exterior windows; a separate telephone cable led directly to the telephone company to avoid tapping; filing cabinets given special locks. To get the public behind him, Dewey gave a series of radio lectures in which he outlined the impact of crime on the citizens of New York. It was these talks that built up the legend of organized crime in the city and led eventually to Luciano being branded a master criminal.

"There is today scarcely a business in New York which does not somehow pay its tribute to the underworld," declared Dewey, "a tribute levied by force and collected by fear. There is certainly not a family in the City of New York which does not pay its share of tribute to the underworld every day it lives and with every meal it eats. This huge unofficial sales tax is collected from the ultimate consumer in the price he pays for everything he buys. Every barrel of flour consumed in New York City pays its toll to racketeers, which goes right into the price of every loaf of bread. Every chicken shipped into the City of New York pays its tribute to the poultry racket, out of the pockets of the public. There are few vegetable or fish markets in the City of New York where merchants are not forced by sluggings, destruction of goods, threats, and stink bombs to pay heavy toll."

Dewey was talking about the protection racket, but there was another lucrative aspect of gang rule that also came to his attention—the "Shylock" business. Taking its name from Shakespeare's Venetian Jew, it was simply money-lending with menaces. The rate of interest was $1 for every $5 borrowed. The gang lenders kept books and sent their collectors to pick up their money every week, many of them walking straight into the officers of borrowers and telling them to pay up. If they refused, a couple of enforcers were sent to beat it out of them.

Dutch Schultz had a considerable interest in the Shylock racket in Manhattan and every day he was in hiding from Dewey he was losing control over his business empire to Luciano and other rapacious gangsters. When he eventually reemerged into the public eye, his clever lawyers managed to get his trial shifted upstate and he avoided conviction, but he still had a score to settle with the attorney.

"Dewey's gotta go," he told a gathering of senior mobsters. "He has gotta be hit in the head."

Luciano and Lansky sympathized with Schultz. The Dewey justice machine was threatening them all, but instinctively they knew that such a high-level hit would bring down on them just the kind of attention they were trying so hard to avoid. Nevertheless, Albert Anastasia of Murder, Inc., was charged with exploring the possibility of assassinating Dewey. The lawyer's daily routine was observed and one criminal observer staked out his home, borrowing a child from a friend so he could pretend to be playing with his son each morning when Dewey emerged from his house. The attorney was accompanied by two bodyguards, but it soon became clear that he always visited a drugstore to make his first untapped phone call of the day while the bodyguards waited outside. All Murder, Inc., would have to do is place a gunman in the drugstore.

When the proposition was placed before Luciano and his allies, they voted it down. It wasn't worth the tremendous grief that would explode over them with Dewey's killing. Dutch Schultz wasn't happy with the decision and vowed to kill Dewey by himself. Schultz had always been a hothead and his defiance of the Mob sealed his own fate. It was the first real test of his authority and Luciano wouldn't be found wanting.

On the evening of October 23, 1935, a black sedan carried three hit men into Newark, New Jersey. They had a deadline to beat. They heard that Dutch Schultz was just thirty-six hours away from blasting Dewey. At just after 10:00 P.M., the three gunmen entered the Palace Chophouse. One of them, Charlie "the Bug" Workman, checked out the restroom. Seeing the back of a man he figured was one of Schultz's bodyguards, he shot him, then strode back into the bar and executed three of Schultz's close associates as they sat around going over the mobster's accounts. But none of them was Schultz. Workman suddenly realized it was the guy in the toilet that was his target. He went back and checked he was dead. But Schultz wasn't dead. He lingered on for another twenty-four hours in hospital before he passed away.

Years later, the assassination plot was revealed to Dewey. He listened stone-faced to the details, reacting only when it was mentioned that his potential killer used a child to cover his stakeout. It was the closest he would ever come to being a victim of the Mob, and the person he had to thank above all for his survival was Charlie Luciano—the man against whom he would now turn all his prosecuting skills.

Dewey wasn't the only new brush to start cleaning up New York. As Roosevelt and his Democrats swept into power in 1933, Fiorello La Guardia stood as mayor of New York City. A Jewish-Italian Republican, La Guardia was not trusted by Luciano and his Tammany Hall cronies and they did everything to halt his rise to office. When they put thugs out onto the street to rig the election, La Guardia, a streetwise man with little physical fear, waded into the action and even took a slug at Luciano when he appeared on the streets to back up his men. La Guardia won the election and wasted no time in condemning Luciano as "Public Enemy No. 1." Journalists accompanied the stocky mayor as he went on regular forays with a fire ax to personally smash up slot machines run by the racket as the most visible way of showing he meant business. The public mood was turning against the Mob.

LUCKY IN HOLLYWOOD

Dewey wasn't the only problem facing Lucky Luciano in 1934. His criminal empire spread all the way across America to the West Coast, but his rule there was coming under pressure from the Mob in Chicago, and they would cause to him to make an almost fatal error.

The appeal of Hollywood to Luciano was obvious—it was a huge narcotics market. Back in 1926, Los Angelinos were already becoming nervous about its impact on their sun-drenched land when newspaper reports declared they had the second largest number of illegal drug convictions in the United States. Morphine and its derivative, heroin, were the drugs of choice in the north and center of the state, accounting for 50 percent of arrests in and around Los Angeles. Marijuana was more popular in the south with mainly Latino users.

"It is plain that society must organize to combat this evil," blared the *Los Angeles Times*. "Like war, its ravages must be checked or it will end by wrecking the present civilization. So great is the profit in peddling the dope that unscrupulous makers and vendors defy the written law. They have found that each recruit to the army of addicts brings others in his train and the secret nature of the traffic makes apprehension of the smugglers extremely difficult."

The other attraction for Luciano, of course, was the glamour. The year after the *Los Angeles Times* warned against the terrors of heroin addiction, a pretty young woman called Thelma Todd arrived in New York. As a teenager, she had won her state beauty pageant and been crowned Miss Massachusetts. Her first job was as a fashion model and then a friend put her in contact with pioneering film producer Jesse Lasky, one of the original founders of Paramount Pictures, as well as the Academy of Motion Picture Arts and Sciences. In New York, he was talent spotting and set up the Paramount School of Acting.

The fun-loving blonde joined the school and within months appeared in her first movie role in *Vamping Venus*. More parts followed, and in 1927 Todd took the railroad to Hollywood where she signed up with comedy filmmaker Hal Roach. She played in comedies opposite Laurel and Hardy and Harry Langdon. The following year, she graduated from comedienne to straight actor, taking leading roles in feature films *Corsair* and *The Maltese Falcon*. By 1933, the twenty-eight-year-old Thelma Todd was a film star—and that was the year she started dating Charlie Luciano.

As always, Luciano had been quick to spot the potential for selling narcotics to Hollywood and had a firm grip on that market by the late 1920s, alongside vice and gambling. Narcotics imported from Europe came through New York and ended up in L.A. His "snow" dealers hung around movie sets and supplied actors with little packets of morphine, heroin, and cocaine. It was fashionable and starlets scooped up the powder with little silver spoons dangling from necklaces or injected heroin with hypodermic needles kept in vanity cases. A few stars became high-profile drug victims, such as silent movie actress Barbara

La Marr, who died from heroin abuse. To take care of business on the West Coast, Luciano appointed Pasquale "Pat" Di Cicco, a theatrical agent very well connected with the movie world. His cousin Albert "Cubby" Broccoli would later go on to produce the James Bond movies, and Di Cicco ended up as a vice president of United Artists Theatres.

By 1933, however, Luciano's West Coast operation had a strong rival in the form of Chicago gangsters who had muscled in on the film business. When Depression-hit Hollywood moguls slashed by half the fees they paid their actors, writers, and film technicians, it caused mayhem, and strikes threatened to bring moviemaking to a halt. Johnny Roselli, a soldier for the Chicago Outfit, came to the rescue of the moguls and, within a week, his hired thugs had crushed the threat of strikes. That favor came with strings attached, and soon Roselli was closely involved with top Hollywood producers, functioning as their Mob fixer and bookmaker. His greatest pal was studio head Harry Cohn and they both wore identical ruby rings as a sign they were blood brothers. This special access encouraged the Chicago Mob to look for richer pickings in Hollywood. By controlling the filmmaking unions and threatening strikes, they planned to extort vast sums of money from the movie moguls.

So far so good, but the film business was not solely located on the West Coast, and several production companies, including MGM, were actually owned by New York–based theater groups. If the Chicago Mob was going to extort money from these businesses they had to ask permission from Luciano and his associates before moving in. To square this, prominent mobster Frank Nitti, who now fronted the Chicago Outfit after taking over from the recently imprisoned Al Capone, invited Luciano for a chat.

In a tense meeting, Nitti outlined his proposal and Luciano listened. The cards were stacked against the New Yorker, as he didn't have the presence in Hollywood that they had in the form of Johnny Roselli, but he bluffed it out and said he would agree to them putting the squeeze on New York–based movie companies, so long as they cleared out of his West Coast drug-dealing business. He also wanted a share of the income from Chicago-controlled nightclubs and restaurants in Los Angeles.

Nitti accepted the share of income, but pontificated over the drugs—it was too big a market to give up. Luciano had little choice but to agree to the overall deal—it was his punishment for taking his eye off the ball. He had let the Chicago mobsters elbow their way into his drug business and now he was paying the price for it. Compared to Roselli, Luciano's representative, Di Cicco, was a bit player. That was why, from 1933 onward, Luciano became a regular visitor to Hollywood—keeping a closer eye on his operation.

In July 1932, Pat Di Cicco had married Thelma Todd in Arizona. She was then at the height of her career, having recently starred in two Marx Brothers' comedies, *Monkey Business* and *Horse Feathers*. But Todd desperately wanted to be taken more seriously and wanted a break from her comedy contract with Hal Roach so she could star in more dramas. When she started talking to United Artists about appearing in the projected war epic *Hell's Angels*, Roach refused to let her go. This was a blow to Todd and she started drinking heavily. It didn't help that her marriage to Di Cicco broke down almost immediately, as he frequently disappeared on business trips for Luciano.

Alone and in need of company, Todd resumed her friendship with a United Artists executive called Roland West. He and his ex-wife, Jewel Carmen, wanted to open a restaurant and tried to interest Todd in their plans over dinner at the Brown Derby. That same night, Di Cicco reappeared in the company of Luciano and joined them for drinks. Todd didn't recognize the gangster but was charmed by him. As her relationship with Di Cicco deteriorated further, Todd started seeing more of Luciano, who journeyed to Hollywood ever more frequently. Soon it was known among her friends that they were sleeping together—she confessed it to her onscreen comedy partner Patsy Kelly. She liked a good time—she dubbed herself "Hot Toddy"—and Luciano kept her supplied with any drug she fancied.

When Todd divorced Di Cicco in March 1934, citing mental cruelty, she was in the mood for creating her own nightspot and joined with West and Carmen in setting up a restaurant on Roosevelt Highway on the way to Malibu Beach. It was to be called Thelma Todd's Sidewalk Café. She didn't invest a penny in the project, but used her Hollywood network to make sure movie stars attended the place and created a buzz around it. It helped that she opened up the second floor of the building for after-hours gambling, which attracted Clark Gable and Spencer Tracy, among others. Luciano gave his blessing to the project. He could see its potential.

Any high-profile activity in Hollywood suited Luciano, as he was finding it hard to compete with the action of the Chicago Outfit. In June 1934, Luciano, Lansky, Siegel, and Lepke joined Nitti and the Chicago mobsters at the biennial convention of the International Alliance of Theatrical Stage Employees (IATSE), the leading Hollywood union. The gangsters sat in the conference hall and applauded as George Browne, a veteran Chicago union extortionist, was appointed president of IATSE—there were no other nominations. It symbolized Nitti's takeover of the movie extortion business, and Luciano was there as a bystander. Luciano was struggling to keep hold of his drug business as Chicago gangsters assaulted his dealers in the fight to control the supply of narcotics on the streets of L.A.

Luciano didn't like gang warfare—he'd brought a definitive end to the Castellammarese conflict so business could carry on—but Nitti was pushing him too far. Bugsy Siegel was keen to start shooting and Luciano considered killing Browne, as a warning to Nitti, but Lepke argued that murdering a trade union leader was too high profile. Instead, they settled on snuffing out the source of their problems. In September 1935, Luciano met Nitti at the Sherman Hotel in Chicago. The two gangster chiefs reviewed the main concerns of their competing financial interests. Nitti could carry on with his Hollywood shakedown, just so long as he kept out of Luciano's California drug market. Luciano told Nitti this was not a discussion but his terms for a settlement. Nitti had twenty-four hours to think it over—if he didn't agree, it would be a declaration of war.

The next day, the two met for lunch, but it didn't go well. Nitti felt he had the momentum in Hollywood. Why should he give it up? Nitti ended the lunch meeting and walked out of the restaurant. Then a car drove past and sprayed him with bullets. Nitti survived the assassination attempt but was sufficiently cowed to give in to Luciano's demands. Nitti stuck to the studio business; Luciano kept his drug racket.

With this success under his belt, Luciano was feeling in an expansive mood. His attention switched back to Thelma Todd's Sidewalk Café. Despite its popularity, it was running at a loss and Todd was forced to use her own money to keep it afloat. She soon found out why it was losing money when her business partner, Roland West, complained to her that it was Luciano's mobsters who were draining them of cash. They wanted him to order alcohol and meat only through them and wanted him to take more than he needed. Their accountant was part of the racket and West blamed Todd for her love affair with the Mob. He wanted her to buy him out. She refused, but said she would have a word with Luciano.

Luciano was always happy to meet the film star and spent the evening of November 25 with her. He told her she should rent out the second floor of the restaurant as a casino, which he could run. Todd wasn't interested, seeing this would only lead to deeper involvement with the New York Mob. When she said that would happen over her dead body, Luciano replied coldly— "That can be arranged."

Todd was heartbroken. It looked like the end of her restaurant as Luciano threatened to swallow it up in his vice empire. Her mother advised her to talk to the police and on December 11, she made an appointment to see District Attorney Buron Fitts six days later. Somehow, Luciano heard that Todd was about to go to the cops and immediately took a flight to L.A. on the thirteenth.

♠

On the evening of Saturday, December 14, 1935, British comedy star Stanley Lupino was hosting a party for Thelma Todd at the Café Trocadero on Sunset Boulevard. At the time, she was living in an apartment above her restaurant but had lost her keys and planned to stay at Roland West's home, just a quarter mile away up two steep flights of steps. She kept her car in his garage and they had a row about her staying with him that night because he didn't want to be disturbed. He told her not to come back any later than 2:00 A.M., otherwise she would find the door locked.

At first, the celebrity party cheered up the actress. "She drank a cocktail before dinner," said Ida Lupino, the comedian's daughter, "and a little brandy and champagne during dinner." But as midnight came and went, her mood darkened. By coincidence, Pat Di Cicco, her ex-husband and a close associate of Luciano, was at a separate event at the Trocadero. He saw her but said nothing to her, he later claimed.

Actor Arthur Prince sat next to Todd at dinner. "During the early part of the evening," he remembered, "she was very gay. Later—I'd say around 2 o'clock—she went over to Sid Grauman's table. He was with three people. When she came back she was terribly depressed." She had told Grauman to phone West that she was on her way to his house. Outside the restaurant, chauffeur Ernest Peters was waiting to drive her back, but Todd seemed very agitated.

"She told me to drive at top speed and not to make boulevard stops. I drove between 65 and 70 miles an hour," said Peters. "Miss Todd was afraid that because she had been the target of extortion notes she might be slain or kidnapped by gangsters."

Peters was the last person to see her alive. On Monday

morning—a full twenty-four hours after this last sighting—
Thelma Todd was found dead sitting in the front seat of her large
Lincoln Phaeton convertible parked in the garage of West's cliffside residence. A maid discovered her. She was slumped forward
with her head on the wheel. The death made front-page news.

"Coagulated blood marred the screen comedienne's fea-
tures," said the *Los Angeles Times*, "and stained her mauve and
silver evening gown and her expensive mink coat when she was
found, her blonde locks pathetically awry, in the front seat of
her automobile." None of the thousands of dollars worth of jew-
els around her throat and wrist was touched.

Later that day, Dr. A. F. Wagner, county autopsy surgeon,
stated categorically that Todd had died early Sunday morning
about 5:00 A.M. "The autopsy showed monoxide poison, to the
extent of 70 per cent of total saturation, in her blood," he said.
"There may have been other contributing causes, but that
definitely was the major factor. The fumes were breathed ac-
cidentally. Either she went to sleep with the motor running or
was overcome before she could help herself."

He explained the blood on her face by saying she probably hit
her head on the wheel when she fell forward. Roland West's testimony to the coroner on December 19 added to this conclusion.

"I went to the garage and rushed in the door," said West, "and
there was Miss Todd lying over there. I put my hand onto her face
and there was blood and I wiped it off on my handkerchief." He
told the maid to get help. "[I] looked to see how much gas was in
the tank and it was almost empty. I know from the position that
she was trying to get out of that car. I know that, because otherwise she would not have been turned in the way she did."

The time of Todd's death was soon disputed, however, as a
friend came forward to say she had spoken to the film star on
Sunday afternoon. Martha Ford, wife of actor Wallace Ford,
talked to her on the telephone. She had invited Todd to a cocktail party.

"Sunday afternoon she telephoned me," insisted Ford. "She

said, 'Darling, do you mind if I bring a guest?' I replied, 'Of course not. Who is it?' 'You'd never guess, and you'll be surprised when you see,' she said. I told her I was dying of curiosity, but she would not tell me anything more. Then she said: 'You know who this is, of course? It's Thelma—your Hot Toddy.' That was a nickname she liked to call herself. Then she said, 'Oh, and another thing—I went to a party last night and I'm still in evening clothes. Do you mind?' I laughed and said to come in anything she wanted, but to hurry. Then she hung up."

Who was the mystery date? Was it Luciano? He was in L.A. that weekend. Several witnesses came forward to say they had seen an attractive blonde in an automobile like hers sitting next to a dark-featured man.

Jewel Carmen, Roland West's ex-wife, gave a statement to the police in which she said she saw a blonde looking like Todd driving in a chocolate brown Lincoln Phaeton on the Sunday evening before her body was found. A mysterious man was sitting next to her. "He was dark, foreign-looking," she said, "wearing a pepper and salt colored fedora hat and coat that matched."

A shop assistant said she had seen Todd four days before her death and she was openly worried about money, paying up front for a hat she had ordered. "You'd better get your money now because I may be broke by the first of the year; a great many changes are going to take place in my life by the first of the year."

The reasons for Todd's financial concerns soon came out in the press. They said she had been the object of several extortion notes and threatening letters. All written on plain white paper of good quality, they bore New York postmarks. Signed "The Ace of Hearts," one of the notes demanded $10,000 from the actress or he would blow up her café. They were followed up by several long-distance phone calls coming from the "Ace."

In the months leading up to Todd's death, two men were arrested in New York in connection with the threatening notes. One of the extortionists was identified as twenty-six-year-old Edward Schiffert, but his parents said he was mentally unsound and shouldn't have confessed to the charge. He ended up in Bel-levue Hospital. The other man, arrested over the summer, had all charges dropped against him. Despite these arrests, the threats kept coming and worried Todd to the point that she dreaded picking up the telephone for a long-distance call.

After her death, the headwaiter of Todd's restaurant said he'd received several phone calls promising to murder him if he spoke out about the case. The maid who discovered the body said a "couple of mean-looking men" approached her and told her not to mention the Mob when giving evidence.

By December 24, there were too many suspicious circum-stances for the police to let the case rest as an accidental death and it became a hunt for murder clues. A further autopsy report said "the throat of the actress bore swellings or bruises such as might have been made by the jamming of a bottle neck or a pipe into her mouth." In addition to this, two of her ribs were frac-tured and her nose broken. The foreman of the grand jury, con-vened to investigate the death, added to the mood of malevolence by saying that "murder by monoxide" might be the conclusion of the case.

The final verdict, however, reverted to the original finding. On the fateful night, Todd's chauffeur dropped her outside her restaurant. She couldn't open the door to her apartment, so she walked up the hill to West's house. It was after 2:00 A.M. West wasn't in his home but sleeping in a bedroom he had in the café. When she got no answer from West's home, rather than walk all the way back down to the café, she spent the night in her car in his garage. Drunk, she kept the motor on to keep herself warm and subsequently died from carbon monoxide poisoning. Ro-land Button, Todd's lawyer, was not happy with the finding and told the district attorney he could prove that Luciano had mur-dered her, but her movie producer, Hal Roach, possibly under Mob duress, leaned on DA Fitts and the matter was dropped.

Thelma Todd's heartbroken mother concurred with the of-ficial version.

"It would be quite natural of her to go to her car rather than inconvenience anybody," she said. "The loneliness of the walk would not frighten her, because she had no fear—none whatsoever. . . . If her face was injured it would be due to her falling over when she became unconscious. I am sure of that because my daughter was happy, very happy, and she had no enemies."

Todd's ex-husband, Pat Di Cicco, echoed this sentiment when he was interviewed in New York. There was no truth to the rumor that they were going to remarry, he told an L.A. reporter.

"It was merely a coincidence that I was at the Trocadero Saturday night when she was there too. We were in two different parties. I merely observed her as she was dancing but I don't know with whom she was dancing."

Was Di Cicco keeping an eye on her for Luciano?

"I have no theory as to the cause of her death," he insisted. "It certainly is confusing. But she had no enemies. There was no reason why she should have committed suicide. And she never took those threatening letters seriously."

Pat Di Cicco was wrong. She took the letters very seriously; and she had the worst of enemies—Lucky Luciano.

If Luciano had the film star murdered to protect his own extortion business in Los Angeles, he had gotten away with it. But the clock was ticking on his own freedom. Other women he had exploited over the years were about to have their day in court when the biggest gang-busting trial came to Manhattan in 1936.

CITY OF SEX

Am writing this letter more for the benefit of the unfortunate women," wrote an anonymous informer in June 1931. "I have a sister whom I saved and is now married happily." The informer had apparently saved her from a life of prostitution and was now telling the Sixty-seventh Precinct police in Brooklyn about a pimp who controlled girls in several "disorderly houses." His business was run from a restaurant on West Twenty-second Street, Coney Island, owned by a woman called Yedis Porgamin, who also had a profitable sideline in buying stolen jewelry and trading in illicit bonded whiskey. The pimp was Louis Weiner, known as "Cockeyed" Louis. "He sends the women to the disorderly houses and receives their pay every Saturday night or Sunday." He and his assistant, Albert Letz, buy and sell women, said the informer. "White Slave girls from out of town 16 or 17 years old. Sells them off to Bethelem, Easton or Lancaster, Pa."

The informer recommended the police put a tap on the

restaurant telephone and directed them to one of the brothels. "Open all hours this is the biggest house in the business," he or she said with some urgency. "Please work on these right away and I hope you don't send men that you can bribe. Once you can land Cockeye Louis and Al Lucks or Yedis Porgamin you break the biggest white slave ring in the country fast and sure because they already pay police protection."

The police took the advice seriously and tapped the restaurant phone, recording the following conversation on September 1, 1931, at 2:40 P.M.

"Hello Lucky, this is Frank."

"Frank who?"

"The sheik."

"Oh hello there Frank, how are you?"

"I am sick."

"Listen Frank, the hell with the women, money and Cockeyed Louis, you take care of yourself. We need you to drive, you know that. . . ."

"Frank" then asked to speak to Louis, but "Lucky" dismissed that.

"Louis is too drunk to talk to you or anybody else so forget it."

A copy of this phone tap and the informer's letter ended up on the desk of Chief Assistant U.S. Attorney Thomas E. Dewey. The reference to "Lucky" may have intrigued him, but it was most likely not Lucky Luciano but the lieutenant of Cockeyed Louis, Albert Letz, also known as "Al Lucks."

The letter did corroborate other information that placed Cockeyed Louis at the center of a prostitution racket in New York State and, by 1935, that was very much on Dewey's mind. When he declared his war against organized crime in July of that year, vice was at the top of his list. "We are concerned with those predatory vultures who traffic on a wholesale scale in the bodies of women and mere girls for profit," he said. It chimed a bell with many fellow citizens who had sent in their own reports of organized vice.

On July 7, 1935, one concerned New Yorker called on Dewey to turn his attention to the homosexual trade of young men. He described it as a "meat market" located in Times Square, a little park behind the Forty-second Street Library, and Fifth Avenue up to Hotel Plaza. "You would find out that the streetboys in New York are mostly not born in this town," he wrote. "They come from Boston, Hollywood, from all the different regions and states of this country. As to their former positions, if they had any, they are sailors, or ushers or bellboys—anyhow come mostly from positions which made them wear a uniform."

It was not just the gay prostitutes themselves who concerned the author of this letter, but the criminals involved with them. "We all will be very grateful to you," he told Dewey, "if you can clean this town from the overabundance of vice. Believe me, that the street boy 'industry' is one of the most dominant vices, because of the different crimes connected with this filthy business."

It was a strong condemnation of just one aspect of the sexual criminal life that infected New York City in the early 1930s, but what really interested Dewey was the organized crime behind mainstream heterosexual prostitution. Letters from concerned citizens provided piecemeal evidence, but he needed to create a much more substantial picture of how prostitution in New York functioned and for that he needed to talk directly to the girls and pimps involved. On February 1, 1936, Dewey triggered a raid on brothels across Manhattan and Brooklyn that pulled in 125 prostitutes, madams, and bookers. By questioning them, Dewey and his investigators—chiefly Eunice H. Carter and Murray I. Gurfein—got just the information they needed.

An important link in the flesh trade was the "booker"— sometimes called a "bookie." He supplied the girls for the madams who managed the brothels. It was the booker who ensured the flow of new girls through brothels throughout the city and the country, keeping regular clients happy with a change of faces. Cockeyed Louis was a booker on a major scale and his son, Al Weiner, took over the business from him. Typically, a booker might handle two hundred girls at a time and would take 10 percent of what they earned. The madam took half—and in 1936 a prostitute might generate around $300 a week.

Surprisingly perhaps, the profits of prostitution had not really interested organized crime in the 1920s, largely because they had their hands full handling the trade in illicit alcohol and narcotics, but with the end of Prohibition in 1933, mobsters began to search for other sources of income. A sign of this pressure being brought to bear on Luciano was recorded in an incident in February 1934.

The police received an anonymous telephone tip-off saying that five men had entered the offices of financial broker Balsam & Co. on Broad Street in New York's Financial District on February 13 at 5:00 P.M. The men demanded several thousand dollars and a percentage of the business in return for their protection. Two of the tough guys were alleged to have been Luciano and Bugsy Siegel, and they intended to put pressure on twenty-five other brokers to join their racket. When the police interviewed Louis Balsam, he confirmed that two men had visited him, saying they were forming a committee to protect brokers in the area, but they did not ask for any money at the time and he could not identify them. Photographs of Luciano and Siegel were shown to other brokers around Broad Street, but none identified them as the racketeers. The police interest was enough to discourage the mobsters from persisting with this enterprise.

Moving in on legitimate business was much harder than putting pressure on illegal activities—victims who were also criminals could hardly go to the cops—so Luciano muscled in on the sex business. Bookers such as Cockeyed Louis and his son Al had been allowed to dominate it for several years, but now senior criminals took an interest and their days of independence were numbered.

Danny Brooks was one of the bookers brought in by the police and he had an interesting story to tell Dewey's team. He worked for Jimmy Fredericks, who was connected with the Mott Street Mob and was a dominant force in the vice trade. He worked out of an office at 117 West Tenth Street. In October 1933, he came to Brooks with bad news.

"I have just lost a decision downtown," said Fredericks.

"What decision?"

"Lucky has given a decision against me."

By that, Fredericks meant that Luciano had made it clear that he was getting into the business of prostitution and Fredericks had to hand over his books to Luciano's associates Abie "the Jew" Heller and David "Little Davie" Petillo. Under the new regime, Brooks would act as both a booker and carry out "bonding." Bonding demanded each girl pay $10 a week. For this money, when the girl was arrested, she would get the service of a lawyer and half her bail paid; her madam would put up the other half of the bail bond. The men who worked together to obtain this money called themselves "the Combination." Brooks wasn't happy with carrying out both of these criminal acts from his own office.

"You have nothing to worry about," said Fredericks, "because this is the toughest thing to convict anybody on."

"I am kind of scared," said Brooks. "I don't know what to do. I want to know who is behind this."

Fredericks said that he was behind it.

"But you haven't any money," said Brooks. "I want to know the truth."

Fredericks said that Abie the Jew and Little Davie were behind the racket, as he'd said before when they took the business directly away from him.

"And who?" insisted Brooks.

"Lucky," said Fredericks.

The October 1933 meeting was a crucial moment. This was when Luciano moved in on the business of prostitution in New York. A week before, several small-time gangsters had come together to form their own bonding Combination. As well as

Jimmy Fredericks, they included Sam Warner, who later described the meeting in more detail. It took place in Alphonso's
Restaurant on Broome Street near Mulberry. Word then got out
about their proposed Combination, and Luciano wasn't happy
with it. He called in all the participants to meet him at the restaurant. He arrived twenty minutes after they'd gathered. As
soon as Luciano entered the room, "all the Italian men stood up
and greeted him just as if he were a general," said Warner. Little
Davie Petillo spoke to them in Italian and then Luciano made
his speech.

"Listen, you fellows are all through; from now on Little
Davie is taking over the bonding."

With that, Luciano walked out of the restaurant. Warner
and the rest were too frightened to say anything. There was a
new bonding Combination in town and that was headed by Luciano with the Mott Street Mob handling its administration. Little
Davie Petillo, Abie the Jew, Tommy "the Bull" Pennochio, and
Jimmy Fredericks were the senior managers charged with en-
forcing it.

Unwisely, Sam Warner and a few of his associates carried on
collecting their bonds for a week after the meeting. Finally, at one
brothel, one of the madams told them that Little Davie wanted to
see them. He told them that if they didn't cut it out, their heads
would be broken. They instantly stopped their operations.

Later, in June 1935, Danny Brooks drove another booker
called Dave Miller to a meeting in Mulberry Street. Jimmy
Fredericks was there and so was Little Davie. Their main topic
of conversation was another judgment from above that took
over Cockeyed Louis's part of the business and gave it to Miller,
but Miller was concerned about his own security if things went
wrong.

"Who is going to take care of me in case of trouble?" he
asked Fredericks. "You know Cockeyed Louis got sent away."

"What are you worrying about?" snapped Fredericks. "You
are always worrying."

"I ain't got no money," said Miller. "I would like to know what this is all about. Who is going to take care of me?"

"We will," said Fredericks.

"Who is we?"

"Davie and Abie and . . . Charlie."

This was just the information Dewey had hoped to get. He wanted to know that Charlie Luciano was at the apex of this particular crime pyramid.

Al Weiner, son of Cockeyed Louis, wasn't happy about the new regime, either. He made a complaint to the police in June 1935 in which he said Luciano was extorting money from him. The official police department report said Luciano obtained the sum of $100 from Al Weiner "by wrongful use of force and fear on the part of the aforesaid Al Weiner by threatening the said Al Weiner to do an unlawful injury to his person."

Luciano would accept no competition in this business.

♠

Confirmation of Luciano's reign of terror came from another source arrested in Dewey's sweep of the brothels—Flo Brown. Also known as "Cokie Flo," a name she detested, she was a morphine addict and madam. She had lived with a series of low-level gangsters in Chicago before deciding to set up her own brothel in Manhattan at 22 West Seventy-sixth Street. In 1933, she was booking with Cockeyed Louis Weiner, but this came to an end when the Combination took over. She bonded with them and opened a new house. She also became Jimmy Fredericks's girlfriend, but this ended badly when she gave him $100 as a Christmas present and he gave her nothing. It only made things worse when she found out that Fredericks had given his previous long-term girlfriend a mink coat.

In spring 1934, Brown said she went with Fredericks to a meeting uptown at a Chinese restaurant on Broadway. Luciano was there with the head of the Mott Street Mob, Tommy "the Bull" Pennochio, and Little Davie Petillo. Brown said that most of the conversation was in Italian, but what she did hear was that Fredericks told Luciano that some bookers were holding out on him—they didn't want to surrender their joints and pay bonds to him.

"I'll tell you what you do," said Luciano. "Bring all the bookers down tomorrow and I will put them on the carpet and we will see that that doesn't happen again."

"Nick Montana is the worst offender," said Fredericks. "He collects bonds and keeps it and then when the place gets pinched they run to me and I don't know anything about it. I am not able to take the girls out because I didn't know they had been paying bond."

"Have them all come down," said Luciano, "and we will straighten the matter out."

Fredericks later told Brown that they "bawled the devil" out of the bookers and that Montana was the most defiant. "Nick thought he would get away with it because he had a brother—big shot in Harlem," said Fredericks. "We didn't care whether he had fifty brothers, he had to kick in just the same." Luciano levied a fine of $500 on every booker holding out on a joint.

Further evidence of how the Combination worked was provided by Mildred Curtis, girlfriend of Tommy "the Bull" Pennochio, also picked up in Dewey's raids. Sitting in the Foltis-Fischer restaurant on Forty-seventh Street in early 1935, she asked Pennochio how the bonding business worked.

"The bookers send the girls to the joints," he said. "We collect ten dollars every week from each girl. In case of trouble we protect them. In case a girl gets in trouble we get them out."

"How do you get the girls to pay the ten dollars?" Curtis wondered.

"We have men go around and collect the money and the bookers turn in all their joints and the madams tell the girls to pay."

Later, Curtis and Tommy the Bull met Luciano in the Hotel Century.

"One of our joints was pinched in the seventies," said

Pennochio, "you know which one I mean. What shall we do about it?"

"Who are the cops?" asked Luciano.

Pennochio mentioned the precinct.

"Oh that is easy," explained Luciano, "we can take care of them."

That was all part of the bonding service.

On one occasion when the police raided several houses, Fredericks swung into action, saying "We've got to get pictures taken of the broken locks. The doors were broken down without warrants. We have to get three or four lawyers to represent the madams and girls. If we have just one, people will realize it's a Combination."

"Who gets the most money of the bunch?" Curtis later asked Tommy the Bull, meaning the profits of the Combination.

"Well, Lucky, he is the boss, gets the most," said Tommy the Bull. "Then I get second and the rest of them are all even." Pennochio acted as the treasurer, keeping control of the total bond money and doling it out to madams when a house had been raided. Extra money was raised from bookers in the form of protection money, pried out of them depending on how much business they were doing.

Pennochio was originally a drug dealer, operating from 72 Mott Street, and had been arrested in 1929 for selling narcotics, spending eighteen months in the penitentiary. He also had a loan shark business. Luciano gave Pennochio permission to enter the prostitution racket.

That the income from bonding was only part of the income generated by these gangsters was made clear when hotel burglar Joe Bendix asked Luciano if he could work as a bond collector for him in June 1935. Bendix had known Luciano for nine years and always brought him his best stolen jewelry.

"You know, Joe," Luciano told him, "it doesn't pay a hell of a lot. It only pays thirty-five or forty dollars a week."

"It doesn't make much difference," said Bendix. "I'm not do-ing anything anyhow. I need the money. It's better than nothing."

"All right," said Luciano, "I'll tell Davie to put you on. See me again. I'm always around."

A couple of weeks later, Bendix saw Luciano at the Villa-nova restaurant.

"I put you on as a collector for $40 a week," he told Bendix. "You know the other collectors only get $35 a week but you are kind of 'high-hat,' so we've got to give you a little more."

♠

Sometimes the madams had to be protected from other gang-sters who didn't fully appreciate the strength of the shield now provided by the Mott Street Mob. In July 1935, one of the bonded brothels was held up by some petty criminals from Williams-burg, Brooklyn. As soon as Jimmy Fredericks heard about it, he got in a car with two other enforcers and drove over to Brooklyn to find the holdup crew. That Fredericks was the chief tough guy in the Mott Street Mob was made clear when Tommy the Bull told his girlfriend that Fredericks was a "gorilla." "If any-body needs taking care of he straightens them out."

When Fredericks tracked down one of the small-time rob-bers, he smacked him, saying, "Didn't I tell you to stay away from these joints—to stay away from joints that are bonded. That they belong to Charlie Lucky. Keep away from these joints."

Of course, Dewey loved it every time someone mentioned that Luciano was behind the entire operation. Luciano got a sense this was happening too much, as bond collectors kept re-ferring to him as the ultimate sanction for what they were do-ing. He had become the top criminal brand and he instructed Fredericks to tell them not to mention his name in connection with the Combination. But it was too late for that.

♠

The life of some of the girls working in Luciano's brothels could be brutal. Pauline Burr was just seventeen when she stayed at the Girls' Service League, a charitable organization helping unemployed young women, in 1935. She was five feet four inches tall, with chestnut hair and an attractive face. She liked walking with a friend around the Lower East Side, where she was introduced to a handsome Italian named Al. She gave him her telephone number. A few days later, a man phoned her saying he was a friend of Al's. This was Patrick Kane and he took Burr to dinner in Chinatown. After a few days of going out together, Kane asked Burr to marry him. She agreed and met him at the Paris Hotel, but when she turned up Kane was not in the room but two other men were.

A friend had accompanied Burr to the hotel and told her not to stay. When Kane arrived, he was furious with Burr for bringing along another girl and told her they had been married that afternoon. When the friend checked with a social worker at the Girls' Service League, she said there was no record of Burr's "marriage." By then, however, Kane had moved Burr to the Alexandria Hotel. There, all Burr's clothes were taken away from her and any pretense of marriage to Kane was abandoned. One October night, five men were brought to her room. She was forced to have sex with all of them. She had entered Luciano's world of prostitution. Burr was taken from hotel to hotel, where she was rented out to men. Kane passed her on to another booker known as Ko-Ka-Mo Joe. If Burr refused to do what he said, Kane threatened to turn her over to the police, telling them she was a bad girl and a prostitute.

A few days later, the forlorn Burr was taken to an apartment on West Fiftieth Street. There she was sold to another booker for $300. She was told to submit quietly to the life of a prostitute, as she could make a great deal of money out of it, but she ran away from the apartment. She went back to Ko-Ka-Mo Joe, who had shown a degree of kindness toward her, and he took her away to Philadelphia. When they returned to New York in

November they were arrested. Joe was held on a charge of statutory rape. When Burr was examined by a doctor, he said "her body is covered with black and blue marks from mistreatment and that her coccyx is injured possibly from sex violation. She walks with difficulty and throughout the interview complained of pains in the back."

Sometimes the men wanted to get out of the business, too. Pete Balitzer was a booker who got into trouble with the Combination. Pete's girlfriend, Mildred, tried to sort it out for him by talking to Little Davie Petillo. She saw him on Mulberry Street.

"What is this I hear about this bonding of houses and the protection of bookies?" she asked him. "Pete is having a lot of trouble with the East Side fellows and I hear that you are interested in it; is that right?"

Little Davie said he was.

"They are asking Pete for a lot of money," she carried on. "He can't pay it. I would like for you to do something about it."

Little Davie shrugged and said Pete had to pay up like all the other bookers. She wanted to know who was heading the operation. "Is Lucky behind this?"

He said he was. Mildred later told Little Davie she was getting married to Pete and he still wanted out of the business.

"He can't get out," said Little Davie, "he owes too much money."

She said it was a shakedown racket and that Pete was ending up borrowing from the Mob's own Shylocks. The money was going around in a circle. Mildred then said she was going to see Luciano directly about the problem.

"It won't do you any good," said Little Davie, "because anything I do is all right with him."

Shortly after they got married, Mildred Balitzer made the journey all the way down to Miami in January 1935 to see Luciano. She saw him at the racetrack and talked to him at the Paddock & Grill Bar.

"You know I am married to Pete now," she told Luciano. "I

want Pete to get out of the business, but he can't get out because of the money he owes. They constantly shake him down."

Luciano said he'd have a word with Little Davie back in New York. Mildred didn't forget and wouldn't give it up. Five months later she met with Luciano at the Villanova Restaurant on Forty-sixth Street. Luciano told her that he'd spoken to Little Davie and there was nothing he could do to help Pete. "When he pays the dough and not until then he can get out."

"That goes back to the same argument," said Mildred exasperated. "He can't get out. He can never catch up. He can never pay." She then changed tack. "You are the only one who can do anything for me. Please do something for me."

Luciano was resolute. Business was business. He said there was nothing he could or would do about it.

"You know the racket," he concluded. "Let them alone."

For Mildred Balitzer that was the end of the road.

Peggy Wilde was a madam of some experience. Her first brothel was on Ninety-fifth Street and Broadway in the early 1920s and there she entertained both Legs Diamond and Charles Luciano. Raised in East Harlem, she had married a musician at sixteen and had a child at seventeen. When the musician left, she set up her sex business. By 1934, the Combination called on her. Johnny Fredericks told her: "You have to bond or you can't run." She said she'd think about it, but over the next two weeks strangers came to her house and harassed her. Other madams advised her to bond and avoid trouble. She did so.

The fate awaiting madams who messed around with the Combination was made clear when Tommy the Bull spoke to Luciano. He told him about a madam who was paying for three girls, but was really running five.

"What should we do about it?"

"Take good care of her," said Luciano, "next week she will know what to give."

"Okay," said Tommy, "I will see [an enforcer] tonight and tell him what to do."

In another instance, when madam Dago Jean refused to bond, Luciano told Little Davie to "go ahead and wreck the joint."

All these women would eventually have their day of vengeance in court and were happy to give their testimony to Dewey and his investigating team. When one Nancy Presser spoke to them, she even revealed a little of Luciano's personal sex life. Nancy had known Luciano for eight years and was one of his many on-off lovers. When she visited him at his hotel room at the Barbizon-Plaza, she told him that she was hard up and thinking of working in one of his brothels. He told her not to work there and if she ever needed money to ask him and he would give it to her.

Presser's best friend was Thelma Jordan and she added a further dimension to this relationship when she revealed the following intimate detail to the investigators: "Nancy Presser told me that Charles Luciano was diseased during the time of her visits to him at the Barbizon-Plaza and that he used to give her money despite the fact that she did not have relations with him."

Throughout this investigation, it is surprising that Luciano's second-in-command, Vito Genovese, was never brought into the picture. According to Nick Gentile, Genovese had been involved in the operation of brothels throughout the 1920s. Perhaps because of Luciano's direct involvement, Genovese had shifted his own interests to other rackets, such as setting up gambling clubs. Gentile was in competition with Genovese in this field and described the services they offered.

"These premises, decorated in an expensive fashion, were located in the section occupied by Chinatown and the lowest element of New York," recalled Gentile. "It was frequented by people of all races: Syrians, Chinese, etc., individuals who lived on the fringes of society, capable of anything, thieves, assassins, who for a handful of dollars, were always ready to undertake any crime whatsoever.

"People, who after being filled with morphine and cocaine,

and after having spent hours smoking a pipe of tobacco mixed with opium, came to pass the time at the gambling tables in order to still feel the ultimate emotion of a game of chance which was protracted until morning, when the first light of dawn showed their faces pale and emaciated; to whom the last glass of whiskey was like a blow of the mallet that was brought down on their foggy head and on their trembling legs."

Police were bought off raiding these clubs by a glass of whiskey and graft, or *la mazzetta,* as it was called.

"When one of the customers of the more dangerous [clubs] would lose and the boys would not know if he was laughing or crying they would call me," said Gentile, "and I would approach him and using a very gentle manner, I would bring him outside to breath [sic] pure air and after that give him a gift of $10 for the next day's lunch and would order my boys to accompany him to his house. This is how the tragic comedy went on."

♠

By the summer of 1935, Luciano was getting irritated with bonding prostitutes. He believed there wasn't enough money in the trade to justify the constant attention it was demanding from him. Flo Brown witnessed his anger at a basement restaurant in Chinatown. She listened as Fredericks told Luciano that some madams were proving difficult and holding out on paying bonds to him.

"Why don't you get the madams together?" said Luciano. "You know I told you before that being nice to them isn't any good."

"Well, you know how it is," said Fredericks. "It is tough now, and I thought if I could talk to them it might be better."

"You can't talk to them," barked Luciano. "They're too stubborn anyway. Get after them. Step on them a little bit."

At this point, Little Davie Petillo reassured Luciano: "We will take care of it."

Later, in the fall, they met again at a Chinese restaurant in the Lower East Side. This time the problem was Dewey and his proclaimed crusade against vice in the city. Flo Brown heard Luciano complain further about the bonding racket, saying it was little money and a big headache. Luciano didn't like his name being mentioned so much by bookers and everyone in the business. Brothel owners would run downtown and try to get to him so they didn't have to bond.

"I don't like the idea of having my name mentioned like that," scowled Luciano. "I'm tired of having these pimps running around to get out of paying the lousy bond."

He knew his personal freedom and prosperity depended on hiding his name from the authorities, and he didn't want every madam in town putting it about.

"Why don't you give it a chance a while," said Little Davie. "We will straighten it out."

"I don't know," said Luciano, "this Dewey investigation [into the vice racket] is coming on and it may get tough, and I think we ought to fold up for a while."

Davie told Luciano he was just fed up because a number of brothels had been shut and the income was going down, but once the heat was off, it would pick up again.

"It would be better if we quit awhile," said Luciano, "and started over again when things were quiet. We could even syndicate all the places like they do in Chicago and instead of three or four combinations having the syndicate as they do in Chicago there would be only one in New York—us."

Davie said he believed that the Dewey investigation would pick up only a few phony bondsmen and they'd be satisfied with that.

"Well, all right then," said Luciano, "let it go for a couple of months and if things are the same we will have to let it drop."

But Luciano had plans for the prostitution business and mused on it over the meal. He could see that sex was like food—a constant demand for it.

"We can take the joints away from the madams, put them on a salary or commission, and run them like a syndicate, like large A&P stores, and there won't be any bonding or booking of houses."

This was the visionary businessman in Luciano, trying to turn his brothels into an efficient commercial concern that dominated the market—just like the A&P supermarkets that first opened in Canada in 1927 that led the food retail sector at the time.

♠

Luciano liked to spend the winter months in Miami, Florida, at the racetrack. Through Lansky, he had been investing heavily in the local gambling rackets. When word got to him in February that Dewey had pulled in a whole crowd of prostitutes, madams, and bookers, he decided to follow Dutch Schultz and disappear. His chosen hideout was Hot Springs, Arkansas, a place renowned for its Mob-backed casinos and amenable lawkeepers. Every so often in the past, he had dropped by and spread money around to ensure an ever ready welcome for himself.

Since February 3, 1936, between eight and ten assistants had worked exclusively on the Luciano case in Dewey's Woolworth Building office, working day and night, weekends and holidays. More than 120 witnesses were in prison and a further 300 witnesses—who were neither prostitutes nor criminals but with some information to give—were questioned. With the mountain of testimony gathered, Dewey was ready to take on Luciano. Copies of all this material still fill sixty-six boxes today in the New York City Department of Records.

Luciano would be indicted with twelve other defendants who were key members of the Combination: Tommy Pennochio, David Petillo, Jimmy Fredericks, Abe Heller, Jesse Jacobs, Benny Spiller, Meyer Berkman, Peter Balitzer, Al Weiner, David Miller, Jack Ellenstein, and Ralph Liguori. Luciano's aliases were listed as Lucky Luciano, Charles Lucania, Charles Lane, Charles Reid, and Charles Ross, the latter names used when he lived in hotels. The first of ninety counts made against Luciano and the other defendants by the grand jury of the county of New York was for the "crime of placing a female in a house of prostitution with intent that she shall live a life of prostitution."

The paucity of other offenses that could be held against Luciano is underlined by the FBI's own file on him during this period. They knew he was a key player in the underworld but had surprisingly little detailed information on his activities. An FBI memorandum dated August 28, 1935, described "Charles Luciana, called 'Lucky'" as "the leading racketeer along Italian lines. Is very powerful and made considerable money in liquor." It had a statement made by an anonymous individual who declared that "Meyer Lansky and Charles Luccio [sic], alias 'Lucky' is the head of the underworld in New York City." Their files said he was the boss of a Lower East Side gang, operated chiefly in beer and liquor, and had business connections with Lepke and other Mobs. It referred to Luciano's trip to Europe with Jack Diamond in the summer of 1930 as part of a conspiracy to smuggle narcotics into the U.S.

Aside from that, the FBI rap sheet said he had been arrested on thirty-five occasions prior to 1936, including minor offenses such as traffic violations. More serious offenses included being charged with felonious assault on December 29, 1926; assault and robbery with a gun on November 17, 1928; grand larceny on October 17, 1929—but on all occasions he was discharged with no further action against him. On February 28, 1930, he was arrested in Miami, Florida, and charged with operating a gambling game, carrying a concealed weapon, and vagrancy, but he was later released. On February 8, 1931, he was charged with felonious assault, but again he got off. Nothing seemed to stick to Lucky. It would be up to Dewey to contrive a better assault on the gangster.

To make the most of his accusations against Luciano, Dewey had ensured the passage of an important piece of New York State legislation that would help him prosecute the mobster for a seemingly minor series of crimes, but ones that cumulatively would pay off with a bigger sentence. It was dubbed the "Dewey Law" and was signed into the books in April 1936.

"Today, crime is syndicated and organized," he explained. "A new type of criminal exists who leaves to his hirelings and front men the actual offenses and rarely commits an overt act himself. The only way in which the major criminal can be punished is by connecting to him those various layers of subordinates and the related but separate crimes on his behalf.

"As the law now stands," Dewey continued, "there is a procedural straitjacket which prohibits the trial of these offenses together (except in conspiracy, which is a mere misdemeanor), though they all coordinate the acts of the master through his subordinates. Although the organization is conceived and functions to prey upon hundreds of men in the same states, each of its offenses must be tried separately before a separate court and a separate jury."

Dewey's Law allowed the joining of numerous similar offenses in one single indictment with an appropriate heavier sentence on conviction. So, Dewey had the law and he had the evidence to put Luciano behind bars for a long time, but come April 1, 1936, he didn't have the accused.

Dewey had a judge issue a warrant for Luciano's arrest based on fleeing New York State to avoid prosecution for extortion against Al Weiner. On April 1, two detectives strode up to Luciano on the boardwalk of Bathhouse Row in Hot Springs. He was in the company of local chief of detectives Herbert Akers. Luciano was put under arrest and taken to the Garland County Jail. Anticipating that Luciano had more than enough money to post bail instantly on a modest sum, Dewey had requested that bail be set at $200,000, but Luciano was one step ahead of him, having a friendly judge set bail at a mere $5,000, which Akers ensured was handed over just a few hours later. Before Dewey even got the news of Luciano's arrest, he was back out on the streets of Hot Springs and thinking about a swift getaway to Mexico.

Dewey next sent out one of his key aides to urge extradition, but his plane hit bad weather and he had to continue his journey by rail. Three days later, by phone and through his agent on the ground, Dewey managed to convince the local judge to order the rearrest of Luciano and this time without bail being set. Dewey also recommended that the no-nonsense Arkansas attorney general Carl E. Bailey make the trip from Little Rock to oversee the case personally—being far removed from the cozy conspiracy in Hot Springs. In the meantime, smart local lawyers hired by Luciano tried to halt his removal to Little Rock. As he waited the outcome of their maneuverings, his cell in the Garland County Jail was made comfortable by Detective Akers, who brought him pillows and sheets from the nearby hotel. To underline his lack of concern, the mobster had a supper of spaghetti and fried chicken in the company of the local sheriff.

The story of Luciano's custody in Arkansas made news around the world. "Luciano is alleged to be the head of the 'Vice Ring' in New York City," said the London *Times*, "and has been described by Mr. Dewey as 'the most dangerous and important racketeer in New York, possibly in the whole country.'"

When Bailey arrived in Hot Springs with a fugitive warrant to take custody of Luciano, the local sheriff refused to hand him over, saying that the prisoner's status required clarification. In retaliation, early on the morning of April 4, the governor of Arkansas ordered twenty Arkansas state rangers to invade the prison at Hot Springs. Armed with machine guns and rifles, they pushed aside the local sheriff and extracted Luciano from his comfortable cell, driving him the fifty-five miles to the state capital. There, he was placed in a less agreeable prison with bail set at $200,000. But still the game wasn't up and Luciano's lawyers put further barriers in front of Dewey. This time, they threatened to appeal to the U.S. Supreme Court to prevent extradition from Arkansas. They presented a new writ of habeus corpus, and the federal judge granted them ten days to apply to the circuit court of appeals. As part of the condition of this process, Luciano's attorneys had to give twenty-four-hours notice of the appeal hearing. On April 16, they forgot to do this. But Dewey didn't forget.

One minute after midnight on April 18, Dewey's men escorted Luciano out of jail and put him on the train to New York. Attorney General Bailey delayed the Little Rock midnight train by fifteen minutes to allow his removal from the state. Handcuffed and bewildered, Luciano was heard to shout out, "I'm being kidnapped!"

The train arrived at Penn Station just before 9:00 A.M. and Luciano was greeted by a mob of journalists and flashing cameras. He told them his name was "Lucania" and he was "sore as hell." A little later, Lucky's current girlfriend, Gay Orlova, dressed in diamonds and fur, was asked by reporters for her comments.

"Lucky was a dear," she told them, "and I don't believe any charges, especially that one about compulsory something or other. It just doesn't sound nice. Not like Lucky at all."

LUCKY ON TRIAL

At 5:50 P.M. on April 18, 1936, in room 139 of the New York County Court House, Luciano and Dewey came face-to-face over the matter of setting bail for the mobster. It would set the tone for the subsequent trial—one of merciless retribution.

The court clerk solicited the plea. "Charles Luciano, alias Lucky Luciano, alias Lucky, alias Charles Lane, you have been indicted by the Extraordinary Grand Jury on four separate indictments, each charging violation of the penal law, section 2460. How do you plead: guilty or not guilty?"

"Not guilty," said Luciano.

Dewey stood up and said bail should be set at a higher figure than the originally suggested $200,000. He argued that since Luciano had been arrested in Arkansas, he had engaged in a costly series of legal maneuvers to avoid facing charges in court and this should be reflected in setting higher bail.

"The business of this defendant is far-flung," explained Dewey, "and brings in, to my certain knowledge, a colossal annual revenue. His interests are, of course, much more varied than those involved in this indictment. It is well known that he is the head of the Italian Lottery, which is a nationwide lottery, which brings in a huge revenue. He is reputed to be, and I believe it to be true, one of the individuals who derives the largest source of revenue from the policy racket in New York City. He is, beyond question, or, rather, his henchmen are, beyond question, actually operating a number of industrial rackets in New York City."

This was the moment Dewey had been waiting for. The case was about so much more than the vice charges Luciano faced—Dewey wanted to portray him as the head of organized crime in New York, and it is this vision of Luciano as master criminal that stuck for the rest of his life.

In the courthouse, Dewey proceeded to list the mobster's illegal income. "His operations include drug peddling," he said, "for which he has once been convicted, and I understand and believe that he is one of the largest importers of drugs in this country. His operations in connection with so-called bookmaking, which he has stated to be his occupation, include not personal bookmaking, as I understand the facts, but being the head of a large syndicate of bookmakers, and the conducting, through his various subordinates, of places where bets may be placed in large volumes by members of the public."

The income derived from all these rackets led Dewey to ask the judge to set a far larger bail of $350,000. Luciano's attorney was Moses Polakoff and he reeled at the size of the figure—a third of a million dollars.

"The sum mentioned by the district attorney is a staggering sum," said Polakoff. "It appears to me that it is attempted to use bail to punish the defendant, and not to ensure his presence here for trial."

Polakoff condemned the "strong-arm methods used by the prosecution" to bring Luciano to court from Hot Springs, but the judge wasn't interested in that. Once he heard Polakoff's case, he followed Dewey's recommendation and set bail at $350,000.

♠

The Luciano trial began on May 11, 1936, and would last almost four weeks. He stood on trial alongside his fellow defendants. It took place at the state supreme court building in Foley Square in southern Manhattan, not far from the Lower East Side. Policemen armed with machine guns and tear gas guarded the corridors and snipers watched the windows. Supreme court justice Philip J. McCook presided over the crowded courtroom. The weather was hot and humid with the temperature on some days getting into the eighties. It took two days to select the jury. It was a sensational event for the city and the daily New York papers were full of the testimony.

Dewey took center stage for what would be the greatest trial performance of his life. He began by admitting the weakness of his case.

"Frankly, my witnesses are prostitutes, madams, heels, pimps, and ex-convicts," he told the jury. "Many of them have been in jail. Others are about to go to jail. Some were told that they would be prosecuted if they did not tell the truth. I wish to call to your attention that these are the only witnesses we could possibly have brought here. We can't get bishops to testify in a case involving prostitution. And this Combination was not run under arc lights in Madison Square Garden. We have to use the testimony of bad men to convict other bad men."

To help the jury understand the complex criminal relationships of the case, Dewey had a chart set up showing the organization of the Combination, with Luciano at the very top of the pyramid, with the Mott Street gang next, headed by Tommy the Bull, and the bookers at the bottom.

At the outset, three of the thirteen defendants pleaded guilty—the bookers David Miller, Al Weiner, and Peter Balitzer— and they turned witness for the state, giving evidence against the accused, but this didn't always go smoothly. Weiner admitted that his testimony had been given on the basis that he would be given leniency and sent to a jail "where I won't be murdered." Another witness, called "Good-Time Charlie," recanted his testimony at the last moment—it turned out later that he had been bribed by the Mob with a gambling concession in the Adirondacks.

It was the prostitutes and madams—like Cokie Flo—who proved to be the dynamite for Dewey's case. They presented a detailed and upsetting picture of the vice business and how the Mob exploited it, with Luciano at the very head of the organization. When Luciano's defense denied that he knew any of his fellow defendants, apart from Petillo, Dewey brought in a succession of witnesses, including hotel staff from the Barbizon-Plaza and Waldorf-Astoria, who swore they had seen him in their company.

After two weeks of listening to a succession of prostitutes place him squarely in the middle of their world, booker Jack Ellenstein also threw in the towel and pleaded guilty. The prosecution case was now over and this left Luciano and eight other defendants to contest the charges. The first of these was Ralph Liguori. He had been accused by prostitute Nancy Presser of supplying her with narcotics and beating her when she didn't bring in enough money. He had threatened Presser and her friend in Dewey's office if they gave evidence against Luciano and the rest. The prosecution further alleged he was the holdup man for the vice Combination, raiding brothels when they failed to pay their bond money. By the time it was his turn to speak in his own defense, Liguori was itching to give the prosecutor both barrels, directing his fire at one of Dewey's assistants, Henry Cole.

"Cole said he knew I had nothing to do with the Combination," said Liguori in the courtroom. "He said 'We don't want you as a defendant. We want to get Lucania.' I said I knew nothing. He said they were going to make me out the stickup man for the Combination. He showed me pictures of Lucky, Betillo [Petillo], Frederico [Fredericks], and Pennochio and said they wanted those four. He wanted me to say Betillo gave me orders to collect $300 from a house. He wanted me to say Lucky and Betillo were there when I went downtown with the $300, that Lucky put the money in his pocket and gave me $10."

It was a strong performance from Liguori and he wouldn't give up his version of events, accusing Dewey and the whole trial of being a setup to get Luciano.

"When I said that didn't happen, " he continued, "he threatened me with twenty-five years. He said if I cooperated they would give me and my girl six months in Europe and protection. He said Dewey was a big man and was going to be governor. He said Dewey prosecuted Waxey Gordon."

Dewey listened to it all with a poker face. Liguori was just a bit player trying to impress his boss. The whole case revolved around the testimony of Luciano and that came the following day, June 2. It was a more measured performance from the top mobster, reflecting his greater gravitas and his belief that the less he said the better—and at first he seemed to be getting the better of the trial.

At 2:13 P.M., Luciano was sworn in and took the stand as a witness on his own behalf. He looked elegant and calm in a cool gray suit. For the defense, George Morton Levy conducted the direct examination, presenting some of Luciano's personal history to the court.

"Is that the correct way to pronounce your name, Lucania?"

"That is right," said Luciano.

"Are your parents living, Mr. Lucania?"

"Everybody except my mother."

Luciano's mother had died the previous August. He explained that his sister lived with his father in White Plains, while one of his two brothers worked as a hairdresser and the other was a presser. At the age of eighteen, after he had served six months of his first prison sentence, he went back to live with his parents briefly. He resumed work at a hat factory for about a year, but his heart wasn't in it.

"I went to work for a crap game," he told the court.

After about three years of that, he started running his own crap games, and this developed into his career as a professional gambler, booking horses—"Go down the track, bet them, and book them"—much in the style of his mentor Arnold Rothstein. This was his line of defense—moving him far away from the dirty business of vice. Witnesses for the defense took to the stand testifying to the fact that Luciano ran a legal gambling establishment in Saratoga, known as the Chicago Club. His partner and front man for this was a lawyer called Jim Leary.

As to his fellow defendants, Luciano didn't know any of them, except for Petillo. The same went for the prosecution witnesses.

"There has not been a witness that got on this stand of Mr. Dewey's, that I ever saw in my life," he said.

"Did you ever say to anybody, in words or in substance, that you were going to raise the price of $2 whores to $3?" asked Levy.

"No, sir."

"Four dollar whores to $5?"

"No, sir."

"That you were going to create an A&P chain store system in the city of New York for whores? Did you ever say anything of that kind?"

"No, sir."

"Did you ever give any orders in connection with any woman to beat her up in any conversations in any restaurants in New York City or elsewhere?"

"No, sir."

"Were you ever paid a dollar in your life by any of these other defendants in this case?"

"No, sir."

"Did you ever take a dollar proceeds from any whore or prostitute, directly or indirectly, in your life?"

"I always gave," said Luciano. "I never took."

No one laughed at the joke.

After nearly half an hour of this, it was Dewey's turn to cross-examine Luciano. The two were now face-to-face, and it would be a long and torturous verbal duel. Dewey started by asking the mobster about his previous convictions, then he wanted some facts about his early life.

"Where were you born?"

"U.S.," said Luciano.

"Where in New York?"

"Thirteenth Street."

This was a blatant lie—Luciano was born in Sicily.

Dewey let this hang in the air and turned instead to Luciano's first criminal conviction for selling narcotics at the age of eighteen.

"How long had you been selling narcotics before you got caught?"

"Oh, about three weeks or a month."

"Where did you get caught?"

"On Fourteenth Street."

"Whom were you selling to?"

"To a dope fiend."

"What was his name?"

"That I don't know."

Dewey moved on to Luciano's subsequent career.

"From 1920 to 1925, did you ever at any time in that entire five-year period earn an honest dollar?"

At that point, Levy intervened with an objection, but the judge said it was a legitimate question.

"Did you have, for one moment during that entire five-year period," repeated Dewey, "any employment with anybody for any purposes except crap shooting?"

"No."

Dewey asked him about his occupation from 1925 to 1930.

"You didn't have a thing in the world to do with any business in the world, except crap shooting and horse race booking, is that your testimony?"

"That is what I did."

Dewey wanted to know if he ever came up with the pretense of a legitimate occupation so he could present it as a front for his gambling business. At this point, under a succession of similar questions, Luciano was knocked off balance and admitted other illegal action.

"Well, I was bootlegging for a while, for about a year and half. . . . And I pretended I had a real estate business."

Dewey seized on the bootlegging admission.

"Somebody else was making it, and you were just selling it, is that it?"

"Just buying the alcohol and selling it, yes."

"Have you any recollection in the world as to who the fellow was who sold you the alcohol?"

"Yes, I have."

"Now tell us what his name was?"

"I am trying to think of his name."

"Was it Dutch Schultz?"

"No, sir."

"Bill Dwyer?"

"No, sir."

Dewey switched tack and got Luciano to admit he owned part of a restaurant on Fifty-second Street and Broadway for six months, eight years previously, and had merely forgotten this one legitimate occupation. Dewey asked him about his claim that he once worked as a chauffeur. Did he drive around Joe Masseria—Joe the Boss?

"No."

"You were a bodyguard for him, weren't you, for some time?"

"Oh, no—never a bodyguard for anyone."

He denied that he had ever told any policemen that he ever was born in Italy—five times he denied his birthplace. At this point, Dewey had a question read out by the judge to underline Luciano's avoidance of the truth.

"I just want to know your philosophy about this. Now if you are under oath, you always tell the truth under any circumstance. Is that it?"

"I am telling the truth now, Mr. Dewey."

The question was read out again.

"I didn't say I told the truth all the time, but now I am telling the truth."

Luciano admitted that the only occasion he lied under oath was about his occupation to get a pistol permit so he could carry a gun around the streets of New York. Dewey exposed further his elastic understanding of the truth by revisiting his arrest for dope peddling in 1923.

"Isn't it a fact that on June 2, 1923, you sold a two-ounce box of narcotics known as Diacetylmorphine hydrochloride to John Lyons, an informer for the Secret Service of the United States?"

"I don't know who they were," said Luciano, "but I was arrested, and if I was charged with them, that I didn't do."

"Didn't you sell the dope to John Lyons on that date?"

"No."

Luciano continued to deny selling dope to the same agent three days later, but did not deny being arrested.

"Isn't it a fact that in your apartment were found two one-half ounce packages of morphine, and two ounces of heroin and some opium?"

"No, sir."

"Isn't it a fact that thereafter you gave to Joseph Van Bransky, a narcotic agent in charge in New York City, a statement that at 163 Mulberry Street they would find a whole trunk of narcotics?"

Levy interceded to object to this line of questioning, but Luciano accepted that that was true.

"You're just a stool pigeon," pushed Dewey. "Isn't that it?"

"I told them what I knew."

"You mean you went to those men and, like a big-hearted citizen, you told them where they could find the trunk?"

"Something like that, maybe . . . what I want to know is where the hell does all this come from?"

Luciano was clearly rattled.

"And you still say you were not engaged in the business of narcotics in the year 1923?" persisted Dewey.

"I was picked up for it, but I was not—I didn't sell them."

Further holes were picked in Luciano's testimony by references to phone calls that he denied making but that were a matter of record. Dewey then wanted to know the kind of men he associated with.

"Do you know a Vito?"

"I know of a Vito, yes."

"Vito who?"

"Vito Genovese."

"What is his business?"

"I think he has got a paper business," said Luciano.

"Where is he now?"

"I don't know, I haven't seen him in maybe seven months, six or seven months."

"Isn't it a fact that he is out of the state of New York?"

"I am in jail," said the defendant. "I couldn't tell you if he is around the corner or he is in China."

Luciano also admitted to knowing Louis Lepke, as well as Bugsy Siegel, who lived at the Waldorf-Astoria.

"I know Bug Siegel having—putting on a couple of shows, and he was interested in a dog track in Atlantic City."

"You were down at his room or he was up in your room at the Waldorf pretty constantly, weren't you?"

"Well, he used to come up to my room, and I went down to his room, yes, a couple of times."

"Almost every day?"

"Not every day, no."

Dewey turned his attention to the ride of 1929, when Luciano was kidnapped and beaten, and got Luciano to admit that he lied under oath to the grand jury about his circumstances at the time. He also admitted he hadn't paid any income tax in that year or the year following. It was not until 1935 that he had got around to filing late returns to the federal government for the previous six years. It was echoes of Al Capone's prosecution for tax evasion.

Luciano explained he never kept any books of record of his income, but he swore that his net income in 1929 was $15,000; in 1930 it was $16,500. In 1931 and 1932, he paid tax on an income of $20,000, although he had not the slightest idea what his gross income or expenses were. He paid the government on the basis of his conscience. He could only guess at his income in the following years.

Luciano's cross-examination by Dewey ended on this financial note at 6:36 P.M.—after four hours of hostile questioning. Levy, Luciano's defense attorney, immediately stood up to get the mobster to explain some of the reasons behind his secrecy and evasion.

"Now, Mr. Lucania, about the use, firstly, of the names Charles Ross and Charles Lane. Was there any particular reason you used either of those names at the Waldorf?"

"Some people, I didn't want them to know."

"A little louder, please," said the judge.

"I says some people, I didn't want them to know where I live."

Luciano explained that he had been taken on the ride in 1929 because some people were extorting money from him under threats and he promised to give them $10,000. He admitted to lying about this to the grand jury at the time. It was not a good end to his testimony. His constant twisting and turning of the truth all came across as very suspicious and, on several occasions Luciano had exposed himself as a relentless and barefaced liar. Newspapers proclaimed Dewey the winner of the courtroom duel. "Dewey Riddles Lucky on Stand," said one headline.

Having failed to present the other defendants in a good light and having failed to knock down the testimony placed before them, some of the defense attorneys used their summing up to attack Dewey. By giving immunity to the prostitutes and pimps paraded before the jury, the special prosecutor was allowing them to go about their illegal business. This was true, but Dewey had already dealt with that, explaining that it was necessary to get bad people to testify against much worse criminals. He admired their bravery in speaking up.

"Gentlemen of the jury, have you ever dealt with sheer, stark, paralyzing terror?" asked Dewey in his closing argument. "You heard Danny Brooks testify that he asked me to put him in some jail where he would not be murdered.

"Then there was Thelma Jordan," he continued, "who was asked by a defense lawyer why she did not tell her story when first questioned in my office. She said, 'I'll tell you why—because I've seen girls cut and burned when they squeal.' They knew they'd made a mistake when they asked that question. They never asked it again."

It was a dramatic end to a sensational trial. The jury retired for a night of deliberations. Early on Sunday June 7, they gave their verdict.

"How say you, gentlemen of the jury," asked Judge McCook. "Do you find the defendant Luciano guilty or not guilty on count number one?"

"Guilty," said the foreman.

Luciano betrayed no emotion. His lawyers had already told him he would be found guilty.

"How say you as to the defendant Luciano? Is he guilty or not guilty on count number two?"

"Guilty."

And so it went on for all sixty-two counts of compulsory prostitution.

Then it was the other defendants' turn—Thomas Pennochio,

Dave Petillo, James Fredericks, Abe Heller, Jesse Jacobs, Benny Spiller, Meyer Berkman, and Ralph Liguori. They were found guilty on all counts.

That afternoon, Dewey issued a statement to the press.

"This, of course, was not a vice trial," he said. "It was a racket prosecution. The control of all organized prostitution in New York by the convicted defendants was one of their lesser rackets. The four bookers of women who pleaded guilty were underlings. The prostitution racket was merely the vehicle by which these men were convicted. It is my understanding that certain of the top-ranking defendants in this case, together with the other criminals under Lucania, have gradually absorbed control of the narcotic, policy, loan shark and Italian lottery syndicates, the receipt of stolen goods and certain industrial rackets."

Dewey ended by thanking his legal assistants and police colleagues for all their hard work throughout the case.

"These men have worked on this case for many months, most of them sixteen and eighteen hours a day, and on a number of occasions as long as sixty hours without sleep."

The conviction of Lucky Luciano was a landmark in U.S. legal history as it was the first against a major organized crime figure for anything other than tax evasion. It was the pinnacle of Dewey's crusade against the underworld. Mayor La Guardia joined in the praise of the young attorney and said it revealed the role of corrupt law-keepers in the rule of the Mob. He said Luciano "could never have run his rackets without the knowledge if not the connivance of some of the very people entrusted with law enforcement. I recommend that at least six public officials commit hara-kiri."

Eleven days later, on June 18, Judge McCook handed out the sentences.

"You are responsible in law and morals for every foul and cruel deed with accompanying elements of extortion performed by the band of codefendants," he told Luciano. "I am not here to reproach you, but, since there appears no excuse for your conduct nor hope for your rehabilitation, to administer adequate punishment."

He sentenced him to thirty to fifty years behind bars. This pronouncement rocked Luciano. He was not expecting such a heavy sentence. He was, in effect, being sent to prison for the rest of his life. His codefendants got lesser sentences: Tommy the Bull and Jimmy Fredericks got twenty-five years each; Little Davie Petillo twenty-five to forty; and Ralph Liguori got seven and a half to fifteen years. It seemed like it was the end of Luciano's criminal career.

♠

The trial might have been over, but the Dewey prosecuting machine kept on gathering evidence against Luciano for the anticipated appeal. A letter dated June 3, 1936, directed the crime crusader toward a notorious house of prostitution at 83 Genung Street, Middletown, Orange County, New York. Called Madges, it was so well known in the area that local politicians frequently joked about it in public and even used it to entertain business associates.

Madges had been around for twenty-six years, said the local informant, and was very well protected by the local police and a few state troopers. In fact, those state troopers were on a "free list" who got taken care of by the girls in the brothel and even recommended out-of-towners to it. Local bartenders and taxi drivers all got a commission for sending customers to Madges. It was a thriving business and seemed immune to prosecution, as anyone of any consequence in Middletown was on its "free list."

Such open corruption may well have appalled Dewey, but what really interested him was the informant's description of who was behind Madges. "For the last few years, this house has been 'controlled' by a syndicate of Luciano. . . . [It] is part of the 'loop,' from New York to Toledo, Ohio. The sale of girls routes through the chain of a Toledo Mob, which is also a subsiduary [*sic*] of the Luciano enterprises."

The letter explained that Madges was managed by Bat Nelson, "who has an interest in Madges place and represents Luciano."

The extent of Luciano's tax mess was confirmed by Tax Field Supervisor Nathan H. Mitchell. On August 20, 1936, he gave a sworn testimony stating: "From my investigation I find that the said Charles Luciano was resident and had his principal place of business in the county of New York, state of New York, during the year 1934 and that for the said year 1934 he had a net income of $20,000, upon which said income, with intent to evade the payment of a tax, he willfully, unlawfully, and fraudulently failed to render, verify, and file an income tax return; and further unlawfully, willfully, and fraudulently failed to pay the income tax which was due thereon, with intent to evade the payment of the said tax. . . ." These accusations hung over Luciano if he dared to challenge the decision of the court, but Luciano had nothing to lose. He was already in jail, effectively for the rest of his life, and he would consider anything to get out.

Nazis in New York

"The whole thing was a frame-up," said Meyer Lansky, twisting the truth to show his support for his closet crime associate. "Dewey had decided to get Lucky Luciano and the only way he could do it was through the girls. They built up a phony case against him and everybody must have known that the girls were lying. They had been told exactly what to say. I never believed a word of it, and nobody who knew Charlie believed it either. But because of his reputation and a hostile judge, the jury was prepared to believe anything."

Lansky shrank away even further from the spotlight and concentrated on building his gambling empire in Florida and Havana, Cuba, both places that were developing into profitable tourist industries. Lansky ensured that Luciano continued to receive his cut of the profits made by the Mob and invested them alongside his own.

With Luciano confined to Clinton Correctional Facility in Dannemora, an isolated maximum-security prison near the

Canadian border, Thomas Dewey scouted around for more gangsters to prosecute. Ice-cold killer Vito Genovese shed few tears
over Luciano's imprisonment and, according to Nick Gentile,
was quick off the mark to suggest that an election be called to
select the new head of their crime family. As its second-in-
command, he obviously considered himself well placed for the
job, but Dewey had other plans for him. The prosecutor linked
him to the murder of a small-time hoodlum called Ferdinand
Boccia in 1934 and, with enough evidence against him for an
indictment, Genovese cheated the law by fleeing to Fascist Italy
in 1937. He was never part of the Sicilian Mafia attacked by
the Fascists, so he managed to make close contacts with Mussolini's regime and set up a criminal network, including drug-
smuggling routes, that would serve him very well during
World War II.

Dewey next went after union racketeer Louis Lepke, forcing
him into hiding. He was also wanted for narcotics smuggling,
and the FBI managed to persuade other mobsters that it was
against their own interests to shield him. From jail Luciano
concurred, and Frank Costello arranged for Lepke to give himself up to the FBI in August 1939 by convincing him that the
Mob had swung a deal with Hoover. It was nonsense and the
less-than-bright Lepke was sent down for fourteen years. Dewey
added a further thirty years to that sentence and Lepke was eventually executed for the murder of a garment industry trucker—
the only top mobster ever to receive the death sentence. Mafiosi
have a ruthless history of using law enforcement to rid them of
troublesome rivals.

When Longy Zwillman was called in for an interview by the
FBI, he didn't hold back on his views about Dewey. He said that
Lepke had remained a fugitive for so long because he distrusted
the New York prosecutor. "It is known in the underworld," said
the FBI report, quoting Zwillman, that Dewey "framed 'Lucky'
Luciano in the White Slave Traffic case; that from his knowledge
of Luciano and from the knowledge of all persons known to him,

Luciano at no time dealt in white slavery. Zwillman stated that in numerous other cases it is known to the underworld that Dewey framed them for his own political glory."

Frank Costello was untouched by Dewey's assaults. "He couldn't touch me because I was legit," he later said. What that really meant was that he could not be linked to any racket within Dewey's jurisdiction in New York. As far as the authorities were concerned, his main source of income came from slot machines in Louisiana—moved there because of La Guardia's attack on them in New York. With Genovese out of the way in Fascist Italy, this lack of attention allowed Costello to move quietly but firmly into the position of senior Mob boss. His connections in political and legal circles were unparalleled, and his discretion ensured he maintained a good reputation among the five Mafia families. He was close to Lansky, Joe Adonis, and Albert Anastasia, and he kept in touch with Luciano in prison, passing on his orders to the underworld.

Thomas Dewey eventually benefited from his formidable crime-busting reputation by becoming governor of New York in 1942. He proved to be a popular politician and was elected to two more terms as governor. He would later stand as a Republican presidential candidate three times, but his youth counted against him in wartime—the nation preferred an older man to lead them against their enemies. Although an infamous headline, proclaiming falsely that "Dewey Defeats Truman," did appear in the *Chicago Tribune* following the close presidential race of 1948.

♠

Life in Dannemora was unpleasant for Luciano. Not only was it bitterly cold and strictly run—dubbed "Siberia"—it was a long way from New York City, making it difficult for his Mob associates to visit him.

Little Davie Petillo, Luciano's codefendant in 1936, was also in Dannemora and formed a gang of Italian criminals. They fought other inmates, stabbing and beating them. Luciano stayed out of the fighting, but in a tense recreation yard confrontation stepped in to bring an end to the conflict. Petillo swung at him with a baseball bat. Another convict defended Luciano and punched Petillo to the ground. Petillo was sent to solitary and Luciano's brokered peace between the prison gangs remained as long as Luciano was there.

John Resko was a fellow inmate who later described Luciano's impact on the prison community. "Life in prison picked up tempo after the arrival of Luciano and his partners," he recalled. "Cons and guards were constantly planning accidental meetings with Lucky. Involved were curiosity, a desire to enhance prestige, or a plea for aid. Everyone around Luciano was approached at one time or another to intercede, to introduce, to pass on information."

Generally, he was called Lucky by fellow cons and guards. His friends knew him as Charlie.

"Though other convicts, with less influence and less cash, availed themselves of special privileges," continued Resko, "wearing outside shirts and tailor-made trousers, having special meals in their cells and hired help, Luciano for one reason or another refused all such favors. The psychology was excellent. He was never pointed out as a big shot because he wore a white shirt or had a guy cleaning out his cell. He was one of the boys. Just another con."

Despite this apparent modesty, money continued to flow into Luciano's coffers on the outside, thanks to Lansky's diligence, and he used it to fund his legal team and their case for a retrial. In early 1937, it looked as though they might be getting somewhere.

Affidavits came to the trial judge from witnesses stating they had testified falsely at the trial. Their recantations came as newly discovered evidence and completely validated the application for a retrial. On January 26, 1937, Cokie Flo Brown stood in a California law office and testified before a notary public for Los Angeles County.

"I was in very bad physical condition," she said of her original testimony. "I don't think I was even able to think at the time." As a heroin addict, she would have testified to almost anything in order to alleviate her suffering.

"On May 5, 1936, I was arrested for soliciting on the streets," she continued, "and was convicted on May 12, 1936, and at the time I testified, I was waiting sentence on that crime. There were also pending against me three other charges in which I was a fugitive from justice. One charge was possessing of drugs, a second, the possession of a hypodermic needle, and the third, of maintaining a disorderly house." Flo Brown declared that the idea for the garage meeting testimony about Luciano came from Mildred Curtis, Tommy the Bull's girlfriend, and she made it up, as well as the Chinese restaurant conversations in which Luciano famously said he wanted to set up brothels like A&P stores. All of it was fabricated, she claimed.

To counter this allegation, Dewey was forced to bring back some of the girls from the trial to testify that they had told the truth about Luciano's involvement with the vice business, despite being terrified of mobster retribution.

"After we had given Mr. Dewey's office our testimony," said Thelma Jordan, "we told the district attorney that after we testified on the stand, we would be in fear of our lives and we had in fact been threatened by Ralph Liguori in Mr. Dewey's office. . . . Mary Morris told me that the Luciano Mob had threatened to torture or kill both of us. I told Judge McCook and Mr. Dewey's office of this conversation. Mr. Dewey's office then agreed to raise the money to send us out of the country."

Dewey was compelled to give his own extensive testimony on the motives and process behind his prosecution case. He denied his office was out to get Luciano.

"Prior to the arrest and testimony given by these witnesses," he explained, "we had no evidence of Luciano's direct connection with this racket; we had made no effort to locate him and did not even know where he was. Toward the end of March, however, the evidence was such that I felt it was my duty to represent the case to the grand jury and attempt to locate Luciano. This was done. After some undercover investigation, it was reported to me that he was either in Miami, Florida, or Hot Springs, Arkansas, having given up his apartment at the Waldorf-Astoria and fled from New York shortly after the murder of Dutch Schultz in October 1935."

No special inducements were offered to the witnesses, insisted Dewey, except for protection from underworld figures.

"It is impossible to picture the fear expressed by almost every witness in this case at the prospect of testifying against these defendants," he said. "Petillo had a reputation as a desperate killer. Wahrman [Abe Heller] and Liguori were widely known for various acts of violence. Tommy Pennochio, alias the Bull, was believed to have murdered a narcotic peddler who had turned state's evidence in the federal courts a short time before the arrest in this case, and at the time of his arrest there was found in his pocket, written in pencil, a careful account of the date of arrest, date of release, date of assault and hospitalization, date of death and date of burial of that narcotic peddler who had been murdered."

Dewey rejected the claim that Flo Brown was in an especially weakened condition when she testified, saying that under the most exhaustive cross-examination she performed very well and her recollection never failed her. "I said at that time that it was my opinion that Florence Brown and Mildred Balitzer were the two most intelligent women in the entire group and also that each had intimate knowledge of the criminal underworld."

Dewey admitted that after the trial he was approached by moviemakers from Warner Bros. looking for inside material on the trial. "I told them that I personally would not in any way participate in such an activity. I would not permit, if I could help it, any dramatization of the Luciano trial as I considered it unfit for dramatization." But he did recommend they talk to Brown and Balitzer. "I also told them that both of these women had repeatedly said that they were going to go straight 'if it killed them' after this trial."

Several of the prostitute witnesses were invited to Hollywood to appear as themselves in movies rushed out to capitalize on the publicity of the trial, including *Missing Witnesses* in 1937 and *Smashing the Rackets* in 1938. Warner Bros. made *Marked Woman* in 1937, their own version of the story with Bette Davis playing a Flo Brown character, while Humphrey Bogart starred as the crusading DA and the Neapolitan-born Eduardo Ciannelli played Johnny Vanning—the Luciano-like mobster.

Despite the recantations of his chief witnesses, Dewey made his argument well, and the case for a retrial was dismissed. In 1938, the case was revisited again by five judges. In their report, they believed the case had been effectively proven. "The appellant Luciano took the stand in his own behalf and testified that he did not know any of the defendants except Betillo [*sic*]. In this, he was contradicted not only by the women witnesses, but by employees of the two different hotels.

"This evidence cogently proves Luciano's connection with this nefarious enterprise," concluded the judges. "His position as head of this Combination did not bring him in direct contact with the victims of this scheme, and he displayed an anxiety that his name be not too openly associated with the bonding enterprise. Thus the evidence against him is not so easily available as it was against some of those lower in the organization, but the evidence produced against him is amply sufficient to warrant the verdict of guilty against him."

The sentence was not overly harsh, either. All the defendants received shorter sentences than the law allowed. "In other words, they got less than they might have gotten." However, only four of the five judges affirmed the judgment. The fifth dissented on the ground "there were material and prejudicial errors committed during the trial which cannot be overlooked, and that the defendants were tried for a crime with which they were not charged in the indictment." This dissension was not strong enough cause for a retrial.

It looked like it was the end of the line for Luciano. His legal team had failed to get him out of jail and there would be no more appeals. It must have been his most depressing moment—realizing he could be imprisoned in Dannemora for the rest of his life. Leo Katcher, the biographer of Arnold Rothstein, visited Luciano in prison shortly after he got the news of his failed final appeal. He told the mobster that he looked surprisingly good for his time in jail.

"Why shouldn't I?" he said. "Lots of work, lots of exercise. No late hours. Just what the doctor ordered. God, how I hate it."

He had a job in the laundry and revealed the calluses on his hands. He still claimed the witnesses had lied against him in the trial and pinned his only hope of getting out of jail on this truth coming out.

"What will you do when you get out?" asked Katcher.

"I'll follow the horses from Saratoga to Belmont to Florida to California. I'll sleep with my windows open so I can reach out and hold the air in my hands. I'll never lock a door again. Whenever I hear a noise I'm going to go in and look at people and watch them. I'll watch women laughing and dancing. I'll laugh and dance too. When I get out, I'm going to be free."

As Katcher stood up to leave, he asked Luciano if he could do anything for him.

"Yeah," he said, "Don't close the door as you go out."

At that point in time, Luciano could have little guessed that political events in faraway Germany—the land he visited with Jack Diamond to set up a narcotics smuggling network in 1930—would conspire to create a world situation that would radically change the future outcome of his criminal career. That dream of freedom would come true. The Nazis were coming to Manhattan.

♠

When it came to extremist politics in the 1920s and 1930s, New York City was just an extension of Europe. So many immigrants thronged the streets of the Lower East Side and other pockets of New York and New Jersey that it is not surprising that the high emotions sparked by events in Italy and Germany should also be expressed on their sidewalks. As early as 1925, the Fascist League of North America was fervently supporting the policies of Benito Mussolini and being attacked for it. In a political meeting in Newark, violence broke out.

"There were yells of 'Here they come!'" reported a local newspaper, "and as the Fascisti reached the center of the hall a half hundred Socialists closed in behind them, some flourishing guns." They fought with knives, razors and sticks, as well as firearms. "The yells of the combatants, punctuated by occasional pistol shots, could be heard for blocks." By the time the police arrived, there were piles of abandoned weapons among the wounded, six of whom were in a serious state from stabbings and gunshots.

Anti-Fascist opposition came from American union leaders. William Green was president of the American Federation of Labor and he spoke out against Mussolini to his five million members.

"Not satisfied with the weapons of a dictator in Italy, he has extended his tentacles of Fascismo into other countries," said Green. "His dictum that 'once an Italian always an Italian to the seventh generation,' prohibits Italian immigrants to the United States becoming naturalized. They must remain Italian citizens to Fascismo. . . . Fascismo and communism have the same fangs and the same poison which it is intended to inject into the political life of our nation."

In Green's view, Mussolini was creating a potential Fifth Column of Italian immigrants of dubious loyalty within the United States.

Italian organized crime was not wild about Mussolini, either, as many of its mafiosi had fled from Sicily in the wake of the Fascist crackdown on the island. Salvatore Maranzano and Joseph Bonanno were just two of these criminal refugees. It meant that the Mafia in New York were more than happy to support anyone speaking out against Mussolini.

Carlo Tresca was a Socialist activist who settled in Greenwich Village and opened up an anti-Fascist newspaper called *Il Martello*—"The Hammer." When a Blackshirt-supporting hoodlum was assigned to kill him, the Mafia intervened. They called Tresca to a meeting where the trembling would-be assassin was pushed down on his knees before him. The mobsters told the killer to kiss the hand of Tresca and forget about the contract on him. It was an early display of organized crime intervening against extremist politics.

The violence at demonstrations grew in intensity and culminated in a murderous meeting on Memorial Day in May 1927. Near the stairs of an elevated station in the Bronx, a group of Blackshirts was gathering when one of their members, thirty-nine-year-old Joseph Carisi, was attacked by a red tie–wearing stranger.

"Carisi had heard the pattering of footsteps," said the newspaper report, "and turned just as the long knife blade came into sight. He shouted for help, and as he looked upward to where his companions were approaching the top of the flight of stairs the stranger stabbed him six times. The blows were delivered with lightning speed and were all within a space of inches and around the collarbone."

Carisi died shortly afterward, along with a second Blackshirt victim on that day. Street battles with anti-Fascists followed, including one involving two hundred Blackshirts in central Manhattan. "Across the broad plaza they ran," noted a journalist, "toward the Hotel Astor, while astonished pedestrians fled for cover before the onrush of whip-waving, yelling Italians. Traffic officers blew their whistles. Motorists clamped brakes."

Such political violence was getting out of control, and the New York police banned all Fascist parades. Mussolini was at first outraged by this murderous assault on his followers, but realizing it was becoming more of an embarrassment than a help to his foreign policy, he withdrew his support for the Fascist League of North America, and it was dissolved just before Christmas 1929. It didn't mean the trouble went away—many Italian immigrants continued to publicly demonstrate their support for Mussolini—but it meant they no longer had an official organization on their side of the Atlantic.

In contrast, American Nazis were only just starting to get into their stride in the early 1930s, and this provoked Jewish gangsters into hitting back.

"My friends and I saw some good action against the Brown Shirts around New York," recalled Meyer Lansky. "I got my buddies like Bugsy Siegel—before he went to California—and some other young guys. We taught them how to use their fists and handle themselves in fights, and we didn't behave like gents."

Lansky's family had fled from anti-Jewish pogroms in Belarus, and he was not going to accept such intimidation in his new homeland. German support for Hitler had been growing in the United States ever since he became chancellor in 1933. Meetings of the German American Bund took place across the United States, where young men and women paraded in martial uniforms with swastika badges.

"There was a house on St. Nicholas Avenue that people spoke of in whispers," remembered one resident of a German neighborhood in Ridgewood, New Jersey. "The shades were always pulled down. On a few occasions the shades went up and on the far wall was a well-lit picture of Adolf Hitler."

Numbers of Nazi supporters grew from the low thousands to more than a hundred thousand within a few years. They organized rallies and noisily demonstrated their admiration of Hitler and the German Nazi party. In 1936, Fritz Kuhn took over leadership of the Bund and campaigned on behalf of a Republican

candidate for president. They received the active support of leading Americans such as the car manufacturer Henry Ford.

In reaction to this, the Jewish establishment in New York
organized its own violent response. New York State judge Nathan Perlman contacted Lansky for help in 1935, offering him
financial and legal assistance if he would take the fight to the
Bund. Lansky was happy to wade in and described their efforts
to disrupt a Nazi meeting in Yorkville, center of the German
community in Manhattan.

"The stage was decorated with a swastika and pictures of
Hitler. The speakers started ranting. There were only about fifteen of us, but we went into action. We attacked them in the hall
and threw some of them out the windows. There were fistfights
all over the place. Most of the Nazis panicked and ran out . . .
We wanted to show them that Jews would not always sit back
and accept insults."

Perlman and other leading Jews were pleased to see this. Italian mobster friends of Lansky offered to pitch in, but Lansky declined, wanting this to be a Jewish-only battle. Max Hinkes was
a soldier for Abner "Longy" Zwillman in Newark, New Jersey,
and he recorded his own assault on a Nazi meeting, when they
tossed stink bombs into the gathering.

"As they came out of the room," said Hinkes, "running from
the terrible odor of the stink bombs and running down the steps
into the street to escape, our boys were waiting with bats and
iron bars. It was like running a gauntlet. Our boys were lined up
on both sides and we started hitting, aiming for their heads or
any other part of their bodies, with our bats and bars. The Nazis
were screaming blue murder. This was one of the most happy
moments of my life."

Such clashes brought unwelcome publicity to Lansky, who
in his desire to beat the Nazis was edging into the spotlight
that he had blamed for Luciano's imprisonment. Jewish newspapers began to describe him as a leading mobster, and none of
his establishment friends could shield him from the attention.

It was this, plus the fact that their bloody assaults on Nazis were starting to garner negative publicity, that led him to halt his fight against the German American Bund.

Fortunately, by 1939 the U.S. government was peering into the affairs of Fritz Kuhn, leader of the Bund, and following a massive rally at Madison Square Garden to celebrate Washington's birthday, he was arrested and jailed for stealing from party funds. A later proposed alliance between the Bund and the Ku Klux Klan came to nothing and the organization disbanded in 1941.

Lansky's experience fighting Nazis in the late 1930s is crucial to understanding underworld events in the 1940s when the United States was at war with Nazi Germany. Alongside earlier battles against American Fascists, it demonstrated that there was a willingness among law-abiding citizens to deploy mobsters in a crusade against anti-American forces.

As Lansky himself put it: "The reason why I cooperated was because of strong personal convictions. I wanted the Nazis beaten. I made this my number one priority even before the United States got into the war. I was a Jew and I felt for those Jews in Europe who were suffering. They were my brothers."

The realization that the U.S. establishment—indeed, even the government—might be willing to associate itself with mobsters to fight Nazis enabled Lansky to forge ahead with his big idea to get his old pal Luciano out of jail. It was a long shot—but it was the only way Luciano was going to grab a fistful of fresh air.

Typical old New York City tenement block on First Avenue, between East 13th and East 14th Streets. The Lucania family first lived in this area when they arrived in New York. It is on the northern boundary of the Lower East Side in an area now called the East Village. To the south of them was Little Italy and Chinatown. AUTHOR'S COLLECTION

Luciano's family home at 265 East 10th Street, New York City. Luciano left home in his teens, but regularly visited his parents here until they moved out in 1933. AUTHOR'S COLLECTION

Police photograph of Luciano as his most powerful. It was taken in 1931 after his arrest for felonious assault. The police record calls him Charles Lucania "Lucky," residing at 265 East 10th Street. NEW YORK WORLD-TELEGRAM & SUN NEWSPAPER COLLECTION/LIBRARY OF CONGRESS

Police photograph of (from left to right) Ed Diamond, Jack "Legs" Diamond, Thomas "Fatty" Walsh, and Charles Lucania (aka Luciano), taken when Luciano was making a name for himself as a bootlegger and gunman.
NEW YORK WORLD-TELEGRAM & SUN NEWSPAPER COLLECTION/ LIBRARY OF CONGRESS

Corner of East 12th Street and Second Avenue, New York City, where Luciano shot Umberto Valenti, gunman rival to Joe the Boss, in August 1922.
AUTHOR'S COLLECTION

Police photograph of a young Meyer Lansky. One of Luciano's most important associates, he oversaw the business interests of the Mob. NEW YORK WORLD-TELEGRAM & SUN NEWSPAPER COLLECTION/LIBRARY OF CONGRESS

Frank Costello in 1935. An early friend of Luciano who became a key figure in the Mafia thanks to his political contacts. NEW YORK WORLD-TELEGRAM & SUN NEWSPAPER COLLECTION/LIBRARY OF CONGRESS

Joe "the Boss" Masseria, a dominant mobster in late 1920s Manhattan. Luciano worked for Masseria until Luciano had him murdered in 1931 and took over his crime family. NEW YORK WORLD-TELEGRAM & SUN NEWSPAPER COLLECTION/LIBRARY OF CONGRESS

Thomas E. Dewey, the young district attorney who put Luciano in jail in 1936. NEW YORK WORLD-TELEGRAM & SUN NEWSPAPER COLLECTION/ LIBRARY OF CONGRESS

The Waldorf-Astoria, the grandest hotel in New York City when it opened in 1931. Luciano lived in a luxurious apartment suite in the Waldorf Towers. AUTHOR'S COLLECTION

Luciano handcuffed to Jimmy Fredericks, one of his
codefendants, during their trial in 1936 for running a
prostitution racket in the city. NEW YORK WORLD-TELEGRAM
& SUN NEWSPAPER COLLECTION/LIBRARY OF CONGRESS

Diagram showing
how Luciano was
linked to the
mobsters running
prostitution in
Manhattan in the
early 1930s. This
was part of the
evidence against
Luciano assembled
by Dewey and
his staff. NYC
MUNICIPAL ARCHIVES

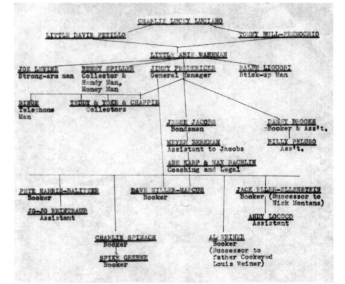

Lieutenant Commander Charles Radcliffe Haffenden was in charge of the U.S. Naval Intelligence operation that used Luciano and his Mob associates to protect the East Coast against German saboteurs. HERLANDS INVESTIGATION

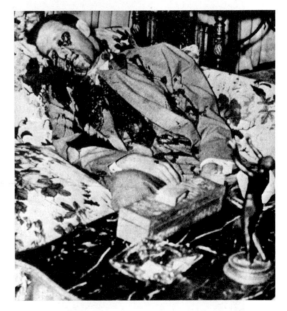

Bugsy Siegel, close friend of Luciano, was killed by the Mob in his Beverly Hills mansion in 1947, for misusing their funds in Las Vegas. NEW YORK WORLD-TELEGRAM & SUN NEWSPAPER COLLECTION/LIBRARY OF CONGRESS

Don Calogero Vizzini was a leading Mafioso in Sicily and was associated with Luciano during the first years of his exile in Italy. AUTHOR'S COLLECTION

The Grand Hotel Et Des Palmes in Palermo was the smartest hotel in Sicily in 1947 and was the favorite place for Luciano to stay when he was on the island. It later hosted an infamous meeting of Mafiosi in 1957 to organize the illicit transatlantic narcotics trade. AUTHOR'S COLLECTION

The legend begins—pulp-fiction–style cover of *The Luciano Story*, first biography of the mobster, published in 1955. AUTHOR'S COLLECTION

TALKING TO THE DEVIL HIMSELF

The Japanese attack on Pearl Harbor on December 7, 1941, was a lucky break for Charlie Luciano. The next day, President Roosevelt took the United States to war against Japan and three days later Nazi Germany and Fascist Italy joined the conflict against the United States. Luciano had been in jail for more than five years and he hated it.

"In the summer it's like a hothouse," he told Lansky. "It stinks like a human being who's never washed in his life. In winter the wind comes right through you and you can see the ice forming on the inside walls. That's why we call it Siberia. It's the worst place in the world. It would be better to be dead than to stay here." But as America entered a brutal world war, there was a chink of light for the mobster. Having thrown away the key on Public Enemy No. 1, it might just be that the authorities now needed his help.

In the first six months of 1942, Nazi Germany put enormous pressure on the transatlantic supply route between Britain and

America. Freed by Hitler's declaration of war on the United States, Axis U-boats torpedoed remorselessly any Allied ship they caught along the East Coast. From the Gulf of Saint Lawrence in the north, all the way down the eastern seaboard to the Caribbean, German submarines sank more than three hundred Allied vessels. In just six days in January 1941, submarine raiders destroyed a ten-thousand-ton merchant ship near Novia Scotia, a Norwegian oil tanker sixty miles off the New York coast, and a U.S. merchant steamer, a Latvian freighter, and a U.S. tanker, all off North Carolina.

On February 23, President Roosevelt admitted in a radio address to the nation the extent of this naval carnage. "We have most certainly suffered losses," he said, "from Hitler's U-boats in the Atlantic as well as from the Japanese in the Pacific—and we shall suffer more of them before the turn of the tide."

The reason why the president was forced to admit this defeat may well have been the most high-profile naval loss of all—the sinking of the troopship *Normandie* just two weeks before in full view of thousands of New Yorkers. This was a very visible blow to American military prestige.

The disaster happened on the afternoon of February 9, 1942. The *Normandie* was a French-built luxury ocean liner that was being converted into a troop carrier for ten thousand American troops crossing the Atlantic to join the war in Europe. Unquestionably, it was a major target for any enemy action. Just over two weeks before she was ready to set sail, a fire broke out in the grand salon of the promenade deck of the *Normandie*. The flames rapidly spread throughout the ship. It was moored in the Hudson River at Pier 88, at West Forty-eighth Street in New York Harbor, and the huge cloud of smoke rising above its three funnels attracted crowds from Manhattan.

"Air raid wardens and auxiliary firemen came from all parts of the city in response to an urgent call," said a newspaper report. "They arrived by taxi, by private automobile and on foot, each with his identifying armband and card. They were quickly pressed into service, along with sailors, workmen, police and ordinary volunteers, to serve as stretcher bearers, to help carry fire hoses and to assist in many other ways. The general scene was one of a war catastrophe."

Some fifteen hundred servicemen and workers were evacuated, but 128 were injured and one died from his wounds. As tugboats sprayed the hull with water, it was thought the fire had been brought under control, but in the early hours of the next day, a new disaster struck. The *Normandie* was listing dangerously.

"A little past 2 this morning," said a witness, "the increasing sag was reflected in clattering sounds from the upper decks, as articles began to topple towards the sea-dipping rail. Tense watchers gasped, hoping the bottom mud would retain its precarious grasp on the keel. But at 2:35, quietly, with little disturbance or noise, as search-lights played upon the great hulk erratically, the once-beautiful ship slipped over on her port side." And there she would stay for four years, rotting in the mud, until she was sold for scrap. In one terrible night, the U.S. Navy's greatest troop-carrying asset—worth $56 million—had been wiped out.

As the hundreds of workmen on board huddled in side-street bars, they talked over the events. Some claimed there had been more than one fire and that was why it had spread so rapidly. Again and again, they kept coming back to the same conclusion—sabotage. It seemed that the fire on the *Normandie* had been set deliberately to knock it out of the war. Official reports denied this was the cause.

Naval authorities spoke to a man who said he saw a worker using an acetylene torch. Sparks from this sprayed around the shield and set light to bales of wood shavings used for packing. This ignited in a flash that reached the ceiling. Another account said that the sparks set alight a pile of life preservers. It was a full eleven minutes before any fire service could start putting out the flames, by which time the fire had a firm grip on the decks. It was the flood of water from fireboats that contributed to its list and turned it over.

Despite this explanation, the sinking of the *Normandie* and its possible connection to enemy sabotage lodged in the popular imagination. Shortly afterward, all lights visible from the sea along the waterfront areas of Brooklyn, Queens, and Staten Island were ordered extinguished for the duration of the war. It was feared that enemy spies were communicating with German U-boats—giving them information on the sailing of ships and their course.

Four months later came the sensational news that the FBI had arrested eight trained German saboteurs in New York and Chicago. They had been landed by German submarines at two locations—Amagansett on Long Island and Ponte Vedra Beach in Florida. The men were caught carrying explosives and more than $170,000, plus maps and plans for a two-year operation of attacks on American war defense factories, railways, water works, and bridges in the East and Midwest. All the spies admitted their intention of sabotage. It could not be any more clear: There was an enemy within.

Further headlines added to the fever of concern. On September 21, 1942, the *New York Times* carried a story pointing the finger at a Japanese naval officer who had been masquerading as an engineering inspector with offices in New York. He had been at the heart of a spy ring in June 1941 conspiring to smuggle examples of American weapons on ships sailing to Japan. But he could just as easily have been planning his own version of Pearl Harbor. It was a chilling thought that only heightened American government anxiety over the vulnerability of the East Coast.

How concerned U.S. Naval Intelligence was about the danger from foreign agents was revealed just twelve years later in a secret government report. Despite reassurances at the time, it said: "The fear of sabotage on the piers and docks and throughout the port was great. In February, the burning of the 'Normandie' at her pier in the North River intensified the fear that saboteurs were active in the port." And this was from the intelligence agency that had full access to the naval investigation that claimed the burning was an accident. Clearly, they didn't believe their own pronouncement on the affair. Added to this was the knowledge that many American citizens had been fervent supporters of Fascism and the Nazis in the 1920s and 1930s. It made for a toxic mix of enemy agents and native collaborators.

As a result of this climate of terror, the secret report concluded: "Naval Intelligence was required to take every possible measure to combat the enemy submarine activity and the activities of any enemy agents along the waterfront."

The war was forcing the government into making an alliance with some very dark characters—among them Lucky Luciano.

♠

"I'll talk to anybody, a priest, a bank manager, a gangster, the devil himself," said Lieutenant Commander Charles Radcliffe Haffenden, head of the U.S. Navy's intelligence staff based in New York. "This is a war. American lives are at stake. It's not a college game where we have to look up the rule book every minute, and we're not running a headquarters office where regulations must be followed to the letter. I have a job to do."

Haffenden was a tough-talking fifty-year-old career officer who had been in the navy since World War I. He was physically fearless and would later volunteer to be beach master during the invasion of Iwo Jima, where he came under heavy artillery fire. Talking straight to a few wise guys would not bother him at all. But the plan he had to execute came from his superiors.

Spooked by the burning of the *Normandie*, senior U.S. naval officers feared for the security of the East Coast. Commercial fishing flects came under suspicion as possibly selling fuel and supplies to enemy submarines. U.S. Naval Intelligence felt confident that they had pro-Nazis under observation, but it was the Italian fishermen who crewed these fleets, sympathetic to Mussolini and the Italian Fascist cause, that worried them. Captain Roscoe C. MacFall was district intelligence officer for the Third Naval District and came up with the plan that was later dubbed "Operation Underworld."

"Naval Intelligence was greatly interested in obtaining information about the possibility that enemy agents might be landed on the coast," said MacFall. "Likewise, Naval Intelligence sought information about enemy submarines in the coastal waters and the suspected danger that enemy submarines might be refueled through fishing boats or ex-rumrunners plying the coastal area and operated by criminal elements or others whose loyalty might be subverted by payments of money." MacFall was talking about the network of liquor-smuggling small boats that had so successfully avoided interception during Prohibition.

It was only a short step for U.S. Naval Intelligence to consider talking to criminal elements based on the waterfront in the great cities—New York especially. To infiltrate the ports, Naval Intelligence agents were placed on trucks, in factories, hotels, restaurants, nightclubs, and bars. To get these jobs the agents needed union cards and these could be obtained only from union officials appointed by organized crime families. It was the Mob that ran the docks.

Captain MacFall understood this and gave the okay to Haffenden and his agents to talk to underworld figures. On March 7 and March 25, 1942, MacFall and Haffenden met with District Attorney Frank Hogan and Lieutenant Colonel Murray I. Gurfein, who ran the DA's Rackets Bureau. Gurfein had been a member of Dewey's original legal team that put Luciano behind bars in 1936. As a result of these two meetings, they were put in touch with Joseph K. Guerin, attorney for Joe "Socks" Lanza, the forty-one-year-old so-called czar of Fulton Fish Market. Lanza's gang had taken over the waterfront Teamsters union, looted their funds, and extorted regular weekly payments from everyone working for them. If anyone knew what was going on along the seaboard, Lanza did. At the time, he was under indictment on charges of conspiracy and extortion, but through the intercession of his attorney and the DA's Colonel Gurfein, a meeting with Lanza was arranged.

Near midnight on March 25, on a bench in Riverside Park on the Upper West Side, Gurfein told Lanza about the fears of Naval Intelligence. "It's a matter of great urgency. Many of our ships are being sunk along the Atlantic coast," he said. "You know the people engaged in commercial fishing. You can find out how and where the submarines are being refueled."

"Sure," Lanza said, nodding, "I'll help the war effort. I got contacts in the fish market and fishing boat and barge captains and seamen all along the Atlantic coast."

A week later, Lanza was ushered into the plush surroundings of the Hotel Astor, where Commander Haffenden had set up his offices. The mobster was told that he was volunteering his help and that no deal had been made with the DA's office. The government would stick by this—having got his assistance, the following year Lanza was sentenced to fifteen years in jail for racketeering.

In the meantime, Lanza proved helpful. He got union cards for naval agents so they could work on boats and monitor the Italian fishing community. The agents installed telephone equipment on the boats and used them as part of a submarine lookout system. Sometimes the boats picked up remains of wreckage— even bits of human bodies—indicative of the savage war at sea. Naval agents also worked on the trucks delivering fish from the coast to Fulton Fish Market, all the time gathering information from gossip and rumor.

By April 1942, Lanza had helped Haffenden as much as he could. Suspicion hung over him because of his pending indictment and senior mobsters were reluctant to talk to him. Lanza went to his attorney and explained this, saying that if Naval

Intelligence wanted to get the complete cooperation of New York's underworld, they had to go the top—and that meant talking to Charlie Luciano.

"If he came into this picture," said Lanza, "I'll get all the cooperation from various people in the City of New York. He'd send some word to Joe Adonis or Frank [Costello]. The word of Charlie [Luciano] would give me the right way."

When MacFall and Haffenden heard this, they shrugged and agreed. MacFall had already crossed the line of talking to criminals and Haffenden could deal with any mobster put his way. Sometimes the collusion brought extra benefits. In the same year, as a result of his underworld contacts, Haffenden was able to defuse a major scandal when the *New York Post* claimed Senator Walsh, chairman of the naval affairs committee, had been spotted in a "house of ill fame" run by a German who was suspected of being a spy by the FBI and charged with trying to get information from navy personnel. It could have been a serious lapse of security, but by talking to the mobsters who ran the brothel, Haffenden furnished the real identity of the elderly gentleman and a damaging scandal was avoided.

So far, in this story, it appears that it was the idea of Naval Intelligence to recruit mobsters and to take this a stage further by talking to gangster No. 1, Luciano. But is this true?

Meyer Lansky was already very aware of what was going on because Lanza was simultaneously reporting back to him on his dealings with Naval Intelligence. "Joe Socks [Lanza] did the right thing by coming to me," he recalled. "Gurfein's move had been even shrewder than he realized, because Lucky and I were close to Lanza ourselves. We got him out of a lot of trouble when he was a boy, and he never forgot how we helped him.

"Lanza told me," said Lansky, "that the Italian people around there [the waterfront] thought that he had a personal motive. They didn't believe him that it was a movement that all Italians should get interested; and he asked me to take him up to Charlie

Luciano, and if Charlie Luciano would send word to these people he thought that resistance would stop."

But is it possible that Luciano and his associates had already set the groundwork for this deal by heightening the government's sense of wartime fear? Is it possible that they could have been responsible for acts of destruction made to look like enemy sabotage? Even more sensationally, were they behind the burning of the *Normandie*?

♠

The Last Testament of Lucky Luciano has long been criticized as more invention than truth, and many of its stories, supposedly from the mouth of Luciano, do not fit in with the facts that we know. But sometimes contained within its pages are nuggets of information that make one wonder where the authors got them from, if *not* from the gangster chief. The book was first published in 1975, four years before the appearance of Meyer Lansky's memoir and two years before the secret government report on the whole wartime affair was widely publicized in Rodney Campbell's *The Luciano Project*.

The Last Testament claims that Luciano himself devised Operation Underworld in December 1941. He pitched the plan to Lansky and Frank Costello. Costello said they had contacts at the Third District headquarters of Naval Intelligence at 50 Church Street and would pursue it. Luciano waited more than a month but got no positive response. He had suggested to Costello that what they needed was a front-page act of sabotage to underline the need for his help. With this in mind, one of his top hit men, Albert Anastasia, came to him with own plan. He said he'd been watching the Naval Intelligence agents on the waterfront, worrying about security, and thought that if something big happened, it would tip them over the edge into doing a deal with anyone.

"Albert figures that if something could happen to the

Normandie," says Luciano in *The Last Testament,* "that would really make everyone crap in their pants. It was a great idea and I didn't figure it was really gonna hurt the war effort because the ship was nowhere near ready and, besides, no American soldiers or sailors would be involved because they wasn't sendin' 'em no place yet. So I sent back word to Albert to handle it. A couple of days later, I hear on the radio where the *Normandie* was on fire and it didn't look like they could save her. That goddamn Anastasia—he really done a job."

It is an incredible claim and would invite derision but for the fact that Meyer Lansky later corroborated the story in his more respected memoirs. He says that after talking to Haffenden, who was still shaken by the *Normandie* incident, he guaranteed there would be more incidents of sabotage on the waterfront. He passed this on to Frank Costello.

"The message went to Albert Anastasia too," recalls Lansky, "and I told him face to face that he mustn't burn any more ships. He was sorry—not sorry he'd had the *Normandie* burned but sorry that he couldn't get at the Navy again. Apparently he had learned in the army to hate the Navy. 'Stuck-up bastards' he called them."

This certainly backs up Luciano's story, and Lansky's memoirs are generally regarded as coming from the mouth of the man himself. However, the reference to Anastasia's hatred of the navy comes straight from *The Last Testament* and there is no other information in the Lansky book to elaborate on the tale first related by Luciano. Generally, Dennis Eisenberg and the other authors of Lansky's recollections are uncritical of *The Last Testament* and quote widely from it. If *The Last Testament* is nonsense and yet they put a story directly from it in the mouth of Lansky, it casts doubt on the veracity of this source, too. Or—the story is true and Anastasia torched the ocean liner. What we do know from the U.S. government's own investigation is that the burning of the *Normandie* was one of the main contributing factors for making them talk to Luciano and his associates.

♠

Negotiations with Luciano began in April 1942. Murray Gurfein arranged a meeting with Moses Polakoff, an attorney who helped defend Luciano against Dewey in 1936. At first, Polakoff wasn't interested in revisiting the Luciano case, but Gurfein underlined the national importance of his proposal.

"We want to set up a network of informants among the Italian element concerning any information about sabotage," he explained. "We want the help of Italian fishermen who operate fishing fleets, concerning any possible enemy submarines off our shore."

Polakoff was a veteran of the U.S. Navy from World War I and was sympathetic to Gurfein's request. "But I don't know Luciano well enough to broach the subject with him," he said. "But I do know a person who I have confidence in and whose patriotism, or affection for our country, irrespective of his reputation, is of the highest."

Polakoff was talking about Meyer Lansky, who had already demonstrated his anti-Nazi credentials by attacking their American supporters in New York on behalf of the Jewish community. Lansky was happy to receive the call.

Over breakfast at the Longchamps restaurant on Fifty-seventh Street, Gurfein, Polakoff, and Lansky met. Gurfein told the mobster that the government was fearful of sabotage and Lansky said he was ready to help, but they had to tread carefully, he warned, because many Italians supported Mussolini and they didn't want to alienate this community. Then the conversation came to the point of the meeting—Lucky Luciano.

"Can we trust him?" asked Gurfein.

"Sure you can," said Lansky. "His whole family is here—his father and two brothers and sister with children." It sounded like a Mafia-style threat, but what he probably meant was that Luciano was rooted in the city and would want to protect it. Lansky was certainly warming to the idea and could see the potential benefits for Luciano. He suggested visiting Luciano in prison in Upstate New York at Dannemora. Polakoff winced.

"Snow's still on the ground up there," the attorney complained, "and traveling is too hard."

They then discussed having Luciano transferred to a more convenient prison. Lansky was delighted, knowing this would please his friend very much—anything to get him out of Siberia. At the end of the meeting, Gurfein emphasized the point already made to Lanza that no payment in kind was to be offered to Luciano for his services. He would simply be doing his patriotic duty. Lansky accepted the proviso. With the ground rules laid, the three walked along to the Hotel Astor, where they were introduced to Commander Haffenden.

The gruff naval officer in his uniform made a strong impression on Lansky. He was well informed on Lansky's criminal career but also about his action against the Nazi Bund. He told the mobster that what he was about to say was top secret and he must keep it to himself. He said a large convoy of American troops was being sent overseas imminently and he wanted them protected—no word was to leak out from the men working on the docks. Haffenden repeated their fear following the burning of the *Normandie*.

"Haffenden told us where we were weak," remembered Lansky. "Where he felt the government needs lots of assistance such as the waterfront; pertaining to loaders of ships; employees on the docks; receiving knowledge as to fishing boats— whatever they do in their movements outside; and he wanted people that could be of assistance in that way so that nothing is brought out to any submarines."

Lansky pledged his support and after the meeting told Frank Costello and Albert Anastasia to cooperate fully with the Naval Intelligence agents. Lanza wondered if they could start charging the U.S. Navy for their services, but Lansky slapped him down, telling him to expect nothing and to pay for his own expenses. He was doing it as a patriot and for the good of his boss— Luciano.

Already the deal began to bear fruit with the transfer of Luciano from Dannemora to Great Meadow Correctional Facility in Comstock on May 12, 1942. Not only did it sound better, it was much more comfortable and more convenient. He had hot water in his cell and decent toilet paper for the first time in six years. Luciano was delighted, even though he didn't know why he had been moved. The transfer was buried within the movement of other inmates, but the commissioner of the New York State Department of Correction was well aware of its purpose when he waived the need for the fingerprinting of Luciano's prison visitors. It was the least he could do, he said, if it saved the life of just one American serviceman.

Luciano's move between prisons did not go unnoticed, however, and the FBI was intrigued by what was going on. No one gave them the full details of the wartime deal and this frustrated their chief, J. Edgar Hoover, who resented being kept out of the loop. The FBI conducted its own report on Luciano in Great Meadow prison, concluding he was "dominated by restlessness and craving for action" but he was "able to get along with his fellow inmates."

Sometime in late May or early June, Lansky and Polakoff took a train to Albany and then drove sixty miles north to Great Meadow, near Comstock. When they turned up, Luciano was surprised to see them. "What the hell are you fellows doing here?" he said. Lansky handed him a package of his favorite kosher food, including pastrami and pickles, with Italian pastries for dessert. While Luciano ate, Lansky explained the government deal to him. He said there was no guarantee of anything, but it had to be of some value in knocking time off his sentence. As it stood, Luciano had no chance of parole until 1956 at the earliest. There was no alternative. Luciano wanted to know what Frank Costello thought of it. Costello agreed he should help the war effort. "We convinced Charlie that it was a duty of us to give assistance," said Lansky.

But still Luciano had one major doubt. He wanted the whole deal kept secret. Since he had been sent to prison, a warrant of deportation hung over him. "When I get out," he said, "nobody knows how this war will turn out—whatever I do, I want it kept quiet, private, so that when I get back to Italy I'm not a marked man." The punishment for breaking the Mafia code of *omerta* was, as always, death. "If he were ever to be deported," said Lansky later, "he might get lynched there."

Haffenden reassured Lansky that everything would be done to keep the identity of those top mafiosi working with the government secret and that each personality would be assigned his own code name so nothing would appear in official documents. In return, Luciano gave the go-ahead for his henchmen to give every assistance possible to Naval Intelligence. Lansky was to be his chief go-between and they had at least twenty more prison meetings on this subject from May 1942 to August 1945. As a result, Lansky could present a very clear guarantee to Haffenden and his team.

"There'll be no German submarines in the Port of New York," Luciano boasted. "Every man down there who works in the harbor—all the sailors, all the fishermen, every longshoreman, every individual who has anything to do with the coming and going of ships to the United States—is now helping the fight against the Nazis."

Other top gangsters visited Luciano in prison, including Joe Adonis, Willie Moretti, and Frank Costello. They were always accompanied by Luciano's attorney, Polakoff, who arranged all visits in advance. According to the agreed arrangements, only Polakoff had to sign the prison register. The visitors were then taken to the prison warden's office, where they would wait until Luciano was brought up from his prison cell. The meetings took place in a large room next to the warden's office. Two guards waited outside the room. The door was locked. Inside, Polakoff sat at the far end of the room so he could not overhear the whispered conversation and usually read a newspaper. The visits took place around 9:30 or 10:00 A.M.

Word was passed on to some of Luciano's toughest enforcers that they were to be deployed in the service of the navy. Johnny "Cockeye" Dunn had a formidable reputation as a racketeer and was sent around dockside bars to see if anyone was blabbing about troop movements.

"Dunn's job was to be a watchdog on the piers," said Lansky, "to have trusted employees amongst the loaders to seek out employees—to make friends with the crew and to stay with them to get reports if there was any bad men around the crowd. He also got friends along the waterfront in the bar rooms. If any of the crews got drunk and they would talk something that you feel is subversive, to report to him."

On one occasion, Dunn got the message that some suspicious characters—possibly German agents—were staying at a waterside hotel. He visited the two gentlemen and they were never seen again. Naval Intelligence was a little worried by these methods and asked him to clear any such incident with them first.

Gangster John McCue was released from Sing Sing after serving ten years for murder and became chief henchman for the president of the International Longshoremen's Association. When any of these workers threatened to disrupt the war effort, McCue broke their arms or legs. Harry Bridges was a no-nonsense union leader from the West Coast. When news spread that he was intent on coming to New York to clean up activities there and organize a strike, Haffenden asked Lanza to sort him out. Lanza personally gave Bridges a beating and later phoned Haffenden to tell him "everything is under control."

At first, some naval agents had their doubts about working so closely with criminals. Lieutenant Anthony J. Marsloe was one of the young Naval Intelligence officers charged with processing the information provided by Luciano. "I felt a certain amount of skepticism," he said, "because I felt that since they had not been good citizens it was doubtful as to whether they would be of constructive service to our war effort." As the war progressed, Marsloe became more of a realist. "Intelligence, as such, is not a police agency. Its function is to prevent. In order to prevent, you must have a system; and the system, in its scope and attitude must encompass any and all means. . . . By any and all means I include the so-called underworld."

But Marsloe had a point—the reality of the situation was that Luciano's alliance with the government not only provided some security for the navy but also enabled him to carry on running his criminal business from behind bars. In fact, it strengthened his authority, as Lansky was allowed to shuttle back and forth to his prison, passing on information and relaying instructions from him.

By buying into Lanza's original statement that Luciano was the chief mobster they needed to talk to, the government was enhancing his reputation as a master criminal. It served their purpose as much as his, or perhaps more so, to show that they were dealing with the most important mobster in order to win the war. They would have to justify this association in due course and they could only do that by making it clear that they were going to the very top—and that was Luciano. From this point onward, government agencies would always regard Luciano as the underworld kingpin and this view of him would continue long after the war ended—whether it was true or not. This wartime alliance was undoubtedly the key event that turned Luciano into an underworld legend.

Soon the scope of this involvement spread beyond the waterside. Haffenden had Lansky place agents in hotels and restaurants throughout Manhattan that were suspected of being used by enemy spies. "One of the places he mentioned was the Pierre Hotel," said Lansky. "He also told me about a place in Brooklyn—some sort of a seamen's club."

In German-populated Yorkville, Lansky hired German-speaking naval agents into cafés and bars as waiters to listen in on conversations. To make their cover even more authentic, these agents sometimes served as collectors for the Mob. "They handed over the money they collected and were always honest in their dealings," said Lansky. "I think this must be the only time the U.S. Navy ever directly helped the Mafia."

To protect the government to some extent, Captain Mac-Fall, chief of Naval Intelligence on the East Coast, shielded his superiors from the full details of this connection. "The use of underworld informants and characters," said MacFall, "like the use of other extremely confidential procedures, was not specifically disclosed to the Commandant or other superior officers as such use was a calculated risk that I assumed as District Intelligence Officer." It would go no further than him and he ensured that the real names of any underworld collaborators never appeared in official wartime records.

Lansky was confident that the government got a good deal out of working with the Mob. He knew his gangsters had complete control of the docks, and by ensuring there was no trouble, naval convoys could carry on their task of delivering supplies to Britain and Russia.

"So," concluded Lansky, "in the end the Mafia helped save the lives of Americans and people in Europe."

By February 1943, however, Luciano was hoping for some payback.

"I won the war single-handed," he later claimed.

A motion was put before the state supreme court to reduce Luciano's sentence. It came before the judge who had originally sentenced Luciano in 1936. Justice Philip J. McCook denied the motion but did hold out the following ray of hope when he referred to Luciano's contribution to the war effort.

"If the defendant is assisting the authorities," said the judge, "and he continues to do so, and remains a model prisoner, executive clemency may become appropriate at some future time."

It was better than nothing. As the war still raged, there was little likelihood of Luciano being deported to Europe, but as the Allies won victories in North Africa, a new battlefront was opening in the Mediterranean. Allied generals looked to Sicily as a stepping-stone to the invasion of Italy. This was Luciano's homeland—the birthplace of the Mafia. Surely there was some way that Lucky Luciano could help directly with the liberation of the old country.

LUCKY GOES TO WAR

Locked in prison, reading daily newspaper reports of Allied victories, Charlie Luciano got impatient. He wanted to be part of the action. If the U.S. government were grateful to him for his help against enemy agents at home, then they'd be knocked out if he got his hands really dirty and stepped forward for active duty. According to Meyer Lansky, he had it all worked out. He would volunteer to act as a scout or liaison officer for frontline troops. He'd put his neck on the line by being parachuted into action—behind enemy lines—and use his considerable influence to win the war for America. Lansky laughed, picturing him landing on top of a church spire. But Luciano couldn't see the funny side—he was deadly serious.

By January 1943, the Allies were on the offensive in the Mediterranean. They had held and defeated the Germans and Italians in North Africa and were now looking to open up a second European front to put more pressure on Hitler, while the German army was fighting for its life against the Soviet Union in Russia. The final decision was made at the Casablanca Conference between U.S. president Franklin D. Roosevelt and British prime minister Winston Churchill. After much debate, the Americans agreed to support Churchill in his desire to invade Mussolini's Italy—the soft underbelly of Nazi Europe. To do this, they would first have to attack Sicily in an operation that would go by the code name "Husky."

Having determined the location of the next Allied thrust, Churchill then had to admit that the Americans possessed an undeniable advantage when it came to dealing with Italians. "In view of the friendly feeling towards America entertained by a great number of citizens of Italy," said Roosevelt in a telegram to Churchill, "and in consideration of the large number of citizens of the United States who are of Italian descent, it is my opinion that our military problem will be made less difficult by giving to the Allied Military Government [in Sicily] as much of an American character as is practicable."

Churchill agreed, but in secret correspondence, his ambassador to Washington, D.C., expressed the fear that Italian-American anti-Fascist agents appointed to Sicily might well turn out to have Mafia links.

"Italian communities in New York were already beginning to lay down the law about administration of Italy," wrote the British ambassador. "Italian communities here had an intimate knowledge and connexion with Huskyland [Sicily] and quite unimportant appointments might have reactions here (for instance it would be known at once if one of our 'anti-Fascist' appointees was a Mafia man as was not unlikely)."

He would not be far wrong. That intimate connection between New York and Sicily could well be a two-edged sword for the Allies.

♠

Having determined the next phase of the war, preparations began for an invasion of Sicily. East Coast Naval Intelligence officers saw an opportunity here to exploit further their connections with Sicilian gangsters. This time, rather than the criminal links confined to the files of his New York office, Haffenden was encouraged to report his contacts to the Washington headquarters of Captain Wallace S. Wharton, head of the Counter-Intelligence Section, Office of Naval Intelligence.

"On the occasions when Commander Haffenden gave names to me," said Wharton, "he told me that he had obtained these names from his contacts in the underworld. The names of the individuals in Sicily who could be trusted turned out to be 40 percent correct, upon eventual checkup and on the basis of actual experience."

Luciano's wild proposal of putting himself in the frontline proved to be true. Lansky told Haffenden about Luciano's suggestion and the commander passed it on to Captain Wharton in Washington. "Haffenden told me that Luciano was willing to go to Sicily," recalled the head of Counter Intelligence, "and contact natives there, in the event of an invasion by our armed forces, and to win these natives over to support the United States war effort, particularly during the amphibious phase of an invasion."

Haffenden argued the case for Luciano, saying he could persuade Governor Dewey to give him a pardon and send him to Sicily via a neutral country, such as Portugal. Full of enthusiasm for the idea, he said that Luciano recommended that U.S. forces land in the Golfo di Castellammare—a favorite Mafia drug smuggling haunt near Palermo and home to many of those mobsters caught up in the gang war of the late 1920s. Wharton seriously considered the fantastic suggestion of sending the U.S. head of organized crime to a theater of war but could see this might well become a scandal after the war and reprimanded Haffenden for a lack of political judgment. He was more than happy just getting information from these gangsters without actually sending them to fight with tommy guns on the beaches of their homeland.

Lieutenant Anthony J. Marsloe had no qualms about dealing with gangsters. "The exploitation of informants, irrespective of their backgrounds, is not only desirous," he said, "but necessary when the nation is struggling for its existence."

He was a law graduate and had served under Captain Mac-Fall and Haffenden since the beginning of the project. Two other members of his four-man team were a practicing attorney and an investigator who would later be tasked with exposing waterfront racketeering. They were now told to speak to all kinds of shady characters in order to get data of use in a projected invasion.

"Because of my personal knowledge of Sicily and the dialects of Sicily," recalled Marsloe, "various personalities, otherwise unidentified, were sent to me by Commander Haffenden. These men were interviewed and photographs, documents or other matters of interest were taken, and in turn given to Commander Haffenden."

Meyer Lansky was actively involved in bringing some of these personalities to Haffenden's office. The naval officers wanted everything they knew about the shape of the coastline and major landing points. "The Navy wanted from the Italians all the pictures they could possibly get of every port of Sicily, of every channel," said Lansky, "and also to get men that were in Italy more recently and had knowledge of water and coastlines—to bring them to the Navy so they could talk to them." Haffenden would then pull out big maps and "he showed them the maps for them to recognize their villages and to compare the maps with their knowledge of their villages."

From his jail cell, Luciano recommended certain people who knew Sicily well, and Lansky escorted them to the Naval Intelligence offices. Socks Lanza helped out, too. "Sometimes some of the Sicilians were very nervous," said Lanza. "Joe [Adonis] would just mention the name of Lucky Luciano and say he had given them orders to talk. If the Sicilians were still reluctant, Joe would stop smiling and say, 'Lucky will not be pleased to hear that you have not been helpful.'"

All the information was sifted and analyzed with much of it ending up on a huge wall map in Haffenden's office with code numbers referring to particular reports from specific individuals. Some of these were major underworld figures who were part of the international network of drug smugglers established by Luciano before he went to jail. Vincent Mangano ran an import-export business between the United States and Italy before the war, which was a cover for his role as key broker between the American and Sicilian Mafias.

That Frank Costello was also involved in this gathering of material was suggested by the testimony of federal narcotics agent George White. He told the Kefauver Senate Committee inquiry into organized crime in 1950 that veteran drug smuggler August Del Grazio had approached him with a deal coming from Frank Costello on behalf of Luciano.

"The proffered deal," recalled Senator Estes Kefauver, "was that Luciano would use his Mafia position to arrange contacts for undercover American agents and that therefore Sicily would be a much softer target than it might otherwise be." Luciano's asking price for all this was freedom from jail and his own travel to Sicily to make the arrangements.

Lansky denied the involvement of August Del Grazio in the wartime dealings. "I never knew of George White and I still don't know of August Del Grazio," said Lansky in 1954. Was he shielding some secret connection? It is interesting to note that Del Grazio, also known as "Little Augie the Wop," was the drug smuggler trusted by Luciano to consolidate his narcotics shipments in Weimar Germany in 1931.

♠

As the days counted down to Operation Husky—the Allied invasion of Sicily in the summer of 1943—it was not only U.S.

Naval Intelligence that woke up to the advantages of having homegrown links with the Sicilian Mafia. Planners for the U.S. Joint Chiefs of Staff—those senior military commanders in Washington—came up with a daring line of action not dissimilar to Lucky Luciano's own suggestion. In their *Special Military Plan for Psychological Warfare in Sicily*, dated April 9, 1943, they suggested infiltrating Sicilian-Americans onto the island so they could link up with dissident organizations and foment revolt against the Fascist authorities.

This included the "Establishment of contact and communications with the leaders of separatist nuclei, disaffected workers, and clandestine radical groups, e.g., the Mafia, and giving them every possible aid," stated the joint staff planners' report.

It would not prove too difficult, as Mussolini had come down hard on the Mafia in the 1920s when he sent to Sicily the tough law enforcer Cesare Mori to subdue and humiliate mafiosi and their families. Many had been tortured, sent to jail, or fled abroad to America. It was this hunger for revenge against the Blackshirts that the American military wanted to utilize. The United States would supply them with weapons and explosives so they could blow up Axis military installations and strategically important bridges and railroads. This extraordinary concept of arming lawbreakers so they could fight against Fascists and Nazis was approved by the very highest military authorities—including General Dwight D. Eisenhower, commanding general of the North African Theater of Operations.

The Americans were not alone in their wish to make contact with the Mafia in Sicily. Their military partners, the British, had their own plans to connect with the Sicilian underworld. The British Secret Intelligence Service produced a *Handbook on Politics and Intelligence Services* for Sicily. In it they identified a figure called Vito La Mantia as head of a Mafia group. They described him as "very anti-Fascist and, if still alive, might supply valuable information: uneducated but influential: was last reported as the manager of a property belonging to the Mafia in

Via Notabartolo, Palermo." It was not a very impressive contact and does not tally with any known Mafia figure quoted in American circles, but it does reveal that it was not exclusively the Americans or their Naval Intelligence that considered utilizing the Mafia in the conquest of Sicily.

♠

On the night of July 9, 1943, American and British landing craft crashed through the waves of the Mediterranean to land on beaches along the southeast corner of Sicily. Ahead of them exploded a curtain of Allied shells and bombs, smashing against Axis pillboxes, crushing any resistance to the landing. Once ashore, troops scrambled across the sand as tanks and trucks were unloaded, building up their strength for the next phase of the invasion. The British were to advance north along the eastern coast of the island from Siracusa to Messina. All the way they would encounter stiff resistance from German soldiers determined to slow their advance, so they could evacuate as many of their own troops across the sea to mainland Italy. The British advance would be measured in blood.

In contrast, the Americans quickly cut across Sicily to occupy the western half of the island and take its capital, Palermo, on the northwest coast. Their casualties were a fraction of those suffered by the British. Had Roosevelt and Eisenhower been right? Had they secretly deployed their Italian-American contacts to somehow ease the progress of their own soldiers? Had underworld links across the ocean instructed the Mafia in Sicily to aid the Americans and discourage Axis troops from attacking them? It has been a long-held belief that that is exactly what happened.

Despite his wishes, Lucky Luciano was not among the seasick Americans staggering out of their landing craft, but Lieutenant Marsloe was. He had swapped his desk job in New York for active service, along with three other Naval Intelligence colleagues, and their mission was to make the most of the information given to them by Luciano's contacts. They were broken up into two teams and Marsloe landed at Gela. The data gathered in New York was of "tremendous help following the landing," said Marsloe, "because we gained an insight into the customs and mores of these people . . . the manner in which the ports were operated, the chains of command together with their material culture."

For Marsloe's colleague, Lieutenant Paul Alfieri, there were more direct benefits. "One of the most important plans was to contact persons who had been deported for any crime from the United States to their homeland in Sicily," said Alfieri, "and one of my first successes after landing at Licata was in connection with this."

This connection began back on the Lower East Side, when a sixteen-year-old kid shot a policeman and was destined for the electric chair. His mother was a cousin of Lucky Luciano and begged him to help her boy escape justice. The mobster intervened and had him smuggled out of the country via Canada to Sicily. There, with his American connections, he became head of his local Mafia family. It was this criminal that Alfieri made contact with in Licata, and the code word he was to give him was "Lucky Luciano."

"Maybe that sounds crazy right in the middle of the war," said Lansky, "but one of those agents told me later that those words were magic. People smiled and after that everything was easy." Even if Luciano wasn't there, his reputation was opening doors.

The young renegade mafioso led Alfieri to the local headquarters of the Italian navy. With the assistance of his armed henchmen, they killed the German guards outside and broke in. They blew open a safe and inside Alfieri found documents describing German and Italian defenses for the island as well as a valuable radio codebook. Secret maps revealed the locations of minefields and the safe routes through them, thus saving many American lives. It was a tremendous breakthrough for which Alfieri was awarded the Legion of Merit—his actions "contributing in large measure to the success of our invasion forces," said the presidential citation. It was a medal that Luciano might well have felt he deserved, too.

But Marsloe, Alfieri, and their colleagues were only four intelligence agents compared to the hundreds of others serving with the army. Their impact on the campaign in Sicily began and ended on the coast. From then on, it was up to the military officers of the Counterintelligence Corps (CIC) to assist the advance of their frontline soldiers into the heart of Sicily, and they did not have the benefit of Luciano's briefings.

Or did they? There is a notorious story that is often quoted as proof that Lucky Luciano's long shadow hung over the fighting in Sicily.

Five days after the Allied landing, on July 14, 1943, an American fighter plane flew low over the small town of Villalba in central Sicily. As its wings nearly brushed the terra-cotta roofs of the buildings, native Sicilians could see a yellow banner fluttering from the side of the cockpit. They swore it bore a large black "L" in the middle of the flag. As the aircraft swooped over a grand farmhouse on the outskirts of the town, the pilot tossed out a bag that crashed into the dust nearby. A servant from the farmhouse hurriedly retrieved it and showed it to his master.

The owner of the farmhouse was Don Calogero Vizzini. A little man in his sixties with a potbelly, he dressed in the usual understated style of a local businessman with his shirtsleeves rolled up and braces hauling his trousers up over his stomach. The image belied his true importance. Don Calo was, in fact, the leading mafioso of the region, and he would later become a major player in postwar Sicily, when he would have direct links with Luciano.

As Don Calo opened the bag dropped by the pilot, he saw at once that an important message had been sent to him by his friend in New York. Inside was a yellow silk handkerchief bearing the "L" of Lucky Luciano. It was a traditional Mafia greeting, and Don Calo knew exactly what he must do next. He wrote a coded message to another mafioso, Giuseppe Genco Russo, and instructed him to give every possible assistance to the advancing Americans. Six days after that, on the twentieth, according to the legend, three U.S. tanks rumbled into the town center of Villalba. Children danced around the vehicles, hoping for sweets and chewing gum. A little yellow pennant flew from the radio aerial of one of the tanks—on it a black "L." An American officer emerged out of the tank and, speaking in the local Sicilian dialect, asked to see Don Calo. The crowd parted as the mafioso made his way toward the tank. He handed his yellow flag with a black "L" to the American, who helped him climb up onto the hull and then disappeared with him into the turret.

The following day, the twenty-first, the Americans braced themselves for an assault against a mountain pass at Monte Cammarata, to the north of Villalba, held by Italian troops reinforced by Germans armed with eighty-eight-millimeter antitank guns and Tiger tanks. But during the night, Don Calo and Russo had worked their magic and their agents had quietly stolen into the Axis camp. By the next morning, the Italian troops had taken the persuasive advice of the Mafia henchmen, dumped their uniforms and weapons, and disappeared into the hills. The few Germans left behind were hopelessly outnumbered and promptly withdrew their forces. Surely there could be no better example of how Luciano and his Sicilian Mafia contacts were helping the Americans win the war in Sicily. It would be—if it were true.

The Villalba tale was first told in 1962 by Michele Pantaleone, a journalist whose family had lived in the town for years. His account was then taken up by the British travel writer Norman Lewis, who repeated it for an English-language audience in his much admired book about the Mafia, *The Honoured Society*. The only problem with this is that Pantaleone was a very biased source. He was a brave campaigner against the Mafia in his country, but he was also a Communist supporter who was in direct competition with the political power wielded by

Don Calo. Added to this was a long-running dispute between the Pantaleone family and the Vizzinis over who owned the rights to a local property. As a result, American OSS agents based in Sicily considered him an unreliable witness.

None of this would matter if only there were other records that corroborated Pantaleone's story. But the daily field reports kept by the U.S. Army as it pushed on through Sicily, reveal a very different picture of the events around Villalba in July 1943. Documents kept at the U.S. Army Military History Institute record that it was a mechanized unit—the Forty-fifth Cavalry Reconnaissance Troop—that entered Villalba on the twentieth. All they found, according to their daily journal, were two small Italian tanks that had been wrecked and abandoned by the retreating Axis forces. Nothing was mentioned of a major body of Axis troops located at Monte Cammarata. Indeed, other U.S. troops were already fifty miles north of Villalba on their way to Palermo and reporting minimum resistance, if any at all. The Third Cavalry Reconnaissance Troop was also operating in the area and their daily journal for the twentieth and twenty-first reports that the road from Cammarata to Santo Stefano was clear. Any minor resistance was quickly overcome as U.S. troops plowed on toward Corleone. None of this verifies the story told by Pantaleone.

A final piece of evidence is provided in the memoirs of Luigi Lumia, a onetime mayor of Villalba. His source was a young man who accompanied Don Calo into the American tank, acting as interpreter for the Mafia boss. According to the interpreter, Don Calo was taken away to be questioned about an incident a few days earlier when an American jeep had come under fire and one of the soldiers was killed. The shots had come from a clump of olive trees near a farm. The Americans shot back and this ignited a field of dry crops. Don Calo nodded sagely, knowing exactly what had happened. The fire had spread, he explained, and set off some boxes of ammunition left by the retreating Italians. It sounded like heavy gunfire, but really it was nothing—the Americans faced no local resistance at all. The explanation sounded farfetched to the American interrogator and he lost his patience with the old man. He began shouting at Don Calo, telling him to get out and walk back to his town. This was an enormous loss of face for the mafioso and he was profoundly embarrassed by the whole affair.

"It was already nighttime," recalled Lumia, "and Calogero Vizzini, tired and browbeaten, was driven back to his house, halfway between the Americans and the countryside. He told his interpreter not to tell anybody what had happened and then lay down in his bed and went to sleep."

Don Calo would have far preferred the tale told by his enemy—Pantaleone—to be spread around, as that made him look more important than the reality of this humiliating clash revealed. Maybe that is why the Villalba legend has endured for so long. It presents Don Calo and Lucky Luciano as far more integral to the American victory in Sicily than they really were.

In truth, it is clear that the American advance in central and western Sicily was too overwhelming and swift for there to be any opportunity or need for the Mafia to come to their assistance. The only direct proof we have of Luciano's influence is on the coast during the initial landing phase with the testimony of the four naval intelligence agents. Beyond that, the mobster's influence was not needed and not called on. That is the truth of what happened in Sicily in 1943. Lucky Luciano might have been itching to get into the combat zone, but there was no need for him.

♠

Despite the truth that Luciano had little impact on the Sicilian campaign, he got his reward for his general wartime assistance from the U.S. government in early January 1946. After spending nine years, nine months in jail, his nemesis Governor Thomas E. Dewey commuted his sentence.

Far from hiding the nature of Luciano's service to the nation,

Dewey made a statement to the legislature in which he said, "Upon the entry of the United States into the war, Luciano's aid was sought by the armed services in inducing others to provide information concerning possible enemy attack. It appears that he cooperated in such effort though the actual value of the information procured is not clear."

A month later, *New York Times* journalist Meyer Berger speculated further on what this aid might be. He claimed that Luciano had been pardoned "ostensibly for help he gave the Office of Strategic Services before the Army's Italy invasion. It is understood that Luciano provided Army Intelligence with the names of Sicilian and Neapolitan Camorra members, and a list of Italians sent back to their native country after criminal conviction in the United States."

The reporter appears to have got his facts wrong, as we know it was U.S. Naval Intelligence that communicated with Luciano in jail, not the OSS. But the reference to the precursor of the CIA is intriguing due to future references to Luciano perhaps playing a role in the Cold War. Certainly, OSS agents were very active in Palermo and had close links with major Mafia figures in Sicily.

Luciano might have been free, but he was no longer welcome in America. In preparation for deportation to Italy, he was moved to a cell on Ellis Island, the entry point to the United States for his family and so many other immigrants thirty-nine years before. Meyer Lansky, Frank Costello, and Moses Polakoff visited him there for their final instructions from him. To comply with government rules that only $60 could be taken out of the country, Luciano gave up the $400 in cash he had on him to Costello. With no limitation on the use of travelers' checks, Costello gave Luciano $2,500 in unsigned checks and explained to Luciano how to sign for them. Three unnamed relatives visited him on Ellis Island, perhaps his brothers and sister.

On February 9, Luciano was escorted by two agents of the U.S. immigration service onto the seven-thousand ton freighter

Laura Keene, which was shipping a consignment of flour. Reporters swarmed around the dockside, wanting a final picture of the king of the underworld. Fifteen journalists were refused admittance to the pier by a menacing guard of longshoremen armed with baling hooks. They'd been provided by the Mafia to keep the media at bay and their boss told the reporters to "beat it."

Six police guards working in pairs watched Luciano twenty-four hours a day in eight-hour shifts during his period of custody on board the *Laura Keene.* Officially, they denied the presence of any liquor or extra food on board for Luciano, but Lansky told a different story.

On the evening before Luciano's departure, all the city's top mobsters gathered on board the freighter for a farewell party. They included Meyer Lansky, Frank Costello, Albert Anastasia, Bugsy Siegel, William Moretti, Tommy Lucchese, Joe Adonis, and Stefano Magaddino. Someone must have bribed the police guards generously. Champagne corks popped and they laughed about old times. "We had a wonderful meal aboard," said Lansky, "all kinds of seafood fresh from the Fulton Fish Market, and spaghetti and wine and a lots [sic] of kosher delicacies." Luciano loved his Jewish food.

"Lucky also wanted us to bring some girls to take along with him on the ship to keep him company. I asked Adonis to do something about that . . . Joe found three showgirls from the Copacabana Club and there was no difficulty in getting them aboard. The authorities cooperated even on that. Nobody going into exile ever had a better [s]end-off."

An FBI report gives yet another version of Luciano's last days in America. An anonymous FBI agent visited him on board the *Laura Keene.*

"I had no trouble whatsoever with the stevedores on the pier or on board the ship," he reported, "nor was I molested or threatened." The stevedores, "chiefly Italians, looked upon Luciano as more or less a hero, and that any word from him requesting that the reporters be barred was all that was needed to have it carried out by the stevedores as an order . . . there would have been bloodshed if the reporters tried to storm the pier in an unauthorized entry."

The agent flashed his ID to the steamship guard and was shown to Luciano's cabin.

"When I entered Mr. Luciano's cabin, I told him that I was stopped by the representatives of the press at the end of the pier and that they would like to interview him. He reacted unfavorably to the idea and he told me that since the press had not been too nice to him in the past, he had no desire to give any statements.

"Mr. Luciano was quartered in a cabin known as the 'gun crew quarters' aft of amidship. In the cabin with Mr Luciano was the first mate who informed Luciano that he would have to remain in the quarters assigned to him, until the 'old man,' meaning the captain, orders the change of quarters."

The FBI agent contradicts Lansky's story of a farewell feast. On Saturday evening, February 9, he was told by guards that Luciano had baked macaroni and steak for dinner. He asked for a cup of tea but was told there was none and he settled for a drink of milk. They stated there was "no evidence of any parties, drinking or visitors to Luciano during the time he was under their surveillance" from midnight to 8:00 A.M. on Saturday the ninth through Sunday the tenth. They denied he had been visited by Albert Anastasia.

The agent returned on Luciano's last day in Brooklyn docks at the Bush Terminal at 6:00 A.M. "Upon my arrival there, I saw a gang or mob of 60 to 80 men and about 20 to 30 cars. I have no idea to their identity or their purpose for being on hand."

When the ship left the pier at 8:50 A.M., a launch followed them for three miles. The agent guessed it was members of the press trying to get one final shot of Luciano. The agent left the ship at 2:00 P.M. when he caught a ride on a fishing ship returning to the Brooklyn docks.

The FBI were generally cynical about the deal with U.S.

Naval Intelligence, and J. Edgar Hoover's suspicions were confirmed when on March 1, 1946, he received a letter from FBI Special Agent E. E. Conroy stating that "Haffenden admitted he was friendly with Costello and had played golf with him" at the Pomonok Country Club in Flushing. To this was added the allegation that "there has been talk around the city that $250,000 would be paid for the release of Luciano from State Prison. This money, however, would probably not go to Haffenden, but rather to others in political circles. It is observed that Haffenden has already been rewarded with the position of Commissioner of Marine and Aviation." This key position gave Haffenden jurisdiction over the docks of the city of New York as well as LaGuardia and Idlewild airports. "When the latter airport is completed there will be a tremendous number of concessions to be leased and the possibilities of graft are said to be great."

A letter dated March 6 from FBI Assistant Director A. Rosen said the newspaper stories about Luciano's assistance to navy and army authorities "might be laid to a fraudulent affidavit on the part of Commander Charles Radcliffe Haffenden." In the same letter, Rosen said that despite Haffenden receiving a Purple Heart for wounds in combat, Special Agent Conroy said that Haffenden had received no such wounds and was "hospitalized as a result of a large gun going off near him thus renewing a stomach ailment."

In a later FBI report of March 13, it was alleged that Frank Costello had Haffenden appointed to his new role, "as it is generally felt that Frank Costello has considerable control in the present city administration." It was said that Haffenden, after returning from Iwo Jima, where he had been wounded, was visited in the hospital by "his good friend" Moses Polakoff and "that Polakoff had induced him, Haffenden, to write a letter to Charles Breitel, Counsel to the Governor of the State of New York. Haffenden explained to the informant that he was not feeling very well and he wanted to do a good turn and he did not see anything wrong about writing the letter on Charles 'Lucky' Luciano."

As the FBI investigation delved deeper, U.S. Naval Intelligence sought to distance itself from the affair by claiming that its files failed to indicate that Luciano had ever furnished assistance or information to them. On April 17, 1946, Hoover expressed a personal interest to Rosen in wanting to know the details behind Luciano's parole. As Rosen explored further, he dispatched a memorandum on April 18, 1946, saying that he had spoken to a key witness for the prosecution in the Luciano trial who admitted that "he had perjured himself when he testified against Lucky Luciano" and "states that considerable opinion exists to the effect that Luciano was not guilty of the charges for which he was convicted and that Governor Dewey's parole of Luciano was motivated partially as an easing of Dewey's conscience." He then added in his own handwriting—"so sorry."

On May 17, Rosen reported that he had received a letter from the office of the chief of naval operations acknowledging that "Luciano was employed as an informant" but "the nature and extent of his assistance is not reflected in Navy records, and further that Haffenden was censured officially for his actions."

Hoover's comment on the whole affair was noted in a memorandum of June 6, 1946, to Rosen: "A shocking example of misuse of Navy authority in interest of a hoodlum. It surprises me they didn't give Luciano the Navy Cross."

Rosen was later informed that Haffenden had paid the price for their investigation, when he was forced to resign as commissioner of the city's Department of Marine and Aviation by Mayor William O'Dwyer in May 1946. The excuse for this was that the mayor had not been satisfied with Haffenden's administration of the position following an item appearing in a New York newspaper. "Unless advised to the contrary by the Bureau, no further action is contemplated by the New York Division in this matter," concluded the FBI.

For the moment that was the end of the FBI's involvement in Luciano's affairs, but Hoover was itching to match Dewey by nailing the mobster. That opportunity would come a year later.

Former New York mayor La Guardia—he had finished his third term in 1945—was less than generous when he heard of Luciano's departure. "I'm sorry Italy is getting this bum back," he told a radio audience and added that he was shocked that Frank Costello should be allowed to visit him on Ellis Island. "What is the limit of Costello's power in the city?" he asked, indicating that that mobster was now the real head of the American Mafia.

The terms and conditions of Luciano's deportation were very clear—if he ever reentered the United States he would be deemed an escaped convict and would be required to serve out the maximum of his original prison sentence. He could never again set foot on American territory. For the forty-eight-year-old Luciano, it might have marked the end of his reign as Mob ruler of New York, but he merely viewed it as a challenge to his ingenuity. There were many points of entry back into the United States, and the authorities couldn't keep him away from his criminal pals.

CUBA FIASCO

After a seventeen-day voyage across the Atlantic, Lucky Luciano arrived in Naples on February 28, 1946. He was required to visit the local police station, where he explained that his stay in Naples would be brief and that he was to be accommodated by a relative. He would then travel on to Sicily, where he would visit members of his family. A reporter asked him whether there was any truth to his working with the American government. "You know I can't talk about those things," he snapped back. That was the last thing he wanted Italians knowing—that he'd been singing to the authorities.

Once in Sicily, Luciano visited his hometown of Lercara Friddi—just fifty miles south of Palermo—and was treated like a king. The main piazza of the town was crowded and a feast laid on for the mobster, featuring dishes cooked by local women. Like an old-style mafioso—like the Mustache Petes he'd executed in New York—Luciano distributed money and was greeted by people bowing and kissing his hand. He also donated money to build a cinema where they could watch gangster movies from America like *Little Caesar*, always popular with the Sicilians.

Luciano enjoyed this reception in his hometown, among members of his family still living there, but he soon had enough of his enforced vacation. He was itching to get back to the United States and make contact with his old friends, especially Lansky and Costello.

"I'm a city boy," he told a reporter. "Italy's dead—nice, but dead. I like movement. Business opportunities here are no good. All small-time stuff."

He said the same thing about Italian horse racing.

"The action at these joints is no good. I need New York. There's the true action. They don't speak my language here," he concluded.

Luciano knew that his continued absence meant that rivals like Genovese would soon muscle in on his territory back in New York. He was also conscious that at forty-eight years old he wasn't getting any younger. He wanted to enjoy his investments and catch up on all the pleasures he'd missed during a decade in jail. Italy just didn't suit him that well. As he endured the dusty heat of Sicily, recoiling at the stink of the sulfur mines his father had left behind half a century before, he plotted his return.

♠

On July 10, 1946, FBI Assistant Director A. Rosen reported that he had received information from the Los Angeles division that exiled mobster Charles Luciano was staying in Tijuana, Mexico. The vicinity of Tijuana was known as the "free zone" because no tourist card or legal permit was needed to enter that portion of Baja California on the border between Mexico and the U.S. FBI Special Intelligence Service (SIS) agents were sent to investigate. They belonged to an elite wartime division of the FBI tasked with tracking down foreign agents who posed a threat to the United States They'd identified some thirteen hundred

Axis spies and prosecuted many of them. With the war over, they were a valuable resource and given the mission to make sure Luciano didn't sneak back into the United States.

The FBI agents searched the whole of Tijuana, giving special attention to the locations Luciano liked to haunt, such as the racetrack, casinos, exclusive hotels, and fashionable nightclubs. They spoke to local gangsters, heard lots of rumors, but got nowhere. Further investigation revealed that the tip-off stemmed from a headline appearing in the Mexico City daily newspaper, *Excelsior*, on March 26, 1946, which ran the story "Vice Czar Intends to Return to Mexico." The reporter claimed that two of the mobster's associates were staying in a prominent hotel in Mexico City in order to establish Luciano in the country. The Mexican journalist was interviewed by the FBI's SIS but could not name the henchmen involved and claimed he got the story from a press release coming from the Associated Press in the United States.

A later AP story quoted in the New York *Daily News* on September 3 said that it had received information from Naples saying Luciano was "plotting a return to power in the North American underworld." It claimed that "Neapolitan stoolpigeons reported to the Italian police that he wangled illegal passage to Mexico on a freighter." In any event, Luciano had disappeared, not having been seen in the previous six weeks since an appearance in Salerno. U.S. Army CID (Criminal Investigation Command) agents compounded the rumors by privately agreeing that "it's very likely he skipped the country, probably hoping to contact some of his old henchmen from Mexico or actually smuggle himself into the States."

A curious story reported in the *New York Journal American* for September 5, 1946, claimed that this was all part of a plot by Luciano to become one of those legends "with everyone declaring he is dead, but no trace of a body." It said that "Luciano would be very happy to have everybody—particularly Government immigration authorities—believe that a sailor who had agreed to smuggle him out of [a South American] port gave him what may be known as 'the Chinese treatment'—in other words, took him aboard ship and, after getting his money, drugged him and dropped him over the side during the night. . . ."

The FBI pursued this lead and found it to be fallacious. Forced to wind up these dead-end investigations, the FBI requested that the State Department ensure that no American consulate ever grant Luciano a visa to enter the United States. The next sighting of the mobster, however, was a hundred percent true.

♠

In early 1947, FBI Assistant Director Rosen passed a memorandum saying that Luciano had been observed by two FBI SIS agents on February 8 in Havana, Cuba, at the Oriental Park Racetrack. He was chatting with various American tourists and Cuban residents while seated at a table in the Jockey Club. Among the Cubans who recognized and talked to Luciano were a wealthy Cuban sugar merchant and a member of a socially prominent Cuban family. He was traveling under the name of Salvatore Lucania and had received his visa through a Cuban congressman who had a financial interest in the local racetrack and Hotel Nacional casino.

Cuba was the perfect playground for Luciano, just an hour's flight from Miami. Meyer Lansky had been exploring its numerous attractions since the early 1930s. With the growth of cheaper, more available air flights, he understood it was the perfect destination for well-heeled American tourists who liked to gamble and dabble in illicit pleasures. To this end, he invested a great deal of Mob money in acquiring underworld assets there. Joseph "Doc" Stacher was an old associate of Lansky and became closely involved with the Cuban operation.

"[Lansky] said we needed somewhere safe to put the cash from the bootlegging," remembered Stacher. "Our biggest problem was always where to invest the money. It didn't appeal to any of us to take it to Switzerland and leave it there just earning interest. What Lansky suggested was that each of us put up $500,000 to start the Havana gambling operation."

Luciano and Siegel, plus a few other mobsters, each put their half-million dollars into the pot, and Lansky took the cash to Cuban military dictator Fulgencio Batista. In return for guaranteeing him an income of $3 to $5 million a year, Batista protected their monopoly on casinos at the Hotel Nacional and Oriental Park Racetrack—the only two places in Cuba where gambling was legal. It looked as though the Mob had bagged its own resort in the Caribbean. But in 1944, a new president, Dr. Ramón Grau San Martín, took over and the native Cuban crime syndicate combined financial power with close political contacts that could ultimately mobilize the army to protect its interests. Always welcoming to outside investors, Cuban mobsters were not completely in awe of Lansky and his Mafia associates and were well aware of where the ultimate power lay.

On February 15, 1947, a photograph appeared in the *Havana Post* showing thirty-two-year-old pop singer Frank Sinatra at the casino of the Nacional Hotel talking to Captain Antonio Arias, president of the casino. The same newspaper claimed on February 23 that Lucky Luciano was seen nightclubbing by New York gossip columnist Robert C. Ruark with Frank Sinatra and Ralph Capone, brother of the late Al Capone.

At the time he was first spotted, Luciano told the *Havana Post* reporter, "This is terrible. I came here to live quietly and now all this blows up in my face." He said he had money saved from better days and had the ability "to get along most anywhere."

Spurred on by the unwelcome publicity, the Cuban secret police picked up Luciano for questioning as he sipped coffee in a Vedado café. The Cuban police revealed that Luciano had $4,000 when he arrived by plane in October and still had $1,000 in his bank account, so they surmised he was receiving an income from somewhere.

Gossipmonger Ruark saved his full fury for the popular singer hanging out with Luciano. "I am frankly puzzled as to why Frank Sinatra, the lean trust and the fetish of millions," he wrote, "chooses to spend his vacation in the company of notorious, convicted vice operators and assorted hoodlums from Miami's plush gutters. This is, of course, none of my personal business. If Sinatra wants to Mob up with the likes of Lucky Luciano, the chastened panderer and permanent deportee from the United States, that seems to be a matter for Sinatra to thrash out with the millions of kids who live by his every bleat."

Ruark said Sinatra spent four days in Havana at the racetrack and casino in the company of Luciano, Luciano's bodyguard, and a rich collection of high-rolling gamblers. He says he was also informed that they attended a party with Ralph Capone, hosted by Jorge Sanchez, a sugar merchant. Sinatra's presence was really not that surprising, as the Mafia were keen on the singer.

"The Italians among us were very proud of Frank," said Doc Stacher. "They always told me they had spent a lot of money helping him in his career, ever since he was with Tommy Dorsey's band. Lucky Luciano was very fond of Sinatra's singing."

Sinatra's concert at the Hotel Nacional was, in fact, a welcome-home party for Luciano, in which all of America's top mafiosi gathered in Havana.

"Everybody brought envelopes of cash for Lucky," remembered Stacher, "and as an exile he was glad to take them. But more important, they came to pay allegiance to him. A number of the younger guys were doubtful about paying allegiance to the old-timer, as they called him, but Meyer backed him a hundred percent and nobody wanted to cross the Little Man."

All the top mobsters flew into Havana to greet Luciano, including Lansky, Frank Costello, Joe Adonis, Albert Anastasia, Joe Profaci, Joe Bonanno, and Vito Genovese. Lansky had many private conversations with Luciano about joint projects. They hoped that Governor Dewey would run for president again in

1948 and that would allow them to contribute to his campaign. Although Dewey had put Luciano behind bars, they believed that his understanding of Luciano's war record meant there might be a bargaining chip there for future relations between the two. Personal enmity should never be allowed to cloud the possibility of business.

Generally, when all the mobsters sat together, they listened to Lansky and Luciano expound on how they wanted to turn Cuba into the Monte Carlo of the Caribbean. It would make Las Vegas look like small potatoes.

But alongside the socializing there were tensions. A strong hostility existed between Luciano and his former underboss, Vito Genovese. Not only was it a matter of personal rivalry, but it also went back to an incident during the war, when Genovese organized a hit on a key opponent of Mussolini in New York—the outspoken journalist Carlo Tresca.

In the late 1920s, Tresca, editor of the anti-Fascist *Il Martello*, had been a favorite of the New York Mafia, who protected him against the Blackshirts. Come the war, however, Genovese wanted to demonstrate the extent of his power to his new Fascist patrons in Italy. When word got through to Genovese that Mussolini was offended by Tresca's constant criticism of him in his newspaper, he put out a contract on the editor. The Brooklyn gunman Carmine Galante was ordered to shoot him down in January 1943. The *New York Herald* described what happened next.

> The Fifth Avenue intersection was dark in the dimout. There was little traffic, and few people were about. As Mr. Tresca and Mr. Calabi [his friend] turned the corner into Fifth Avenue the killer suddenly materialized in the dimout, whipped out a gun and shot four times. Two bullets went wild, but one struck Mr. Tresca in the head, passing through his cheeks, and another lodged in his back. He fell into the Fifth Avenue gutter, the oversize

hat he customarily wore dropping beside him, and he was dead when Mr. Calabi bent over his friend.

The gunman ran across Fifteenth Street to the getaway car and sped off toward Union Square. Luciano was furious when he heard of this abuse of Mafia power. He strongly disapproved of Genovese's new loyalty to the Fascists—these were the allies of Hitler and the wartime enemies of the United States. He later offered to give up the names of the Mob assassins who killed Tresca in return for his outright parole and permission to stay in the United States. The U.S. government refused.

Some sources say that a face-to-face meeting between Luciano and Genovese in Cuba ended in blows, but this seems unlikely. Despite Luciano's distaste for Genovese's wartime record and suspicion of his ambition, he probably followed the Mafia dictum of keeping your friends close but your enemies closer.

There was one item of personal business, however, that could not be ignored. Bugsy Siegel was Meyer Lansky's oldest mobster friend. They had grown up together and formed their own gang. Lansky criticized his hotheaded approach to problems—Siegel was too keen to reach for the revolver—but Lansky had managed to remove him from causing trouble in New York by sending him to the West Coast. There, he took care of their business in Hollywood and their new investment in Las Vegas.

Lansky was backing Siegel's creation of a luxury casino in the desert called the Flamingo. It was costing the Mob a million dollars, but word had got through to Lansky that Siegel was overspending by many more millions. Every made major mobster had given a contribution to this Las Vegas project, and they were not happy to hear rumors that Siegel's girlfriend, Virginia Hill, was skimming off money from the construction budget and stashing it in a Swiss bank account.

Lansky did everything he could to shield Siegel from the wrath of the Mob, explaining that the casino would bring in millions more, but all they could see was that one of their own was ripping them off. Eventually, it was Luciano, during a lavish celebration for Sinatra, who told Lansky the brutal truth.

"Meyer, this is business," said Luciano, "and Bugsy has broken our rules."

Lansky tried to excuse Siegel by saying he was under the influence of Virginia Hill.

"They're like two teenagers in love."

Luciano wasn't interested. Time was running out for Siegel.

But the clock was ticking, too, for Luciano, and shortly after the grand gangster gathering, to a soundtrack sung by Sinatra, Luciano was under arrest. His flagrant enjoyment of his freedom in the company of top celebrities and criminals, just ninety miles from Florida, was just too much for the U.S. authorities.

♠

Once arrested, Luciano was escorted by the Cuban secret police to Tiscornia immigration camp, where they allowed the FBI to question him. During the interrogation, Luciano admitted that he gave information pertaining to the war effort to Commander Haffenden of Naval Intelligence. This was a subject of continuing fascination for the head of the FBI, J. Edgar Hoover, as he felt he had been misled and sidelined by this secret deal between the Mob and the navy. Although he knew that something fishy had been going on between them that had ended in Dewey granting him parole, Hoover did not know the exact details and this continued to annoy him.

It partly explains why the FBI sorely wanted to be involved at some stage with Luciano, having so far failed to make any major contribution to curbing his activities. With him temporarily under arrest, they wanted to make the most of this opportunity to talk to him. Interestingly, their report says that Luciano also admitted passing on wartime information to Murray I. Gurfein, who later became a lieutenant colonel in the OSS.

Further questioning revealed that Luciano had arrived in Cuba on October 29, 1946, by air from Italy on an Italian passport issued in the name of Salvatore Lucania with a six-month visa granted by a Cuban chargé d'affaires in Rome. This had been facilitated by a Cuban congressman. Luciano's passport also contained visas issued in Rome by consuls for Venezuela, Bolivia, and Colombia. Cuban immigration records confirmed that the Cuban congressman had stated that he knew Luciano personally and guaranteed him as "a person of democratic ideals who had sufficient financial resources to prevent him from becoming a public charge."

Luciano first stayed at the Hotel Nacional and then rented a furnished house at 29 Calle Thirty, in Miramar, a wealthy suburb of Havana. His servants and neighbors called him "Mr. Charley," and some claimed he was going to marry a Cuban girl to gain Cuban citizenship. The FBI gave a physical description of Luciano in 1947 as five feet nine and three-quarter inches tall, 145 to 150 pounds, slim, wavy, heavy dark brown hair turning gray, dark chestnut eyes, and tattooed on both arms.

Luciano told the FBI he was managing a gambling concession at the Jockey Club and the Hotel Nacional. His New York associates there were identified as Meyer Lansky, Bugsy Siegel, and Frank Costello. FBI research concluded that Lansky had been involved with the operation of the Oriental Park Racetrack Casino since 1939. His official business title in 1947 was recorded as vice president of the Emby Distributing Company at 525 West Forty-third Street, New York City. He also had connections with the Elaine Produce and Food Company, the Lansky Food Company, the Paruth Realty Corporation, and Crieg Spector & Citron, a retail grocery organization. Lansky was noted to be spending the winter season in Florida and making regular visits to Cuba.

Following a second interview with the FBI, Luciano admitted he wanted to buy shares in gambling concessions for the baccarat and craps tables at the Oriental Park Racetrack and the Hotel Nacional casino but the deal had never been completed. He said that "gambling in Cuba was so deeply involved in politics that he wanted no part of it." This hinted at the fact that the local syndicate was no pushover and was flexing its muscles to any foreign mobsters on the make. It was true that Lansky had a comfortable relationship with the Cubans, but that didn't necessarily mean they were going to roll over for Luciano.

At the same time, the Cuban weekly magazine *Tiempo en Cuba* ran a leading article that identified Cuban congressman Dr. Indalecio Pertierra and Carlos "the Goat" Miranda as running crooked gambling in Cuba. It said that Pertierra ran the gambling at the Hotel Nacional casino and Jockey Club with the assistance of Luciano, Lansky, and Charles Simms—calling them card sharks. Pertierra was the brother of a former president of the Cuban senate who was reported to receive a cut from the gambling concessions. The magazine warned:

> If you go to Havana, keep out of the races. Beware the gamblers. . . . Under the view of tolerably suspicious police and soldiers, and surrounded by killers, bouncers and gorillas, the cheaters are dividing thousands of dollars every night. Any time that a police official dares to intervene, he will be immediately transferred to another district.
>
> Recently, a group of American tourists intoxicated with highballs and daiquiris went to the Jockey Club roulette tables to try to win back what they lost at the races. Two Cuban friends, who knew the situation, tried to dissuade them. But the Americans insisted and began to lose immediately. On the last play, they won and should have received $442 but only got $342. The Americans protested and immediately two strong arm men were called and recommended that they leave.

When they returned home, the Americans reported the incident to the mayor of Miami and the tourist authority. "With this type of publicity," concluded the magazine, "Havana will soon equal the reputation of Chicago during the time of Torrio and Capone."

American tourists also told the Cuban tourist police they believed the tables were fixed at the casino at the Hotel Nacional and Oriental Park Racetrack and said they had seen dice being palmed by American gamblers running the craps tables.

Other local press in Havana claimed that Luciano had links with at least twenty prominent Cuban officials. Luciano told the reporters he had no intention of running narcotics on the island, but a U.S. Treasury representative at the American embassy in Havana was not so easily reassured. He said he had received information indicating that Luciano might well be attempting to establish himself in the trafficking of illegal narcotics.

Clearly, the FBI was more than happy to gather as much information as they could from Luciano while he was in custody in Cuba, but was not sure what to do with him next. It was up to another U.S. government department to insist on firmer action being taken. On February 22, the FBI received a radiogram informing them that the U.S. Federal Bureau of Narcotics (FBN), headed by Harry J. Anslinger, was taking the action needed to get Luciano out of Cuba. It would cause a diplomatic crisis.

The FBN informed the Cuban government they would cut off all shipments of legal narcotics to Cuba until Luciano was expelled from the country. The decision made headlines throughout the island. With all this negative publicity, Luciano agreed to return to Italy rather than wait for deportation proceedings. The FBI had no evidence that Luciano was involved in illegal trafficking of narcotics, but a special representative of the Treasury Department arriving at the U.S. embassy said he had "definite proof."

In retaliation to the American threat, Cuban Liberal Party representative José Suarez Rivas proposed: "I am going to request the president of the Congress to ask President Grau to suspend shipments of sugar to the United States until Jose Martinez, who has been expelled from Cuba and is head of a sugar black market in the United States, and who at present is living in Miami, Florida, is deported from the United States to Catalonia, Spain, which is his native land." It never happened.

The Cuban press generally supported their government's decision to deport Luciano, although they would have preferred a more diplomatic and less threatening approach from the United States. Antigovernment papers claimed the affair revealed the corrupt state of the police force, while left-wingers denounced American "imperialism." On one weekly radio program, Senator Eduardo Chibas accused Senator Francisco Prio Socarris of protecting Luciano. The next day, this resulted in a fistfight on the floor of the Cuban senate between Chibas and Socarris. It was rumored that a duel would follow to settle the matter of honor.

On February 27, President Grau signed a decree classifying Luciano as an undesirable alien in Cuba in view of his past criminal activities and ordered his deportation. The American embassy then advised the Cuban Ministry of State that no actual embargo on shipments of narcotics had been put into place despite the threatening statements of agents of the U.S. Federal Bureau of Narcotics.

However, Colonel George White, a senior federal narcotics agent, continued to brief the press with negative stories about Luciano. In the *Washington Post* for March 14, a gunman suspected of killing James M. Ragen, owner of the racing National News Service, was linked to Luciano. White further disclosed that the "slayings of Carramusa and Ignacio Antanori [narcotics case witnesses], killed at Tampa, Florida, early in 1945, had been arranged by Luciano, former New York crime head." It all helped to sway public opinion against the mobster.

An FBI profile on Bugsy Siegel put further flesh on the Ragen case by explaining that Ragen had been targeted by New York gangsters because he ran the wire service business, which communicated all news of racing results throughout the country. As the FBI noted, the Mob was "attempting to take over the wire service and if they are successful in so doing will extort tribute from every bookmaker in the United States."

At 1:00 P.M. on March 20, 1947, Luciano accepted defeat and set sail on the Turkish boat, SS *Bakir*, destined for Genoa via the Canary Islands. He said he intended to return to South America after getting back to Italy, or perhaps even disembarking at the Canary Islands to catch another ship. His anger was directed at the American authorities that put the pressure on the Cubans to kick him out. He suggested Venezuela or Mexico as possible destinations, claiming his "original intention in coming to Cuba was to be near his friends and relatives who resided in the United States."

FBI chief Hoover personally sent messages to South American embassies, including Rio de Janeiro in Brazil, warning them against Luciano's arrival.

After his voyage back to Italy from Cuba, Luciano spent nine days in jail in Genoa. He was then sent under the escort of two armed carabinieri to Palermo, where he spent nine more days in jail. From there, he moved to Rome, where he set up a fancy apartment. Luciano's dream of settling in a country near to his old friends had been blown apart. He was furious. From now on, he was restricted to operating in Italy.

Twelve years after the Cuban fiasco, the corrupt regime backed by President Batista collapsed in the wake of a Communist revolution and the Mafia lost all their valuable gambling investments—a hit that would cost Luciano 25 percent of his future investment income.

Cold War Warrior

The Grand Hotel et Des Palmes, halfway along the stylish Via Roma in central Palermo, was the smartest hotel in Sicily in 1947. Its marble-and-mirror deluxe rooms entertained the richest businessmen in town. On July 5, Mr. A. E. Watkins of the British consulate filed a report on Charles Luciano, saying he was staying at the hotel.

"This bandit, or ex-bandit, is very much in the public eye," noted Watkins. "He has two luxurious American motor cars; dresses and lives expensively, and is often to be seen in the company of an elegant but vulgar Italian-American woman."

Watkins went further. His job was to pick up on local gossip and sketch in the relationships between important people.

"I am told, on good authority," he said, "that some of the leading members of the Mafia have called on him at the hotel on more than one occasion. Rumour has it that he is now in somebody's pay working against the communists."

In the same report, Watkins mentioned that the notorious

Sicilian bandit Salvatore Giuliano had issued a manifesto in which he pledged to switch his activities from his usual law-breaking to an assault on the Sicilian Communist party. Giuliano called on his fellow Sicilians to oppose the "Red gangsters"—"Those men who want to throw us into the lap of that terrible Russia where liberty is a chimera and democracy a legend must be fought." The CIA couldn't have put it better!

The British consulate officer wondered at the veracity of the so-called manifesto and believed it might have emanated "from an interested party under the assumed name of Giuliano." He then concluded that this event might well be linked to his comments on Luciano also being deployed against Sicilian Communists.

It is tantalizing material that has never been picked up in any other book on Luciano, and there is a dimension to it that seems highly possible—that Luciano was a Cold War agent. His wartime work brought him very close to government intelligence agencies, so the avenues of contact were already there, and Luciano's own personal views were bluntly anti-Communist.

Added to this are two further connections. The OSS, forerunners of the CIA, had established close links with the Mafia in Sicily through their agents in wartime Palermo. Luciano had a personal link to the OSS through Lieutenant Colonel Murray I. Gurfein, who had been part of the team that first put Luciano in contact with Naval Intelligence. Luciano also had a strong relationship with chief Sicilian mafioso Don Calogero Vizzini, who three years earlier had tried to kill Girolamo Li Causi, the leader of the Sicilian Communist party when he came to Villalba to give a rabble-rousing speech. Li Causi was at the top of Giuliano's hit list and posed an even greater threat to postwar Sicily now that the Communist movement had grown in strength.

To understand this web of Cold War conspiracies into which Luciano ventured, it is important to understand the shifting interests of the Americans in Sicily since World War II.

♠

Having punctured the myth that Luciano and the Mafia directly helped the Americans conquer Sicily, there is another equally strongly believed legend that it was the Americans who put the Mafia back into power after their long subjugation under Mussolini and the Fascists. It is a belief held even by local Sicilians, but the truth is somewhat different. At first, the invading Americans and British saw the Mafia for what they were—a criminal organization that grew rich off the back of its own intimidated people.

With the Fascists gone from their island, Mafia gangs thought they could get back into business, but the Allied authorities—known as AMGOT (Allied Military Government of Occupied Territory)—were intent on establishing law and order. Major General Francis Rennell Rodd was the British head of AMGOT and he knew exactly what the Mafia was all about. "The aftermath of war and the breakdown of central provincial authority," he observed, "provide a good culture ground for the virus."

By "virus," Rennell meant the Mafia. He came down hard on the black market and any racketeering. When he heard a wealthy landowner had been stabbed to death for refusing the advances of the local Mafia, he had the suspected murderers arrested and put on trial before a military tribunal. Unable to threaten local jurors, the two Mafia hit men were found guilty and shot by a firing squad.

This official attitude was matched by several high-profile operations against Mafia bases. Aided by a major who had special knowledge of breaking up racketeering gangs in New York, the U.S. Third Division stormed a Mafia fortress near Palermo in September 1943 and arrested two leading mafiosi.

"The Mafia, Sicilian extortionist gang that fascism tried for years to rub up," said the *New York Times*, "has been smashed from the top. . . . It follows that breaking the Mafia gang means breaking the black market."

Of course, the power vacuum left by removing Fascist authority in Sicily meant that many anti-Fascist replacement figures were, in fact, local mafiosi. Lord Rennell admitted this, saying the Allies "have fallen into the trap of appointing the most pushing and obvious person, who in certain cases are now suspected of being the local Mafia leaders. . . . It will take quite a long time for the Allied Military Government to weed out the good from the bad." Although he said this, clearly his intention was not to hand government back to criminal organizations. A major incentive in this drive against the Mafia was that they were irritating AMGOT by giving support to a Separatist movement in the island.

For years, Sicilians resented the heavy hand of central Italian government and dreamed of becoming an autonomous nation. Under Allied rule, some Sicilian politicians believed their opportunity had come to push the case for becoming separate from mainland Italy. Top mafiosi could see the potential for establishing an independent criminal kingdom and strongly backed the movement. Don Calogero Vizzini was a leading proponent of Separatism and deployed his henchmen to battle against their opponents—including both Monarchists and Socialists.

While the Allies were directly in control of the island they tried to keep a lid on these activities, but when they handed back rule to the Italian government in 1944, the conflict broke out into open warfare. Vizzini and his like-minded mafiosi recruited bandits such as Salvatore Giuliano to form a Voluntary Army for Sicilian Independence, called EVIS. Throughout 1945, armed with captured German weapons, including armored cars and tanks, and dressed in khaki uniforms, the bandit army attacked police bases in Sicily and killed a number of carabinieri. The situation became so serious that the Italian government was forced to send its own troops to fight the Mafia-backed campaign for independence.

At one stage the arrest of Don Calogero Vizzini was suggested as a way of decapitating the Separatist movement, but a chilling warning was passed on by an intermediary to the Italian government. "This intermediary has declared that because of the threatened arrest of Vizzini," noted an American intelligence report in February 1945, "the Maffia [sic] has threatened to order active participation by the Sicilian Maffia on the side of the EVIS and the outlaw bands. Because of their known power, this would mean real civil war in Sicily." Vizzini's proposed arrest was said to have been provoked by the confession of an EVIS rebel stating that he had been personally recruited to the bandit army by Vizzini to fight against the carabinieri. Instead of arrest, Don Calo was advised to get out of Palermo.

Neither the Americans nor British condoned this action and just wanted to see an end to the Mafia. So, contrary to popular myth, the entire wartime policy of the Americans and the British toward the Mafia was one of irritation and suppression. By the time Charles Luciano was deported to Italy in early 1946, however, the political map was beginning to change.

♠

Setting up his office in the plush rooms of the Grand Hotel et Des Palmes in Palermo, at the top of Luciano's list of people to see was Don Calogero Vizzini. Don Calo had taken control of much of the black market in western Sicily and was trading back and forth with mainland Italy. He was the Sicilian end of the black market empire established by Vito Genovese during his period in Naples.

Until the summer of 1943, Genovese had ingratiated himself with the Fascist regime, supplying heroin and other drugs to many of its prominent figures, but his comfortable accommodation with the Fascists came to an end when the Allies invaded Sicily. Suddenly, Genovese was on the losing side. Having recovered from the shock, he quickly seized upon this as a new criminal opportunity that could bring in much more money than his small-time deals under the Fascists.

Genovese volunteered his services as an interpreter and local fixer to the American officers that arrived in Nola, near Naples, where he lived. Indeed, some of them were so impressed with his abilities that they wrote him letters of recommendation. "He would accept no pay," said Major Holmgreen, "paid his own expenses, worked day and night and rendered most valuable assistance to the Allied Military Government."

Genovese certainly worked night and day—lining his own pocket. With such close contacts inside the U.S. Army, he was able to corner the market in stolen Allied goods. His Camorra—Neapolitan Mafia—gangsters stole American military trucks, drove them into army supply depots, loaded them up with food, cigarettes, and medicine, and then transported them to dealers in the black market. Some of these goods were shipped from Naples to Sicily, where they were distributed by Don Calo. A U.S. Army report estimated that 65 percent of the income of Neapolitans was derived from the black market in stolen American goods and that one-third of all supplies and equipment brought into Italy by the Allies ended up in criminal hands. To remove goods from American bases on such a vast scale demanded a number of inside personnel on Genovese's payroll. Some of these corrupt military personnel could have been very high ranking indeed.

A name that comes up again and again in conjunction with the Mafia infiltration of the U.S. Army is Colonel Charles Poletti. He'd been a rising star back in legal circles in the United States. Indeed, at the age of just thirty-eight he had been the youngest Italian-American to rise to the post of lieutenant governor of New York under Thomas E. Dewey. In 1943, he was appointed American senior civil affairs officer in Palermo, but almost immediately got a reputation for dealing with senior Mafia figures in Sicily, many of them closely involved with the Separatist movement.

Lord Rennell, head of AMGOT, was none too keen on him and refused to recommend him for promotion to the post of administrative director, saying he was "most unsuitable for this appointment." One of Rennell's colleagues was more explicit, saying Poletti "has clearly run Sicily with enthusiasm and gusto though the shadow of Tammany Hall may have been thrown lightly across the Island."

In 1944, Poletti was appointed to a senior position in the Allied Military Government in mainland Italy. This brought him into the realm of Vito Genovese, and the mobster made sure he was on board. It is interesting to note that in *The Last Testament of Lucky Luciano*, the only reference to Poletti comes from Luciano, who calls him "one of our good friends."

Further evidence of Poletti's role as high-ranking shield to the Mafia came with the arrest of Vito Genovese in August 1944. Plucky twenty-four-year-old U.S. Sergeant Orange C. Dickey took on the task of tracking down the mobster—with little help from his senior colleagues. A former member of the Camorra first put him on to Genovese's role as king of the black market in southern Italy. Dickey then arrested two Canadian soldiers who had deserted to drive trucks for the mobster.

As Dickey gathered his material to make his move on Genovese, he sent a request for information to Colonel Poletti's office in Rome, but the Allied Military Government (AMG) denied having any knowledge of Genovese being employed by them. They then confused matters further by identifying him as an ex-prisoner ten years older than the real gangster.

Accompanied by two British soldiers, Dickey courageously arrested Genovese in Nola. In jail, Genovese denied any knowledge whatsoever of the black market in Italy, but when Dickey searched his apartment he found a number of official AMG passes giving him access to U.S. Army fuel and food supplies. Having put Genovese behind bars, Dickey needed to know what he should do next with him. Should he put him on trial by the military authorities or send him back to the United States to face civilian justice?

Dickey traveled to Rome to get the advice of Colonel Poletti, but when Dickey arrived at his office, the American chief

administrator seemed reluctant to see him. Bizarrely, on one occasion he appeared to be sleeping at his desk, then on another day
his office was filled with people and he was too busy to see the
young sergeant. Outside the office, a senior official told Dickey to
steer well clear of the case, as neither Poletti nor he wanted to be
involved with it. With such criminal reluctance from Poletti to
prosecute Genovese, Dickey was left to oversee his extradition to
America. Genovese tried to bribe the young man with $250,000
to forget about the whole business, but Dickey persisted and accompanied him back to Brooklyn by ship.

Having made sure that the major witness against Genovese's involvement in a murder back in the 1930s was dead, the
mobster was delighted to be going back to America. "Kid," he
told Dickey, "you are doing me the biggest favor anyone has ever
done me. You are taking me home." Once he was back in the
United States in June 1945, and with little evidence against him,
all charges were dropped against Genovese and he was free to
resume his position as a major Mafia boss.

Since Genovese had been arrested and taken back to America
just eight months before Luciano arrived in Sicily, it would have
been natural for Luciano to take over running his side of the
black market business, but there is little evidence that he did.
The fact that Luciano disappeared to Cuba so soon after his arrival in Italy suggests that he did not have Genovese's contacts or
authority over a racket that was probably running pretty well
under the control of local Camorra and Sicilian gangsters. He
certainly did have contacts with Don Calo, but these may have
been more political than commercial, as subsequent events would
reveal. The whiff of collaboration with American government
agents hung too strongly over Luciano for Don Calo to perhaps
risk any criminal dealings with him.

♠

U.S. intelligence-gathering agencies stayed on in Sicily after
the war had ended. In Palermo, agents of the Office of Strategic

Services (OSS) had established close links with leading mafiosi on the island. At first, the OSS had been committed to undermining the Separatist movement, but curiously they believed it was the British who were behind it, as they suspected they wanted to continue their imperial dominance of the Mediterranean after the war. The British, however, were convinced it was some corrupt Americans, Poletti among them, who were helping the Separatist mafiosi by placing them in senior political positions.

Into this maelstrom of politics and crime stepped the familiar figure of Nick Gentile. Cut out from a more senior role in the Mob in the United States, which he felt his status as fixer had deserved, he turned to dealing in narcotics. In 1937, he was arrested for heroin trafficking and broke bail to flee back to Sicily, where he became a senior mafioso. He was a key contact for Luciano when he arrived in Sicily and helped organize the island's narcotics trade with America. He was also perceived to be a valued *consigliere* when it came to political matters, and Prince Umberto turned to him when the Italian royal family feared that the Separatist Mafia was anti-monarchy.

A military intelligence report from January 1946 records a secret meeting in which Gentile was reluctant to tell them the "name of the American Colonel who allegedly informed him that the policy of the United States was to retain the monarchy in Italy." It would be surprising if this American colonel was not Poletti. Shortly after this unofficial statement of American strategy, Poletti was released from his job in Rome and returned to the United States.

But the Mafia could not fix everything. Despite Don Calo giving his considerable support to the bandit Giuliano and his armed campaign against the Italian government, national elections in June 1946 brought a shocking defeat for the Separatist party. Cleverly, the mainland government had outmaneuvered the Separatist appeal by granting autonomy to the island. While the Separatists received only 8 percent of the vote, right-wing support switched to the Christian Democrats.

Many mafiosi now saw the Christian Democrats as the realistic opposition to the growing tide of Socialism in their country and shifted their patronage and influence toward them. A year later in April 1947, the Communists and Socialists won 30 percent of the Sicilian vote against 21 percent gained by the Christian Democrats. Suddenly, with the Separatist cause annihilated and the Christian Democrats looking like losers, right-wingers began to panic. It was a situation that the CIA, formerly the OSS, had already feared.

"It is of vital strategic importance to prevent Italy from falling under Communist control," said a CIA report of 1947. "Militarily, the availability to the USSR of bases in Sicily and southern Italy would pose a direct threat to the security of communications throughout the Mediterranean."

In the face of Cold War terror, U.S. agents abroad could see that their own interests coincided with those of the Mafia. Rather than viewing them as an irritation and hindrance to internal security, they now viewed the criminals as an international asset. For the first time—because it never happened in wartime Sicily—the Mafia were recruited to further American foreign policy in the Mediterranean. Their joint aim was to stop a Communist breakthrough in the Italian national elections in 1948.

The bandit Giuliano rallied to the cause and announced his new adherence to the anti-Communist crusade in May 1947 by ordering his henchmen to open fire on a peaceful gathering of Socialists enjoying a picnic near the village of Portella delle Ginestra. After just three minutes of gunfire, eleven people lay dead, with fifty-six wounded. A month later, Giuliano published his call to arms in the Sicilian press and followed through with a campaign of terror. Socialist headquarters were bombed and several Communists killed.

A month after that, rumor linked Luciano, residing in Palermo, to the anti-Communist cause. Considering his close relationship with Don Calo and other influential mafiosi such as

Nick Gentile, it would not be surprising that Luciano should be expected to use every aspect of his high-level contacts within the U.S. government and its intelligence agencies to help support a campaign of murder against the Communist threat on the island.

It would not be the first time the CIA deployed organized crime to help influence foreign politics. In the same year, their agents made contact with members of a Corsican syndicate in France. Their mission was to break a Communist-organized strike in the docks at Marseilles. The Corsican mobsters murdered a number of strikers and business returned to normal. The criminal alliance was repeated in 1950 when Marseilles dockworkers threatened the supply of war materials to Vietnam.

In Sicily, the violence worked. By the time the 1948 general election came around, in the areas terrorized by Giuliano and his henchmen, the votes for the Christian Democrats more than doubled. The threat of a Communist takeover had been thwarted in Sicily. The CIA was delighted and so were the Mafia who had risked the wrath of the Communists by backing a right-wing party. It was the beginning of a long relationship between the Mafia and the Christian Democrat party. It resulted in decades of corruption at the very highest level of Italian politics, but it suited the Cold War concerns of America very well.

In the wake of the Christian Democrat victory, Luciano was on the winning side and should have thrived in Italy, but with little more to contribute to U.S. foreign policy, it appears that he was rapidly dropped by any friendly government agents and, instead, became a bogeyman for the Federal Bureau of Narcotics.

As for Giuliano—the hero of the moment, the frontline warrior of the Mafia with film-star good looks—he, too, was betrayed. Expecting his prize for securing victory over the Communists—such as a pardon or some kind of involvement with the new establishment—he got nothing. He had served his purpose and was left out in the cold. Feeling double-crossed, Giuliano returned to looting and kidnapping, but as he grew more brazen, he launched assaults on the barracks of the carabinieri. This was too embarrassing for the government and they sent a military force to hunt him down.

In the end, it was the Mafia that got Giuliano. Tired of his headlining atrocities, they wanted to sink back into the shadows now that they had the access to the power they craved. Two years later, in July 1950, Giuliano was hiding out in small town in southwest Sicily called Castelvetrano. As he emerged from a brothel in the early morning, he was confronted by vengeful carabinieri.

"He at once opened fire on them," reported the London *Times*, "but fell riddled by bullets from police tommy-guns. Beside his body was found a submachine-gun, a German revolver, and a telescope. On one of his fingers was a large diamond ring and his belt was fastened with a gold clasp."

The carabinieri had been tipped off by the local Mafia. No one person was bigger than the Mob—a lesson that even Luciano would have to learn.

NARCOTICS OVERLORD

War stimulated the illicit trade in drugs. Throughout World War II, Japan and Japanese-occupied Korea became a major base for producing heroin. Nazi Germany devised many new synthetic drugs. Wounded soldiers needed painkillers and both during the war and immediately afterward, there was a lively trade in black market drugs. The last flight of popular bandleader Glenn Miller, which disappeared midair in late 1944, was organized by Lieutenant Colonel Norman F. Baesell and reputedly involved the smuggling of ampoules of military-use morphine to newly liberated France.

As Nazi Germany collapsed, Wehrmacht supplies of drugs entered an extensive underground network where even concentration camp survivors were caught with pilfered narcotics. The chaos that followed the end of war shielded the activities of criminals. Added to this was new technology that allowed the extraction of opium from the whole plant rather than just the flower, and morphine could now be produced directly from dried poppy plants rather than from opium. All this saw output increase dramatically.

Before the war it had been the job of the discredited League of Nations to coordinate international action against drug barons, but in 1945 a new institution took over this role—the United Nations. Early UN reports portrayed a world on the brink of a drug addiction epidemic. Amidone was identified as one of the new synthetic drugs that offered morphinelike euphoria. "An able but unscrupulous chemist," said one report, "with equipment and materials available in the open market, could undoubtedly produce substantial amounts of these drugs secretly. One factory alone could flood the whole world with these toxic substances."

It was a potential gold mine for criminal gangs with a massively enlarged market desperate for new and old highs. Lucky Luciano was well aware of this, particularly as he now resided in a country recovering from the ravages of war and with a heady mix of administrative chaos, Allied occupation, and efficient black market suppliers. And yet, if Luciano thought he could dominate the demand for postwar drugs, he was in for a surprise. Many other suppliers were already in charge of large chunks of the market.

The UN identified four main sources of opium production: Mexico, Iran, India, and Turkey. Of those, Mexico was by far the most important, with at least 50 percent of the farmed opium turned into morphine or heroin. An investigation by the Mexican government in spring 1947 found that 4,500 fields of opium were being cultivated and that thirty to forty landing strips had been built to handle the illicit movement of narcotics into the United States and elsewhere. Clearly, this was the main conduit of opium-derived drugs into the United States, and it dwarfed any imports from Europe. There is no known link between Luciano and the Mexican drug traffickers.

The international flow of drugs received an extra boost in 1949 when the Communists won control of China. They inherited a drug empire that had been cynically exploited by the

Nationalists to raise money for their cause. The U.S. Federal Bureau of Narcotics (FBN) estimated that some 670 tons of raw opium was being produced and stored in southern China with at least four tons of it passing every month through Hong Kong on to the Pacific Rim with a good portion of it entering the United States.

Harry Jacob Anslinger was commissioner of the FBN at this crucial time, and had been its boss since its inception in 1930, when he was appointed to the post at the age of thirty-eight. Like his crime-busting colleague J. Edgar Hoover, he dominated his organization for more than three decades, finally giving up the office in 1962. He became a relentless foe of Lucky Luciano—who dubbed him "Ass-linger"—and hounded him throughout the late 1940s and 1950s. Anslinger was behind the U.S. government operation to get him thrown out of Cuba.

In 1953, Anslinger's biggest concern was how Communist China was using its stash of opium as a Cold War weapon. When he addressed the UN Commission on Narcotic Drugs in April of that year, he said, "There can be little doubt of the true purposes of Communist China in the organized sale of narcotics. Their purposes include monetary gain, financing political activities in various countries, and sabotage. The Communists have planned well and know a well-trained soldier becomes a liability and a security risk from the moment he first takes a shot of heroin."

It is very interesting to note that when this statement came to the attention of the British embassy in Washington, D.C., they were less than impressed by Anslinger's warning. In a departmental comment attached to the front of the statement, they made the candid remark that much of his statement was based on Chinese Nationalist propaganda and they understood that "Mr Anslinger is under pressure in Washington and having to fight to keep his job, partly because of his lack of success in combating juvenile delinquency in the US and partly for domestic political reasons."

Like all veteran bureaucrats, Anslinger knew he had to

maintain the appearance of master criminal enemies of the state in order to justify his budget and departmental existence. This may help to explain why Anslinger directed part of his anger at Lucky Luciano in Italy—a high-profile mobster whom the public had heard of and could fully appreciate why the FBN might be concerned about his activities.

There are some references in contemporary newspapers to Luciano being involved in smuggling narcotics from Europe to America, but it is certainly not on the massive scale of either the Communist Chinese or the Mexicans.

In January 1948, the New York *Daily Mirror* reported that federal authorities seized the biggest cache of contraband opium since 1941—fifty pounds of opium in raw gum form and ten pounds of opium with a value of $300,000, but with a street value when cut of more than $1 million. It was discovered when customs agents boarded the French freighter *Bastia* at Pier 28 in the East River. The ship had called at North African and southern European ports, including Naples, before it arrived in New York.

The drugs were found hidden in three burlap sacks in heavy tar-paper wrappings floating in a lubricating oil tank beneath the floor plates of the engine room. Their smell had been disguised by the inclusion of twelve bottles of French perfume. The link to the exiled Sicilian mobster was made by Deputy Surveyor Herman Lipski, head of the customs enforcement division. "We have positive information in our files that Luciano is involved directly or indirectly in all transportation of dope from Italian and French ports," he said. In the two years since Luciano's deportation, they had been searching all ships from the Mediterranean and had seized some $10 million worth of drugs in just the previous year.

Anslinger's conviction that Luciano was masterminding drug trafficking from Italy was based on pretty flimsy evidence. On June 25, 1949, Italian-American Vincent Trupia was stopped at Ciampino airport just outside Rome. He had arrived from Germany—Luciano's old drug-smuggling territory—and was catching a plane to New York. One piece of his luggage had a false bottom and it was found to contain 6.8 kilograms of cocaine, worth 15 million lire ($50,000). The FBI was informed, but no one was caught waiting for Trupia in New York. U.S. authorities suspected Luciano of involvement and under their pressure the Rome police searched his apartment and he was jailed for nine days.

"If somebody slips on a banana peel," he complained to the press, "the cops call me in to find out if I'm selling bananas."

The Italian police wanted him to give up his associates and suggested a whole raft of local criminals they linked him with.

"The way they talk about my 'lieutenants,'" he snapped, "I got more than the army."

Such wisecracking did not endear him to Rome's police force, but one of their police chiefs shortly afterward admitted to a journalist that charges against Luciano were "pure inventions."

Luciano agreed.

"Italy has one of the best police forces in the world," he said, "and if they had anything on me they'd arrest me."

They didn't have anything on him, but they banned him from Rome for three years and he moved to Naples. Luciano hated the southern city, calling its inhabitants "dirty Neapolitans," and did everything he could to get back to Rome, where he had several properties.

An FBI investigation into the criminal activities of Longy Zwillman—a longtime Jewish associate of Luciano—quoted the *Newark News* when it reported a raid on the Casablanca Club on May 16, 1950, for handling heroin. Thirty-one federal indictments were handed down prior to the raid. Small-time hoodlum William Margo, arrested in the raid, was reported to have contacted Luciano in Italy through his girlfriend. Zwillman opened the Casablanca Club with his own money but ownership was passed on to Zwillman's former chauffeur.

In 1951, Giuseppe Dosi was the agent at the Italian Ministry of the Interior charged with the Luciano case. He looked at all the evidence gathered by his police force and could see there was very little to act on. When he wrote a memorandum to Anslinger he had to admit that "in spite of the strict and continual surveillance of which [Luiciano] is the object, nothing has been found against him."

Anslinger declined to believe Dosi and dispatched FBN Special Agent Charles Siragusa to Rome to further investigate Luciano's activities. A former wartime OSS agent born to Sicilian immigrant parents, Siragusa was an accomplished investigator. He discovered that Joe Pici was Luciano's criminal lieutenant. An underworld informer told Siragusa that Pici had made several drug deliveries to the United States and had supplied trafficker Frank Callace, who, with his uncle, was arrested with three kilograms of heroin in Rome on April 6, 1951. This was confirmed in an International Criminal Police Commission (ICPC) report of June 1952 in which it said that Pici and Callace had been sentenced several times previously for drug trafficking and had been deported from the United States. "Furthermore," said the report, "among the accomplices of these persons were a certain 'Lucky' Luciano and others."

Siragusa's informer—who put the finger on Pici—was later revealed as Eugene Giannini, a drug dealer for the New York Tommy Lucchese family, who was arrested in Naples in 1950. He had been turned by the FBN in 1942 when he received fifteen months in jail for trafficking heroin. In 1950, Giannini was tasked with smuggling penicillin and other medical supplies into the Italian black market, along with counterfeit U.S. currency. He met Luciano in Naples and fed little bits of information to Siragusa. When he was arrested by the Italian police for dealing in fake dollars, he despaired at the filthy conditions in prison and elaborated on his knowledge about Luciano's connections with drug trafficking—anything to get him out. He made the fatal error of putting his thoughts in writing.

"I've given you a lot of information," he wrote in a letter to the FBN. "I gathered all this information the same way that got me into the jail that I am in now—by just mingling with people who are doing these things."

He mentioned linking Pici and Callace with Luciano but denied his own involvement with narcotics smuggling.

"I was being investigated for being mixed up with junk," he said. "Well, you can look until doomsday. All you find is talk, talk—what I spread around to make friends—but actual facts you will never find because there aren't any."

Giannini was right there. The problem for him was that he was trying to be too clever, trying to use Luciano's reputation to his own advantage. Finally put on trial in Italy, Giannini was acquitted for lack of evidence and flown back to the United States.

But word got out that Giannini had been squealing. Tony Bender, faithful lieutenant to Vito Genovese, summoned veteran Mafia hit man Joe Valachi to a meeting in Greenwich Village in September 1952.

"Gene [Giannini] has been talking to the junk agents," said Bender. "The old man [Genovese] has got the word personally from Charley Lucky. Charley says Gene is the smartest stool pigeon that ever lived. He has been talking to the junk agents for years. He has got to be hit, him and anybody with him."

Valachi subcontracted the hit to three East Harlem gunmen, and a few days later Giannini was shot in the head, his body found in a gutter outside 221 East Tenth Street. At the time he was planning to import six kilograms of heroin into the United States from his brother-in-law in Italy. Giannini's death was no great loss to the FBN, as his supposed inside information was far less important than the heroin he was smuggling into the country.

Despite all these stories, no definite link could be made with Luciano. Certainly, his notoriety attracted the attention of people who wanted to deal in drugs. During the time he lived in Naples, he met a cigarette-smuggling countess who wanted to progress to narcotics and a rich Englishman with a yacht who volunteered his boat for drug-smuggling purposes. Luciano dropped them both once he learned of their ambitions. An Associated Press release from Naples said Luciano was under constant surveillance by Italian police and was interviewed by them on November 29, 1952. With attention like this, Luciano probably suspected everyone of trying to set him up as a narcotics dealer.

An indication as to how desperate Siragusa was getting to pin something on Luciano came with the disappearance of Lorenzo Rago, mayor of Battipaglia, on the evening of January 20, 1953. Ostensibly a wealthy landowner with his own canning factory, Rago also led a double life as a backer of cigarette smuggling and possibly other substances. One theory was that a delivery of contraband cigarettes had been intercepted by the Italian Coast Guard and been jettisoned into the sea, resulting in the loss of 20 million lire for the mayor. Rago had complained and been eliminated by the smuggling gang.

It seemed pretty straightforward, but Siragusa was convinced that Luciano had to be involved somehow and found an ally in Giovanni Florita, head of the local police in Naples. Florita was keen to remove Luciano from his vicinity and asked his superior in Rome for permission to expel the gangster from Naples and confine him to his home village of Lercara Friddi in Sicily. Rome refused, so Florita continued to harass Luciano by depriving him of his driving license and passport. The police chief also imposed an 8:00 P.M. curfew on the mobster. Luciano's lawyers appealed against this measure to the Ministry of the Interior, but they were turned down on the grounds that Luciano was known to frequent racetracks and clubs with a view to resurrecting his contacts with the underworld and narcotics trafficking.

To link Luciano with the Rago affair, Siragusa recruited another low-level drug peddler called Francesco Scibilia who had been deported from the United States. Scibilia claimed that Luciano was linked to Rago because the mobster had lent him 150 million lire to invest in his cigarette-smuggling racket. Rago, apparently, had pocketed most of the money and Luciano retaliated by having the mayor kidnapped in Tangiers. Scibilia supposedly proved the truth of all this by presenting a business card that belonged to Rago's brother with 48,000 lire scribbled on the back—the sum presumably for his ransom.

This unlikely tale was enough for Siragusa and Florita to devote much police time and effort to following up and further harassing Luciano. In the end, it turned out that Scibilia had obtained the business card when he bumped into Rago's brother on a train in Calabria—and the sum of money jotted down on the back of the card was the value of some stolen watches. It was no more sinister than that! A furious Luciano instructed his lawyers to sue Scibilia for libel.

The sad truth of this story, as far as Luciano was concerned, is that if he truly had the mafioso power claimed for him by Siragusa and Florita, he would not have been so easily targeted by the Italian police. His influence within the Italian government would have protected him. The same is true if he was making millions of dollars smuggling narcotics. He would have used this wealth to better protect himself from pretty minor harassment by the police. Florita was obviously finding it very easy to pick on Luciano. This alone proves that Luciano's power during this period must have been greatly diminished and was nowhere near that ascribed to him. It served the purposes of everyone to make a bogeyman out of Luciano—because they knew very well he wasn't that terrifying in reality.

Luciano's criminal impotency was revealed in an anecdote told by local mafioso Antonio Calderone, who recalled an incident in the Agnano hippodrome in Naples toward the end of the 1950s. There, in full public view, a low-level Neapolitan hoodlum slapped Luciano. It was a gross insult to the veteran mobster and the disrespectful criminal was soon after murdered, but the moment was considered emblematic by Calderone as the end of American influence in his country. This scene was later dramatized in Franceso Rosi's movie about Luciano. Clearly, the old gangster might still have powerful friends in America, but he lacked any serious respect among the Italian mafiosi.

Siragusa was delighted when an undercover agent revealed to him that Luciano was "so frightened of my influence with the Italian police that he never even drives through the city of Rome during his frequent trips from Naples to Santa Marinella, where he owns some property." The mobster said that "rather than driving though Rome, he leaves the main highway and takes a detour." This had little to do with Siragusa—if Luciano violated his ban from Rome, he faced six months in prison.

With so little to go on, when it came to making a connection between Luciano and the international drug trade, the FBI could only draw on the paltry evidence gathered by the FBN. In an FBI monograph on the Mafia written in July 1958, they quoted the FBN, saying "there exists a realm of cooperation and coordination between Mafiosi in the United States and the Mafia in Sicily in the illicit traffic of drugs." They pointed the finger at Nick Gentile, who jumped bail in 1937 to flee to Italy and was closely linked to Luciano. They also mentioned Joseph Pici as an intimate of Luciano, who was known to smuggle heroin into the United States for the Kansas City Mob.

Nick Gentile was a senior narcotics dealer. He even admitted to his involvement in a major drug-smuggling ring in the United States. Back in the mid-1930s, he had contact with Charles La Gaipa, a supplier of narcotics from Sicily. La Gaipa proposed to Gentile that he organize drug handlers in Texas and Louisiana. In their first year working together, they would clear $100,000. At this stage, Gentile was part of the Mangano family, and he claimed that Albert Anastasia was a member of the drug syndicate he put together.

In 1937, Gentile suspected that his girlfriend was an undercover agent and soon after the FBN swooped on his organization. "In one night alone they arrested 75 narcotics dealers that were operating from New York to Texas," he recalled. He fled to Sicily, where he reestablished his drug-smuggling business until he was turned by an FBN agent in 1958. Gentile would have been a prime candidate for Luciano to work with, but Luciano's high profile in Naples discouraged Gentile, who was terrified of being arrested again.

"During the talks between my lawyer and the judge of New Orleans [where he was arrested]," recalled Gentile, "the judge said, thinking I did not understand English, 'What's the use of reducing bail when once in New York the court will throw the book at him—by adding tax evasion, and white slavery that will bring such a sentence that he will never be able to get out of prison, as was the case with Lucky Luciano and for the same reason Lucky was condemned for 30 to 50 years?'"

With such a reputation for being framed up, it is understandable if Gentile had wanted to steer well clear of doing business with Luciano in Italy.

Meyer Lansky visited Luciano in Rome during the early part of this period, although he later denied he had planned any such meeting. He was on a general vacation, touring southern Italy with his new wife in June and July 1949, in which he visited Palermo, Capri, Naples, and Pompeii. At the Kefauver hearings in 1951, he was asked to explain exactly what happened in Rome. He said his meeting with Luciano had come about by accident thanks to the Italian press.

"He called me when I was about to ready to leave Rome," Lansky said. "As far as I knew, he was in jail. And I said 'How the hell did you know where I am staying?' He says 'Well, I got it from the paper, and I traced you through Naples, Hotel Excelsior.' Because I had my itinerary made up with Cook's Tours."

Luciano went to Lansky's hotel.

"He came up to see me and he says 'Do you want to have dinner with me?' He invited me to dinner, and I said 'OK.' I couldn't very well refuse him."

Over dinner, Lansky claimed nothing was said about business in America.

"Just he told me how he was being crucified, and what

happened to him. And I told him, I says 'You have nothing to kick about; look at the way I am being crucified.'" Both were suffering from too much attention from the authorities.

Lansky was then asked if he had any knowledge of any money or assets of any kind that were given or sent to Luciano since he left the United States.

"Not that I know of," said Lansky.

Lansky was very aware of the increased interest shown in him and Luciano by Anslinger's agents. That summer just before he sailed to Italy, they burst into Lansky's penthouse apartment overlooking Central Park.

"I invited them in," he recalled, "but the way they behaved I had the impression they were going to smash the place to pieces. They cross-examined me about my trip to Europe. For some reason they had it in their heads that I was involved in narcotics."

Lansky understood that this was part of a publicity campaign by Anslinger to win positive headlines for the FBN.

"It was a game," said Lansky, "but a nasty one for Teddy [his new wife] and me. It gave the authorities a lot of publicity, but I was outraged. They knew I never touched drugs in my life."

But Lansky was playing a publicity game of his own. As his friend Doc Stacher revealed: "Meyer knew that Charlie felt out of things in Italy, and there were some signs that his influence wasn't as strong as it used to be. That was unbearable for a man like Charlie. Meyer decided to demonstrate his friendship for Lucky by planning a trip to Italy, and for once he let it be known that he wouldn't mind if the news got out."

Lansky claimed that FBN agents followed him throughout his European trip and even tried to bug his hotel rooms, but all that attention suited him just fine as it demonstrated to the criminal fraternity back home in the United States that Luciano was still worth visiting. Maybe this also explains why the continuing FBN harassment of Luciano had its upside for the mobster because it made him still look like a Mr. Big.

In 1950, the New York Police Department reported that

Luciano was receiving transatlantic telephone calls several times a week from leading mafiosi, including Frank Costello, Vincent Mangano, and Joe Adonis. The calls were made early morning, discussed various areas of criminal administration, and lasted roughly twenty minutes. In 1956, Joe Biondo—his old friend from the East Fourteenth Street days—was identified as the Mob's go-between, traveling back and forth to Italy to keep Luciano informed on Mob matters and to pay him his slice of the profits. At the beginning of Luciano's exile, this is said to have amounted to $25,000 a month. Frank Costello was said to keep him well supplied with cash as well, and one delivery from him amounted to $70,000.

This was the money that Luciano actually lived on in Italy—not the profits of any mythical drug dealing. He lived on the dividends of his previous decades of racketeering, when he was a real gangster chief and not the fake mobster he had now become.

♠

Although it suited Anslinger's political purposes to cast Luciano as a narcotics overlord in Italy, the truth of the situation reveals a more complex network of criminality. Turkey was the nearest source of opium into the Mediterranean region and this entered Italy via Yugoslavia. Much of it then passed through north Italian cities such as Milan and Genoa and continued to Marseilles in the south of France. Luciano's supposed associate, Joe Pici, got his heroin from Milan. The other big seizure of 1951 comparable to that grabbed from the Callaces was a raid on a secret laboratory run by a Frenchman in which three kilograms of basic morphine was discovered. Further investigation showed that he was connected to heads of the Marseilles underworld already renowned for dealing in drugs and American cigarettes—the notorious French Connection.

Only one major drug seizure was linked to Sicily: 5.8 kilograms of heroin found at Alcamo in March 1952, just south of Castellammare del Golfo in the northwest of the island. It had arrived by train from Rome and was intended to be sent on to the United States. This was, undoubtedly, a Mafia organized trade. The four other major heroin seizures of that year were all in the north of Italy.

More significant than all these cases was the illicit trade in drugs from legitimate wholesale chemists in Turin, Genoa, and Milan, which between 1948 and 1952 amounted to a staggering 1,100 kilograms in total—900 kilograms of which was heroin— and led to the arrest of seven Italian businessmen. An ICPC report of May 1952 declared that "since the close of hostilities, hundredweights of kilos of morphine and of heroin were diverted in Italy from lawful manufacture, and that the distribution of these constituted the principal source of supply to the French black markets in drugs, and more especially the American ones." This was known as the Schiapparelli case, after the name of the Turin-based pharmaceutical company.

FBN agent Siragusa reported that it was these corrupt factory bosses who had supplied known associates of Luciano with heroin, but, again, nothing stuck to him. Siragusa spent most of his time dealing with the really important suppliers in Turkey and the Middle East.

In 1956, the ICPC revealed that the Italian police had been working with the FBN to break a major drug-smuggling ring that operated across several Mediterranean countries, including Lebanon, Egypt, Italy, France, and then on to the United States. In Italy, the network was run by a Jerusalem-born Italian called Giorgio Morcos who ran his operations from a villa in Rome. He converted base morphine into heroin. When his villa was raided, he was found to have forty-seven kilograms of hashish, one kilogram of morphine, fifty grams of cocaine, and thousands of travelers' checks stolen from American tourists in Rome.

None of the ICPC reports for this period credit Luciano with more than peripheral involvement in heroin trading—he's certainly not portrayed as the master crook of the drugs business.

And yet the illusion persisted that somehow he was the shadowy presence behind all narcotics smuggling in Italy.

In 1954, the Italians accused the American and British military authorities in Trieste of allowing their territory to be used as a transit point between Yugoslavia and Italy for illicit drug trading. From 1947 to 1954, Trieste had been declared an independent city under the protection of the United Nations.

The British Home Office dismissed the accusations by saying "In view of the notorious Schiapparelli case, it seems incredible that the Italian government would be so foolish as to take such a brazen line . . ." It then concluded its letter to the British embassy in Washington, D.C., by saying "there is abundant evidence of organised and wide-spread illicit trafficking in Italy itself and some reason for suspecting that it is controlled, partly at any rate, by Italians expelled from the United States, eg 'Lucky' Luciano, a notorious racketeer and trafficker."

As the British disputed the role of their military authorities in the supposed drug trade in Trieste, they called upon the head of the Venezia Giulia Police Force to give his candid version of the battle against drugs in Italy. He said that the FBN agent based in Rome was most useful and that, contrary to the critical comments of the Italians, who liked to shift the blame for their failures in drug policing to an alleged conspiracy based in Trieste, it was the Italian police force that was dragging its feet.

"On May 8, '53, a certain Pertusi was engaged in a drug transaction in Trieste," said the British police report. "Upon hearing that his two accomplices had been arrested, he fled to Rome. We made constant efforts to obtain the return of Pertusi to Trieste, but all was in vain. Rome Police replied that he could not be located. However, reliable sources advised us that Pertusi was physically in Rome and had been in contact with the Guardia di Finanza [a military police force charged with stopping drug trafficking]. Nevertheless, Pertusi was tried here in absentia, sentenced and later amnestied. Pertusi returned to Trieste when he learned the amnesty had been granted. So far as I am concerned, his crime went unpunished."

From this incident, it seemed that the Italian police always preferred to blame outsiders for bringing illicit drugs to their shores. This view was solidly expressed by Luke Monzelli, a lieutenant in the carabinieri tasked with following foreign crooks.

"What is it that makes Americans think that the simple act of deportation will solve the problems of gangsters whose activities they cannot abolish because of 'insufficient evidence'?" complained Monzelli. "When they unleashed Luciano in effect they appointed a clever man the Chairman of the Board of an international drug cartel. . . ."

When the Americans deported more gangsters in the 1950s, they merely provided Luciano with more soldiers, argued Monzelli.

"They could not be denied their cards of identity or Italian passports. So they fanned out, under Luciano's direction, to Marseilles, to Munich, to Tunis, to Hamburg, to Frankfurt, to London. A couple stayed at home, travelling constantly as Luciano spun his spider's web with the help of these fellow-Mafiosi who set themselves up in their cities as merchants and importers."

It was all Italian mythmaking. In reality, it was their own homegrown crooks that proved to be the biggest operators. In March 1956, after coming under sustained international pressure, Italy finally banned heroin production on its own soil.

In 1973, FBN agent Charles Siragusa played himself in Italian film director Francesco Rosi's movie *Lucky Luciano*, an impressive film biography of the mobster. In this, Rosi refers to Luciano buying his heroin from Schiapparelli and selling it on to the United States via Marseilles. One scene shows Anslinger at the UN blaming an Italian delegate for allowing his country's legally manufactured heroin to pass into the mobster's hands. Rosi wrote the screenplay himself, based on Siragusa's comments, and this has undoubtedly added to the legend of Luciano as the narcotics overlord of postwar Italy.

♠

Joseph Bonanno returned to Sicily in October 1957. It had been thirty-seven years since the Fascists had chased him out of the island, but in that time he had survived the Castellammarese War and risen to become head of one of the five main Mafia families in New York. He adored his Sicilian background— conducted much of his business in the dialect at home—and delighted in his return visit.

"I don't mean to degrade the United States," he said. "I am an American citizen and it's a great country. But when I revisited Italy I felt as if I had returned to high civilization."

The Christian Democrat minister for trade had a red carpet rolled out for Bonanno at Rome airport. It didn't come better than that. The cabinet minister was a childhood friend of Bonanno from Castellammare and had ridden the wave of Christian Democrat success—thanks in part to the electoral influence of the Mafia who helped put them in power. Bonanno stayed in a grand hotel in Rome overlooking the fashionable Via Veneto. From there, he traveled directly to Palermo in Sicily. He makes no reference at all to meeting Luciano—obviously, not sharing Lansky's desire to add to the old mobster's luster by paying homage to him in Naples.

In the Sicilian capital, Bonanno admitted to meeting "men of honor," who showed him around a city being disfigured by corrupt Mafia-backed building projects. According to his own memoirs, the only incident that disturbed him was a clash with a disrespectful waiter. He ended that by smashing a glass jug of water over the man's head.

In truth, this was no vacation. Bonanno was on a business trip and, according to Mafia legend, it was one of the most momentous of the postwar era. At the Grand Hotel et Des Palmes on Via Roma—Luciano's favorite hotel in Palermo—he chaired a meeting of American gangsters and their Sicilian counterparts. Bonnano was backed up by his second-in command, Frank

Garofalo, and senior family members, Carmine Galante and John Bonventre, plus other key American mafiosi. The Sicilians were headed by Don Giuseppe Genco Russo, who had taken over after the death of Don Calogero Vizzini in 1954.

One of the minor Sicilian gangsters attending the meeting was Tommaso Buscetta. He later became a key informer against the Mafia and liked to talk up his status within the underworld. He denied there ever was a formal conference in the Grand Hotel et Des Palmes, but does say that he sat down with both Bonanno and Lucky Luciano at a dinner in October 1957, along the waterfront in Palermo. He further claimed that it was Luciano who set up the whole meeting. Buscetta is the only source for this, and Luciano's role as fixer for the Mafia gathering is not attested by any other primary witness, least of all Bonanno.

It seems very unlikely that Luciano did in fact attend such a meeting in Palermo. His every movement was watched by the Italian police and American agents, and his presence in Palermo would only have attracted unwelcome attention. Also, in the light of previous incidents in Italy throughout the 1950s, it appears that Luciano's power had been in serious decline ever since Lansky had felt it necessary to pay him a morale-boosting visit back in 1949. He was no longer a major player in the international Mafia and Bonanno would have put little value on seeing him. With the death of Don Calo three years earlier, Luciano had lost his most powerful contact in Sicily. Younger and more aggressive mafiosi were on the rise and they had no interest in old-timers.

It was at the Palermo meeting in 1957 that Bonanno forged a transatlantic alliance between the American Mafia and the Sicilian Mafia. They agreed that the Sicilians would organize the export of heroin to the United States. Much of this would pass through the little ports of northwest Sicily—such as Castellammare del Golfo, Bonanno's birthplace—under the guise of food exports destined for America. The prime motive for this shifting of responsibility to the Sicilian Mafia for drug trafficking was the introduction of the draconian U.S. Narcotics Control Act of 1956. This threatened forty-year maximum prison sentences for anyone convicted of dealing with drugs.

By the time Bonanno arrived in Sicily, one in three of his crime family had been arrested on drug charges. If they carried on like that, there would be no one left to run their other criminal enterprises. Bonanno had little choice but to hand over the business to his Sicilian colleagues. It also underlined the point that if Luciano had truly been overlord of a narcotics smuggling network, as Anslinger and his FBN agents wished to portray him, then surely he would have been the obvious person to organize this. Instead, he was sidelined by Bonanno and the Sicilians who ran it themselves.

The truth is that Luciano's power within the Mafia has been steadily draining away ever since he was kicked out of Cuba in 1947. His high profile made him useless within the organization as everything he did attracted too much heat. His New York friends still held him in high regard—because of the old times—none more so that Meyer Lansky and Frank Costello, but that couldn't make up for his real lack of authority. American government agents liked to ascribe tremendous power to Luciano because it suited their purposes—they knew where he was and could do something about him—but this was just a publicity game.

All that said, Luciano's American friends still wielded considerable power within the United States, and when it came to a falling-out among the mafiosi, Luciano could still help to deliver a killing blow—especially when it involved his longtime rival, Vito Genovese.

GENOVESE'S GAME

In Washington, D.C., before a Senate Special Committee to Investigate Crime in Interstate Commerce, Salvatore Moretti, a New Jersey racketeer and brother of Willie Moretti, was asked to testify about his criminal associations.

"Do you know what the Mafia is?" asked Counsel Rudolph Halley.

"What?" said Moretti.

"The Mafia? M-A-F-I-A?"

"I am sorry, I don't know what you are talking about. . . ."

"You never heard that word before in your life?" persisted Halley.

"No, sir, I did not."

"Do you read?"

"Nah—as I says before, I don't read very much on account of my eyes."

By the end of what became known as the Kefauver Committee hearings, everyone in America knew what the Mafia was. It was the process that Luciano and Lansky had feared most—full nationwide coverage of their activities in every newspaper and on television. The chairman of the committee was the soft-spoken forty-seven-year-old Democrat senator from Tennessee, Estes Kefauver. What had concerned him was the corruption of political life by organized crime. Once many fellow Democrats in Chicago and New York caught a whiff of his investigation into their relationship with the Mob, they probably would have liked to order a hit on the six-foot-three-inch senator.

The committee of five Democrat and Republican senators sat from May 10, 1950 to May 1, 1951, and examined more than six hundred witnesses, including mobsters, politicians, and policemen. Meyer Lansky and Frank Costello were the most senior gangsters interviewed. Costello famously refused to have his face televised, so the camera focused lower down on his anxious fingers in what became known as the "hand ballet." Many of the witnesses took the Fifth on the grounds that their answers would incriminate them, but the quiet, insistent questioning of Kefauver mesmerized many into letting slip nuggets of information.

By the end of the process, Kefauver concluded, "A nationwide crime syndicate does exist in the United States of America, despite the protestations of a strangely assorted company of criminals, self-serving politicians, plain blind fools, and others who may be honestly misguided, that there is no such combine."

Among the "plain blind fools," the senator probably meant J. Edgar Hoover, who had consistently downplayed the existence of the Mafia. Kefauver identified it as "a shadowy, international criminal organization" and said that there were two main factions in New York and Chicago, with the East Coast Mob led by Frank Costello, Meyer Lansky, and Joe Adonis.

Kefauver reserved his praise for the crime-busting activities of Harry J. Anslinger and the Federal Bureau of Narcotics and it is a little surprising to see that he took their angle on the importance of Luciano to the syndicate.

"The Mafia today actually is a secret international government-within-a-government," said Kefauver. "It has an international head in Italy—believed by United States authorities to be Charles (Lucky) Luciano."

It was a breathtaking statement that relied mainly on Anslinger's questionable evidence. Unable to talk to Luciano, the committee spoke to many of the key players involved with him. They wanted to know more about his rumored secret deal with the government during World War II, but Governor Dewey refused to testify before them. They spoke instead to Moses Polakoff, his attorney, who confirmed some of the details regarding the prevention of sabotage in the New York docks. FBN agent George White contributed his information about narcotics smuggler August Del Grazio offering to act as go-between with Luciano to help make Sicily "a much softer target than it might otherwise be." The full details of Luciano's wartime deal came out four years later in the Herlands Report, which thoroughly investigated the alliance between U.S. Naval Intelligence and organized crime.

Lansky admitted to maintaining links with Luciano, seeing him off at Ellis Island, then meeting again in Havana and Rome. Costello let slip that he bumped into Luciano, sharing a car ride with him to the airport in Cuba.

"What did you talk about?" asked Counsel Halley.

"Just his health and what not," said Costello, "and that is about all."

Lower-level mobster Mike Lescari revealed a little more, saying he had taken $2,500 in cash to Luciano in Italy. "I just thought he might need it," he added.

It all really amounted to nothing, but still the committee liked to persist with its notion of Luciano as a criminal mastermind.

Bizarrely, Senator Charles W. Tobey berated Moses Polakoff for doing his job as Luciano's defense lawyer.

"How did you become counsel for such a dirty rat as that?" said Tobey. "Aren't there some ethics in the legal profession?"

"Minorities and undesirables and persons with bad reputations are more entitled to the protection of the law than are the so-called honorable people," said Polakoff. "I don't have to apologize to you."

"I look upon you in amazement," sneered Tobey.

"I look upon you in amazement," said Polakoff, "a Senator of the United States, for making such a statement."

The smart retort had little effect on Tobey, who concluded: "There are some men who by their conduct in their life become a stench in the nostrils of decent American citizens, and in my judgment Lucky Luciano stands at the head of the list."

Lansky was later dismissive of the legal attacks on him.

"Committees like the Kefauver Committee," he said, "pointed the finger at me. Yet why is it that with the great power of the United States behind them, they were never able, or willing, to put me up in a court of law and accuse me with the proof that I was a so-called master-criminal?"

The Kefauver Committee was more successful in establishing the links among mobsters, corrupt politicians, and policemen. Former New York mayor William O'Dwyer was shown to have a close working relationships with Frank Costello and Joe Adonis and as a result of this failed to tackle the rampant racketeering within his city. Costello was the real casualty of the hearings. He talked too much and looked nervous. The national exposure he received meant he could no longer enjoy his cozy relations with senior politicians and his era as powerbroker for the Mob was over. Kefauver, on the other hand, came out of the hearings as a political star and was selected as a presidential running mate in 1956.

♠

In retrospect, it all started to go wrong for Luciano and his associates in 1947 in Cuba. Intended as a grand reunion of all the great gangsters from the 1930s with Luciano as their honored leader, it turned out to be a disaster for the chief mobster. Not only did it expose the limits of his power and his inability to outsmart the U.S. government—Anslinger's FBN in particular—it also demonstrated that the cohesion of the top bosses that had served them so well for the better part of two decades was breaking down.

Although their businesses were based on close friendship since the 1920s on the Lower East Side, the pressures of their multimillion-dollar businesses superseded their amity. Bugsy Siegel was the first to go. Neither Meyer Lansky nor Lucky Luciano could do anything to protect him. Sure, he was the author of his own fate, but if Lansky and Luciano had been at the top of their game—as they were in the early 1930s—they could have fended off the demands for his blood, but the other heads of the Five Families no longer deferred to their old capo.

Frank Costello, also close to Siegel, took some of the blame for losing so much Mob money in Las Vegas, and Luciano did his best to shield him from the wrath of the other families. Costello's lawyer, George Wolf, was given the gist of the conversation between the two in Havana.

"You got to get the money up somehow," Luciano told Costello. "Otherwise I can't hold them back."

"I'll get it," said Costello.

"Meanwhile, you retire as head of the Commission. Genovese takes over."

Costello agreed.

"But I told the boys—and they agree—as soon as you get the money back, you take over again," said Luciano. "I want you there."

"What happens to Bugsy?" asked Costello.

"Him I can't help."

On the evening of June 20, 1947, Siegel was sitting on a chintz-patterned sofa in his Beverly Hills mansion reading the *Los Angeles Times* when the glass of the large picture window shattered under the impact of seven bullets from a thirty-caliber army carbine. One smashed his nose and a second ripped out his right eye, flinging it fifteen feet across the floor. The dead body of the once Hollywood-handsome hoodlum looked a bloody mess.

With Luciano back in Italy and both Costello and Lansky cowed by the assault on their close friend, it was clear that there was a new dominant figure in the American underworld. That was Vito Genovese—the man who Luciano said should take over from Costello while he sorted out the money problems.

Ever since the forty-eight-year-old Genovese had come back to America from Italy in 1945—courtesy of the U.S. government—he had been determined to reassert himself and take over what his old boss Luciano left behind. Even among other mafiosi, Genovese had a mean reputation. He fell in love with a married woman, Anna Petillo, in 1932. Her husband was later found strangled. The two men who killed him also disappeared. Genovese never liked to leave loose ends to any crime and was renowned as a dependable hit man.

Luciano chose him as one of his top four henchmen to kill Joe the Boss. In an anecdote told in *The Last Testament of Lucky Luciano*, the mobster was musing in jail how best to end World War II when he came up with the idea of assassinating the Nazi leader. His associates looked at each other—then laughed.

"What the hell are you laughin' at?" snaps Luciano. "We've got the best hit man in the world over there—Vito Genovese. That dirty little pig owes his life to me and now it's time for him to make good on it. He's so fuckin' friendly with Mussolini and that punk son-in-law of his, that Count Ciano, he oughta be able to get close enough to Hitler to do it."

It was not such a farfetched idea. Bugsy Siegel was rumored to have visited Rome in 1938 with his girlfriend—the Countess di Frasso—and shared a villa with top Nazis Hermann Goering and Joseph Goebbels. The Jewish gangster was just itching to finish off the strutting Nazis as they walked around the garden of the villa but held back because of the potential repercussions for his lover.

When Genovese was returned to America, he still had the charge of murdering Ferdinand Boccia hanging over him. The chief witness to the killing was Peter La Tempa, serving time in jail. Shortly after news came through to him of his extradition to the United States, friends of Genovese made contact with the prison authorities holding the witness. When he woke one morning with acute kidney stone pain, he was given sedatives strong enough to "kill eight horses." With La Tempa dead, there was little evidence against Genovese and he walked the charge.

"By devious means," said the judge, "among which were the terrorizing of witnesses, kidnapping them, yes, even murdering those who could give evidence against you, you have thwarted justice time and again."

Genovese was a formidable foe adept at playing a deadly game of chess with his rivals. Luciano knew Genovese wanted to step into his shoes after he was exiled to Italy, but he trusted Frank Costello more to look after his own concerns. Luciano depended on the flow of money from his investments in the United States, and only Lansky and Costello could be trusted to deliver this. Luciano wanted Costello to remain in charge of affairs, but recognized Genovese's seniority by letting him take over the business while Costello paid back Las Vegas money to the Mob. Costello—ever the great politician of the syndicate—also worked hard to pay full respect to Genovese, but this wasn't clear enough for the wannabe boss of bosses.

"Vito should have understood that from the way Frankie handled a charity dinner he gave at the Copacabana in 1949," recalled retired mafioso Angelo Torriani. "Frankie was great for that sort of thing. He loved showing off what a great guy he was in public, and so when he gave Vito Genovese the place of honor at that dinner, that man should have known that he was aces, that he was tops, that he was being treated like a capo should be. Maybe that was too quiet a way for Vito to get the message. He wanted things down in black and white."

Joe Valachi, a gunman for Genovese, was also aware of the tension.

"It was a bad time for us," he said. "Everyone was a little nervous. I felt at any moment I could get hit with a shotgun blast." He blamed it on Genovese's maneuvering. "Vito is like a fox. He takes his time," Valachi said.

Genovese began his move against Costello by bringing Carlo Gambino, a rising mafioso who was hungry to take over his position close to him. He next made a move against Willie Moretti, a childhood pal of Costello, and master of his own army of sixty gunmen in New Jersey. It was Moretti who had become godfather to the young Frank Sinatra and got him out of a contract by putting a gun into the mouth of his bandleader, Tommy Dorsey. By 1950, Moretti was suffering from advanced syphilis and his rambling monologues were seen to be a threat to the discretion of the Mafia. When he was called before the Kefauver Committee, many mobsters grew nervous. In the event, he talked freely but gave very little away, declaring he couldn't be a member of the Mafia because he didn't possess a membership card.

But he kept on talking to the press, and Genovese used this to get at Costello, accusing him of a lack of judgment by constantly shielding Morretti. Valachi remembered his insistent conversations on the subject: "He says it is sad about Willie and that it ain't his fault. He is just sick in the head, but if he is allowed to keep talking, he is going to get us all in a jam."

On the morning of October 4, 1951, Moretti sat down to a meeting with three other men in Joe's Elbow Room Restaurant at 793 Palisades Avenue in Cliffside Park, New Jersey. When the wife of the owner and the waitress went into the kitchen, they heard gunfire. When they came out, they saw Moretti sprawled on the floor with blood pouring out the back of his head over the hexagonal patterned linoleum. The other men were gone.

Frank Costello's lawyer knew the significance of the murder. "Everyone in the underworld knew that Frank was Willie's protector. The murder of Willie was a violent announcement that Frank's power as the king was under direct threat."

The problem for Costello was that his power was already fading because of his appearance before the Kefauver Committee. He was no longer invisible and soon other law enforcers exploited his vulnerability. Two trials followed in which Costello was charged with contempt of Congress. At the second trial he was found guilty and sentenced, at the age of sixty-one, to eighteen months in prison. He was then pursued by IRS investigators, and in 1954 he was sentenced to five years in prison for tax evasion. He appealed, of course, but if he wasn't in jail, he spent most of his time in and out of court. It was no way to run organized crime, and this played effectively into Genovese's hands.

With the death of Moretti, Costello had sought a new enforcer and encouraged Albert Anastasia, Luciano's old hit man. He allowed Anastasia to murder Vincent Mangano and take over his crime family in 1951. But the power went to Anastasia's head and he put a contract out on a Brooklyn salesman called Arnold Schuster just because he didn't like the way Schuster boasted on TV about his role as prime witness against a bank robber. The murder of Schuster brought a lot of heat on the Mafia, and Genovese used this concern about the kill-crazy Anastasia to lure other mobsters away from him, including his underboss Carlo Gambino and Joe Profaci.

So far, Meyer Lansky had managed to stay out of the growing antagonism between Costello and Genovese—he was too busy building his gambling business in Cuba—but he always knew Genovese was bad news for Luciano and his friends. He believed it was Genovese who was behind the apparent suicide of Longy Zwilllman, another old-time crime boss who, in February 1955, was found hanging from a wire in the basement of his New Jersey home. When Lansky visited Luciano in Italy, he had told him about his misgivings, finally convincing Lucky of their rival's devious plans.

"You were so against Vito even in those [early] days," Luciano told Lansky, "that I thought you were being unfair to him. OK, Little Man, you handle Vito as you think best. I know you'll wait for the right moment."

But it was Genovese who finally made the big push against Luciano's key associates. Surprised by Frank Costello's sudden release from prison over the IRS case, pending an appeal, Genovese hastily put together a hit. On the evening of May 2, 1957, Costello had dinner with Philip Kennedy, a former baseball player and head of a modeling agency. They shared a cab back to Costello's apartment at 115 Central Park West, and as he said good-bye to his friend, a powerfully built man scurried past him into the lobby of his apartment building. When Costello walked into the entrance hall, the big man pulled a gun and said, "This is for you, Frank."

Costello raised his arm to shield himself from the point-blank shot, but blood spurted out from the wound on the side of his head. It looked as though Genovese had achieved the ultimate blow against the old Luciano family—the death strike he had long dreamed of.

Miraculously, Costello survived the assassination attempt, the bullet merely grazing the side of his head. Everyone knew that Genovese had ordered the hit—he was the only mafioso of the stature to order such a high-ranking assault. It was a tremendous gamble, too. To slay the king and then fail to finish him off could bring the whole wrath of organized crime down on him. Joe Valachi and other Genovese gunmen were summoned to an urgent meeting.

"We were told we got to get ready," said Valachi. "There could be war over this." Genovese retreated to his Atlantic Highlands mansion with a small army of loyal soldiers.

But nothing happened. Genovese had played the game too well and was too strong to be punished. Instead, Costello had to endure the humiliation of facing his assassin in court—Vincent "the Chin" Gigante—and saying nothing. Costello didn't recognize him, he told the jury. At the end of the trial, Gigante was acquitted and walked over to Costello. He shook his hand and said, "Thanks, Frank."

Six months later, Genovese sought to wrap up the loose ends of Costello's demise by taking on his strong-arm man. On October 25, 1957, at 10:15 A.M., Albert Anastasia strolled into his favorite barbershop in the Park Sheraton Hotel on Seventh Avenue. He took chair number four and told the barber to give him a haircut. The barber draped a cloth around the gangster's neck and switched on some electric clippers. Anastasia shut his eyes and relaxed.

A couple of minutes later, two men entered the barbershop with the lower part of their faces hidden behind scarves like old-fashioned robbers. One of then told the shop's owner: "Keep your mouth shut if you don't want your head blown off." The gunmen stood directly behind Anastasia, who still had his eyes shut—half asleep in his chair—and opened fire at the same time.

"Anastasia leaped forward with the first report," said a front-page story. "His heavy feet kicked at the foot rest and tore it away. He landed on his feet, weaving. He did not turn around to face the killers. He lunged further forward, still facing the mirror. The second spurt of bullets threw him against the glass shelving in front of the mirror. He grabbed for the shelving and brought a glass of bay rum to the tiles with a shattering crash. He took two further shots. Then the last shot—so the police figure it—took him [in the] back of the head."

The gunmen said nothing as they fled. They dropped their guns—one in a trash basket near the West Fifty-seventh Street subway station. This time, the assassins had made sure their victim was dead—they didn't want to face his vengeance.

Within hours of the shooting, Frank Costello went to see the dead man's brother, Tony Anastasio, and they hung on to each other, weeping. Costello was a broken man. He had no defense against Genovese and immediately went into retirement, handing over most of his criminal assets to the victor.

To Luciano in Naples, it looked as though Genovese was

systematically wiping out anyone related to his old crime family. Who would be next? Lansky? Luciano himself? Although with his power severely reduced and many of his powerful friends gone, Luciano set about planning his revenge and in this was aided by a distinctly nervous Lansky.

♠

Genovese wanted a coronation to celebrate the beginning of his reign as boss of bosses and he chose a stone hilltop mansion at Apalachin in Tioga County in Upstate New York as the venue. He wanted a gathering of the top mafiosi from around the country. He wanted them to recognize him as their leader and accept a period of peace under his rule. It was the culmination of more than three decades of ambition. They met in the house of Joseph Barbara, a lieutenant in Stefano Magaddino's Buffalo family. In the middle of nowhere, surrounded by wooded countryside for miles, it seemed a perfectly discreet place for such a meeting.

The list of some sixty mobsters who turned up on November 14, 1957, less than three weeks after Anastasia's killing, included many senior figures such as Profaci, Gambino, Magaddino, Miranda, Galante, Lucchese, Giancana, and Bonanno—although Bonanno later denied he had ever been there and claimed he had opposed the meeting. More significant, however, were the gangsters who refused to turn up. Frank Costello said he was under constant surveillance after the attempt on his life. Meyer Lansky was unwell and had to stay in Florida for his health. Obviously, Luciano wasn't there. What happened next was recorded with glee by the newspapers of the time.

"Elaborate preparations had been made for the meeting," reported the *New York Times*. "Nobody was likely to go hungry. The host had ordered $432 worth of special cuts, including 200 pounds of choice steaks, twenty pounds of veal cutlets, whole hams and other meats. The approximately sixty guests came in Cadillacs, Chrysler Imperials, Lincolns and other high-priced cars."

Joseph Barbara had rooms in two nearby motels booked for his guests. All this activity in a sleepy little hamlet aroused the interest of local state trooper Sergeant Edward Croswell. Within a short time after the arrival of the fleet of grand cars, the state troopers had thrown a cordon around the mansion and moved in before the meeting had barely got under way. In a panic, some senior mafiosi were reduced to scrambling out of windows and fleeing through the woods. It was a very undignified exit for men in their fifties and sixties and was a complete humiliation for Genovese. Why had he not organized the meeting at a location where the Mafia had bought the connivance of the local police? Costello would have done that—as would have Luciano.

No one was arrested, but the combined criminal records of the guests were noted. They insisted they were there to pay a visit to Barbara, who had had four heart attacks since January of that year. It was a surprise there were no more heart attacks during the raid. A month after Apalachin, the press was still wondering about the purpose of the mysterious gathering. "The general opinion of law officers is that it was convened because of the murder of Albert Anastasia," said one report. "It is believed that the Apalachin conference had probably met to discuss changes in the combine's future operations."

Government agencies started a feeding frenzy of investigations. Immigration peered into the background of the Apalachin guests, whether they were aliens or naturalized citizens. The state tax department reexamined their income tax returns. The state parole board checked to see if any one of them had violated their parole conditions. Twenty-seven of the Apalachin gangsters were subpoenaed to appear before three days of public hearings.

"The sensational publicity created by Apalachin affected me tremendously," said Joseph Bonanno, "because up to then I had been relatively inconspicuous. Publicity can maim and destroy." Barbara had a fatal heart attack and his estate was put up for sale. "The bad publicity generated by Apalachin helped

destroy any hope of an intelligent examination of my Tradi-
tion," claimed Bonanno. "Instead, the publicity perpetrated a
myth . . . the myth of the 'Mafia.' " In fact, it put even more
pressure on the FBI to put all its efforts into taking apart what
it dubbed the "Cosa Nostra."

In Naples, when Luciano read the newspaper reports, he
cracked up with laughter. It couldn't have happened to a nicer
bunch of people, he sneered. But years later, it emerged that
Luciano and Lansky were not mere passive observers of Genovese's failure. They were active participants in it.

"Meyer and I were invited [to Apalachin]," recalled his close
friend Doc Stacher, "but he sent word that as it was November
he did not want to make the journey north from Miami. He was
suffering from flu at the time. In fact, none of Lansky's closest
friends went to the meeting."

What he did do was tip off the local sheriff about the meeting.

"Nobody to this day knows that it was Meyer who arranged
for Genovese's humiliation."

It was an accomplished strike against their enemy—the
Mafia had always been willing to use the police as a weapon
when it suited them—but it was only just the beginning of their
revenge on Genovese.

According to Stacher, Lansky set a trap for Genovese using
the Federal Bureau of Narcotics. One of his couriers, Nelson
Cantellops, had been imprisoned for dealing drugs on the side
and had been sent to Sing Sing. Lansky was furious with him but
let it be known, through Nelson's brother, that he would forgive
him if he did one job for him. That task involved asking to talk to
an FBN agent in prison and then spinning him a very precise
story. Cantellops agreed and told the agent about how Genovese
was organizing a major smuggling ring of narcotics from Europe
to the United States.

"Cantellops was very well briefed," said Stacher. "He named
Vito and 24 others. He gave exact details of where and how the

drugs were imported, because Meyer had this information from his spies in the Genovese organization. The Narcotics Bureau was delighted with this information and in exchange got Nelson out of Sing Sing. Nelson was the main witness when Genovese and all his partners were convicted on narcotics charges."

In 1959, Genovese was sentenced to fifteen years in prison and died behind bars ten years later. Luciano and Lansky had got their revenge. Nelson Cantellops was rewarded with a $100,000 dollars and a job for life. It was said that his prize money was put up by Lansky and Luciano, along with Costello, who specified that he wanted Vincent Gigante nailed alongside Genovese as part of the narcotics setup—the incompetent gunman got seven years. Carlo Gambino, who had visited Luciano in Italy, apparently turned on his first Mafia patron and put up the final $25,000 of the money in an act of solidarity with the old fellows. Gambino eventually came out of the affair as head of his own family. Cantellops later died in a barroom brawl.

Genovese never knew the details of the plot against him but suspected something was not right and, believing one of his top aides was involved, had Tony Bender assassinated. He also wanted Valachi, whom he suspected was part of the setup, killed, and that's when Valachi turned stool pigeon for the state.

Lucky in Love

Igea Lissoni was twenty-six years old when Lucky Luciano first saw her. She later claimed a Milanese fortune-teller had told her she would meet the man of her dreams in Capri and she found him there in a vast suite taking up half a floor of the island's best hotel. That was her mythologizing of the event. In reality, the beginning of their affair was more prosaic.

It was in early 1948 at a dinner party in Milan that Luciano met the love of his life. Until that point, he had been happy to hang out with good-time girls and prostitutes, but this woman was different. She was elegant and refined and remained his close companion in Italy for the next ten years.

Lissoni was a dancer. She came from a middle-class Milanese family and had been trained at ballet from an early age. She progressed to the La Scala Opera House, where she performed in their ballet company, but the leading roles eluded her. "I realized I could never become a prima ballerina," she later admitted, "that I did not have enough talent. So I began to dance in nightclubs, hoping I could some day dance in films and perhaps become a star. My family was scandalized, of course, but I could wrap Papa around my finger."

She also charmed Luciano, who considered her a "lady to the tip of her toes," but he was too shy to make a move at their first meeting. Back in Rome, he arranged to attend the first night at a nightclub where she was dancing. He asked her on a date. She refused, but he persisted, and she eventually moved into his Rome apartment in June 1948.

"She's the only girl I ever loved," said Luciano. "There was something about her that was special. If all broads were like her the world would be a terrific place."

It was her intelligence that beguiled him and he acted like the perfect gentleman around her—no swearing, no volcanic outbursts of anger at the persistent harassment of him by Anslinger and U.S. agents. She was blond when Luciano first met her, but in later photographs she is shown as a head-turning brunette. When Luciano was pulled in for questioning following the drug-smuggling arrest of Vincent Trupia at Rome airport, Lissoni wanted to visit him in jail and take him little cakes.

"I'm lonely in this big apartment," she told reporters, revealing an early talent for saying the right things in public. "Charley was always so gentle and kind. Why, oh, why don't they stop this persecution?"

When Luciano was kicked out of Rome, they moved to Naples. Lissoni wanted to have a family with Luciano, but the mobster was reluctant to bring children into a world overshadowed by his villainous reputation.

"I didn't want no son of mine to go through life as the son of Luciano, the gangster. That's one thing I still hate Dewey for, making me a gangster in the eyes of the whole world."

Added to that was the fact that Luciano was never that close to his family. He had triumphed in the underworld away from them—unlike other mobsters who had a ready-made gang in their own brothers. He had kept his family life very separate

from his criminal world, probably because his father disapproved so strongly of his ill-gotten gains. As a young man, his
strength had been his friends—not his family—and he had no
wish to surround himself with children and remind himself of
a far from happy childhood.

In Naples, they lived together in a penthouse apartment at
Via Tasso 464 with a spectacular view across the bay toward
Mount Vesuvius. Luciano had originally bought the block but
sold off all the apartments, except for the penthouse—and he
would have sold that for $16,000 if he'd got permission to go
back to Rome. They exchanged wedding rings but did not get
married. They both liked to dress stylishly and expensively and
spent hours sitting in the best restaurants and bars. They regularly went to the races where Luciano invariably won. The races
were usually fixed, and Luciano would settle up with bookies in
town—never dealing in cash at the track. In the evening, after
supper at home, they might go out to watch a movie.

When Lissoni wasn't around, Luciano still liked to flirt
with other women—but God help him if she found out. On one
occasion, she burst into their favorite haunt—the San Francisco Bar and Grill, which he owned—as he chatted with another woman and pulled a twenty-two caliber pistol from her
handbag. Luciano was embarrassed and told her to stop making
a scene.

"If I ever see you even flirt with another girl," she said, glow-
ering, "you'll get this."

An alternative version of this story came from an undercover
FBN agent who had got friendly with Luciano. One evening they
were at the Snake Pit nightclub in Naples when Lissoni walked
in looking for him. Luciano told her that she had disobeyed his
orders by coming into the low-life club and slapped her. This
was probably his place to hang out with other women and he
didn't like her intruding. Later, Lissoni complained to the undercover agent, saying she was a civilized European, not a Sicilian, and was unaccustomed to being slapped. The next time

Luciano beat her in public, she said, she would kill him with a pistol she kept in their apartment. Still, they stayed together.

Luciano couldn't help attracting attention. He was possibly the most famous gangster in the world. In Naples, he became something of a tourist destination for Americans on holiday. U.S. sailors coming into port would seek him out to sign autographs, while journalists were keen to get a scoop by interviewing him. One Italian-American merchant sailor regularly brought him cartons of his favorite brand of Viceroy cigarettes. Luigi Parigi, a New York labor union official on a holiday to Italy, gave him twenty-five tailor-made shirts, but they were the wrong size and he sent them back. Luciano liked to keep himself looking smart, and each day started with a visit to his favorite barbershop in Naples's main railroad terminal.

He was still a magnet for showbiz stars. Jimmy Durante sent him a check for $250 for undisclosed services. When Frank Sinatra was on tour in Italy, Luciano visited him at the Hotel Terminus in Naples. He later said he was tempted to tell the singer to go back to his first wife, Nancy, rather than chase after Ava Gardner, but considered it better not to interfere in Sinatra's private affairs.

Rumors abounded that he was still able to give authorities the slip. In February 1956, FBI chief J. Edgar Hoover was sent a clipping of Dorothy Kilgallen's Broadway column. It cited underworld gossip that Luciano had been in the United States at least nine times and that it "cost him a cool $100,000 each time." In December 1957, the Seattle office of the FBI received a message from a man with an Italian accent who said he was living in Tacoma, Washington.

"Luciano came ashore from a boat somewhere on the West Coast," said the Seattle report. The informer said "he hated Luciano's guts. He had done some time for Luciano in the pen and wanted to see the s.o.b. get what was coming to him." The agent was inclined to pay more attention to this because "there was no noise in the background and the caller did not sound incoherent or drunk," but the director assured him that Luciano "was and has been continuously in Italy."

In 1956, Italian senator Lina Merlin accused Luciano of being involved in prostitution. She told a newspaper: "I have information showing that Lucky Luciano has shown more than just a passive interest in this highly lucrative operation. He still holds all the strings in Marseilles and New York and Naples."

The senator was the author of a law named after her that sought to outlaw government-licensed brothels in Italy. "There are 725 houses of ill repute between the Po Valley and Palermo," she said, "and each one is inhabited by misery." She estimated some two to three million Italian women lived by prostitution and that some of these were being trained in government-licensed brothels for export to the United States, Latin America, the Middle East, and Far East. "To make them more amenable," she said, "the women are introduced to the dope habit." The gangs who transported these women and the drugs were "among the world's richest and most influential organizations" and even had tentacles behind the Iron Curtain.

Throughout this period, Luciano was under constant surveillance and had to report regularly to the Italian police. He had to ask permission every time he left the city. In December 1958, the appellate court of Naples reviewed Luciano's case at the request of the prosecuting attorney of Naples, who was requesting authority to continue police surveillance and investigation of Luciano, but the appellate court upheld an earlier decision by the Naples court denying police the authority to continue surveillance. It declared that insufficient evidence had been produced to indicate that Luciano was "engaged in illegal activities or activities inimical to the best interests of the Republic of Italy."

Despite this, an Italian police statement in 1958 maintained that "Luciano spends more money than he appears to earn here and that he has contact with shady characters who go back and forth between Italy and the United States."

Luciano's happiness ended in October 1958 when Igea Lissoni died from breast cancer at the age of thirty-six. He accompanied her body back to Milan and was said to have wept at the funeral—the first time any of his friends had seen him cry. Shortly afterward, a magazine interview with him described the sixty-one-year-old mobster as a "tight lipped individual who is in the habit of answering the most searching question with a stony-faced silence. . . . His life is a quiet one and his greatest desire is to forget and be forgotten."

After the death of Lissoni, only the conviction of Vito Genovese lifted Luciano's spirits. During this period, he was visited by Federal Bureau of Narcotics agent Sal Vizzini. Despite no evidence whatsoever to validate their continued interest in him, the FBN considered it well worth investing taxpayers' money to keep the old mobster under close surveillance. Vizzini arrived in Naples in April 1959 pretending to be U.S. Air Force major Mike Cerra. He made it clear that his bosses still considered Luciano number one on their international list of criminals.

"His tentacles were long and his influence powerful," enthused Vizzini in his 1972 memoirs. "The Narcotics Bureau, and the Justice Department, knew he was still making decisions for the Mob, that he was still receiving large shipments of money from the States, and that he was still engaged in directing much of the world's narcotics traffic."

It was a case of yet another law enforcement agent magnifying Luciano's reputation to suit his own purpose—this time to tell a real-life adventure story. His arrival came shortly after a three-part series was broadcast by New York radio station WMCA profiling Luciano. It quoted the FBN saying that Luciano was "the guiding genius behind the expansion of the international dope traffic." It also repeated Anslinger's statement to Congress that Luciano was one of the top men in the Italian-American syndicate and that he bought opium in Turkey, had it refined in Italy, and then sold it on to the United States.

Despite finding little evidence of this narcotics trafficking,

Vizzini's account of his time with Luciano is an interesting insight into how the old mobster spent his last few years. The Sicilian-born Vizzini got on well with Luciano, having been introduced to him by a waiter turned informer at the San Francisco Bar and Grill. Luciano was glad for the company. He took Vizzini to the races and chatted away with him in bars. He was still bitter about being exiled from New York.

"Just six months, that's all I want, three months in New York and three months in Miami. Then they could bury me," he told Vizzini. "I'd still be there if it wasn't for that son of a bitch Tom Dewey. He framed me, Mike, and that's the God's truth. I never took a dime from a woman in my life, let alone from a prostitute."

Luciano was constantly accompanied by a large bodyguard called "Momo," armed with a nine millimeter Browning automatic, who took an instant dislike to Vizzini. In a nightclub, they ended up having a fight and the FBN agent disarmed the hulking giant with a karate chop to the throat. A little later, Vizzini got to the point of his mission and made a reference to a wad of $100 bills Luciano pulled out of his pocket in the San Francisco Bar and Grill.

"Where do you get that kind of money around here?" he asked.

"Not in Italy, that's for sure," snapped Luciano.

Luciano wasn't making a fortune in Italy from illicit heroin smuggling. He was still living off the money his friends continued to send him from the United States, and that was getting to be less and less as they came under pressure themselves. He was always thinking of little business projects, but these usually came to nothing. On one occasion he told another undercover agent he was considering buying up vacant lots and building public garages on them.

The contrast in fortunes between Luciano and other mafiosi was shown when Joe Adonis, who ran rackets and gambling in New Jersey, agreed to accept deportation to Italy in 1956 rather than go to jail for perjury. He retired to Milan, where he lived in a grand style on his accumulated fortune. Adonis had been one of Luciano's gunmen back in the late 1920s when he helped kill Joe the Boss. Occasionally, he met with Luciano in Naples, but the men fell out soon after, partly it seems because Adonis flaunted his wealth and never asked if he could help out his one-time boss.

When Vizzini wasn't visiting Luciano, he was on far more important business tracking the real narcotics traffickers from Turkey to Marseilles. They were the ones making the big money.

♠

That Luciano was still regarded as a menacing figure in Italy is revealed by a curious anecdote regarding the celebrated singer and movie star Mario Lanza. As a young man brought up in Philadelphia, Lanza developed a beautiful tenor voice. During the war, he toured with the U.S. Army's Special Services unit when he got his first show business break singing at a party for Frank Sinatra. After a breathtaking performance at the Holly-wood Bowl in 1947, he starred in several musicals. But he was a difficult performer, plagued by weight problems and an un-healthy lifestyle, and he was eventually dropped by Hollywood. He resurfaced in Italy, where he toured and made movies. In 1959, he met Luciano in Naples.

Ever mindful of good publicity, Luciano thought it would be a great idea if the golden tenor sang at a charity gala he was or-ganizing in Naples. When the temperamental Lanza failed to appear for a rehearsal, it is said that two of Luciano's henchmen visited him to ensure he would not back out from the concert.

Unable to cope with this pressure and not wanting to perform at all, Lanza checked himself into a clinic in Rome, claiming he had to lose weight rapidly for the good of his health. Luciano was furious. A few days later, when Lanza's chauffeur came to see him on October 7, Lanza was found in a coma with an empty intravenous tube pumping air into his arm. Attempts to revive him failed, and the thirty-eight-year-old Lanza was pronounced dead later that day. No official autopsy was performed, but it was said he died from a heart attack.

The principal source of this story is Mario Lanza's daughter, Colleen, who was eleven years old when her father died, but she recalled the accusation coming from the driver. When they lived in Rome, she suggested that Lanza had contact with some underworld figures.

"Sometimes there were strange, unusual and shady people around the house who Daddy did not approve of," she recalled, "and he tried to get them out of his home. Often it became quite a violent confrontation."

The day of her father's death in the clinic in Rome was traumatic.

"There were many questions about how my father died. I think he was murdered. The chauffeur was in his room—he disappeared and was never found again. He was so totally dedicated to my father that he slept on a cot beneath his bed while he was in the hospital. He awoke suddenly, he said before disappearing, and found Daddy with the intravenous still in his arms and nothing but air bubbles going into his vein. My grandmother forbade me to discuss such things while she lived, but now it really doesn't matter anymore."

Later writers have blamed Luciano and his associates for this death as punishment for the severe embarrassment caused to the mobster by Lanza's no-show in Naples.

♠

Toward the end of the 1950s, less money was coming through to Luciano. Castro coming to power in Cuba in 1959 put an end to his share of the Mafia casinos in Havana, which he reckoned cost him a quarter of his income. He depended very much on the money sent to him by his friends. Looking at alternative means of income, he saw there was possibly good money to be made from selling his own story. Movies were starting to appear about his contemporaries, and he began to think about his legacy. *Al Capone*, starring Rod Steiger as the Chicago gangster, appeared in 1959, twelve years after Capone's death. It was made in a semi-documentary style, telling of the real rise and fall of the mobster, ending with his conviction for income tax evasion. A year later came *The Rise and Fall of Legs Diamond*, with Ray Danton as the New York hoodlum. In the same year appeared *Murder, Inc.*, based on the book by Burton Turkus and Sid Feder, with actors playing Anastasia and Lepke.

Previous gangster movies had been based on Capone and other leading mobsters, such as Luciano, but had avoided using their real names, creating characters loosely based on them and their crimes. No one wanted to stir up the rage of the Mob. Ben Hecht wrote the story for *Scarface*, the movie modeled on Capone in Chicago in 1932, and he remembered being approached by two of Capone's henchmen holding a copy of the script.

"Is this stuff about Al Capone?" asked one of the heavies.

"God, no," said Hecht. "I don't even know Al."

"Never met him, huh?"

Hecht insisted that he had left Chicago before Capone came to power.

"If this stuff ain't about Al Capone, why are you callin' it *Scarface*?" reasoned the gangster. "Everybody'll think it's him."

"That's the reason," struggled Hecht. "Al is one of the most famous and fascinating men of our time. If we call the movie *Scarface*, everybody will want to see it, figuring it's about Al. That's part of the racket we call showmanship."

In the event, it was very clearly based on him—even featuring a re-creation of the St. Valentine's Day Massacre.

Bamboozled by Hecht's answer, the gangster said he'd pass it on to Al. He then wondered about the motive of the the film producer Howard Hughes.

"He's got nothing to do with anything," said Hecht. "He's the sucker with the money."

"OK. The hell with him."

In the wake of the Kefauver hearings at the beginning of the 1950s, there was a public taste for more realistic renditions of how the Mob worked, stories that pulled fewer punches and weren't afraid to name names. After all, despite what the FBN thought, Luciano was now crime history—not a contemporary criminal mastermind. In 1953, in the organized crime thriller *The Big Heat*, Luciano is even mentioned as an example of how not to conduct underworld business. The Mob boss in the movie is called Mike Lagana, and he talks to one of his gangsters about how crime has changed since the 1930s.

"We've stirred up enough headlines. Things are changing in this country," says Lagana. "Never get the people steamed up— they start doing things. Grand juries, election investigations, deportation proceedings, I don't want to land in the same ditch with the Lucky Lucianos."

Luciano probably thought it was time to tell his own version of events. An early reference to him wanting to make a movie about his life came in an issue of the Havana daily newspaper *Alerta*, November 25, 1952, which said that the gangster was going to spend $300,000 on the project.

It was in 1959, however, that Luciano met the film producer Barnett Glassman. Luciano had already spent some of his time in Naples writing a screenplay and showed it to the producer. It portrayed him as a middle-aged gambler who'd been set up by the corrupt Dewey, wrongfully sent to prison, and was now settled in Italy, where he was much respected for his charity work. He had been considering who should portray him.

"Pity Humphrey Bogart is dead," he said. "Boy, that would have been the man to play Luciano. Now, maybe, George Raft— he's about the only tough type left"—or maybe Marlon Brando, who'd starred in the much revered gangland movie, *On the Waterfront*, to play a younger Luciano.

Not surprisingly, Glassman was unimpressed by Luciano's efforts and recommended a professional screenwriter. It took two drafts before Luciano realized he had to reveal more of the

truth about his criminal career to make it an interesting project. The whole enterprise took on more urgency when Luciano
visited his doctor later that year. He'd been complaining about
pains in his chest and arms, and the doctor confirmed he had a
dangerous heart condition.

FBN agent Sal Vizzini, under his guise as Major Mike Cerra,
visited Luciano during this period. He was told that Luciano
had been ill and he was invited to see him at his apartment at 8
Strado Parco Comela Ricci, overlooking the harbor. He looked
thinner than Vizzini remembered. He was living with a twenty-
four-year-old shopgirl called Adriana Rizzo. His doctor had told
him to take plenty of bed rest and give up smoking, drink, and
sex. He could do all that but the last. He remembered something his old Sicilian associate Don Calogero Vizzini had told
him.

"He was over seventy and still had to have a girl every day.
He knew what to do with them too. I told him he was about to
kill himself. He looked me right in the eye and said . . . 'pussy
is a million times sweeter than honey and I want it till the day
I die'—I agree with him."

Agent Vizzini was given a tour of the modern apartment and
noted some of the books in Luciano's library. They included *The
Traffic in Narcotics* by Harry Anslinger, *Brotherhood of Evil* by
Frederic Sondern, and *The Luciano Story* by Sid Feder and Joachim
Joesten. *The Luciano Story* was the first major biography of Lu-
ciano and was cowritten by the author of *Murder, Inc.,* the book
that exposed the inside story of the hit men who worked for the
Mob in the 1930s.

The publisher of the *The Luciano Story* sent a copy to the FBI
in January 1955. Because *Murder, Inc.,* had "contained derogatory remarks concerning the FBI and attributed false statements
to the Director," the FBI decided not to acknowledge receipt of
The Luciano Story until "we have had an opportunity to make
a complete review of it in the Crime Records section." The subsequent analysis described it as a "readable account," which

used much of the material contained in *Murder, Inc.* "Of the nine references to the Director or the FBI throughout the book, none appears to be of a derogatory nature."

In fact, the FBI took pride in the fact that the author said Luciano felt no antagonism toward the director, directly quoting the mobster as saying: "Hoover's no friend of the hoodlums or the underworld. I like him because he never makes an announcement about what he's gonna do. He never says a guy is tied up in a racket, and he's gonna grab him for it. None of that yakity-yak. A guy does somethin'. Hoover grabs him. No announcements. He don't shoot his mouth off. He's got efficiency!"

Luciano had also read Ed Reid's *Mafia,* an exposé of the business dealings of the Cosa Nostra, first published in 1952, but he called it "a pack of lies."

As agent Vizzini looked in detail at some of the other objects in Luciano's library, he noticed a painting of a beautiful dark-haired woman hung on the wall—it was Igea Lissoni. Later that evening, they talked about the rumored movie of his life. Luciano complained that he'd been offered only a "lousy" hundred grand plus 10 percent of the profits. Vizzini said Luciano hadn't been very impressed by the *Al Capone* movie.

"They made Capone look like an ignorant bum," said Luciano. "Nobody knew Capone better than me and, believe me, he was no ignorant bum. Everything in that picture was phony, except maybe how he got rid of the competition."

While film producer Barnett Glassman was making a movie in Spain he met a wannabe producer called Martin Gosch. He only had one movie credit on *Abbott and Costello in Hollywood,* but Glassman took him on as his assistant. Gosch was keen to meet Luciano.

"Gosch saw Charlie a number of times in the next couple of years," said Glassman, "but Charlie never talked to him about his Mob activities or anything like that. You couldn't get twenty words out of Charlie unless he really trusted you, and he didn't care much for Gosch."

They just chatted about the script, but all the time Gosch was keen to take on the project himself. According to Glassman, Luciano phoned his brother in Christmas 1961 to say that Gosch wanted to cut out Glassman and he didn't like it.

"Tell Gosch, I want to see him," Luciano is supposed to have said. "Tell him I'm going to lay it on the line to him, that I don't want to ever have anything to do with him, I never want to see him after I tell him what I think of him."

Gosch saw his relationship with Luciano somewhat differently. In February 1961, he showed Luciano a final version of the script they had been working on and he approved it, signing a contract for $100,000 and a percentage of the profits. Shortly afterward, however, Thomas Eboli, lieutenant for Vito Genovese while he was in jail, arrived in Naples. Despite several movies about every other mobster being made, Eboli supposedly told Luciano that the Mob back in New York did not want to see his film get made.

"I'm as good as dead," Luciano then told Gosch. "And maybe you too."

Supposedly, Meyer Lansky was the key figure behind this request. This seems odd, as Lansky hated Genovese and Eboli would never have spoken for him. According to Gosch, it was then that Luciano softened his disappointment at ending the film deal by telling him that he could take down his life story and turn it into a book to be published ten years after his death.

Almost a year later, Eboli's brother Pat arrived in Naples to tell Luciano that the movie project had so upset the ruling mafiosi that they had ordered his execution. The only thing that could save his life was if he sent the original script, with his signature of approval on it, to New York so that the bosses had this in their possession. This is Gosch's story and seems more like a fairy tale. Why did the Mob bosses think that possession of an easily copied script would stop the film being made? But apparently, Luciano agreed to the deal and this was why he set up a meeting with Gosch at the Naples airport in January 1962.

According to Glassman, the meeting was called so that Luciano could sack Gosch from the project and give him a piece of his mind about betraying his colleague. Luciano's phone was being tapped at the time and, shortly after he arranged for Gosch to fly in from Madrid, his apartment was raided by Italian police who suspected he might be seeing a narcotics smuggler from Spain. Gosch dressed up this story by saying that Luciano was being set up in a fake drug bust by associates of Genovese looking for vengeance. The source for much of this tale was investigative journalist Jack Anderson, who wrote an article for the *Washington Post* in early 1962 entitled "The Last Days of Lucky Luciano."

Anderson was fed a story by FBN agents that went like this: Eight months before his final meeting with Gosch, in May 1961, a Miami couple called Henry and Theresa Rubino arrived at Luciano's apartment in Naples. They were looking for a restaurant to buy and Luciano was their adviser, having invested in a few over the years. They visited several nightspots together with Luciano and his girlfriend, Adriana Rizzo. A month later they went back to Miami to sell their own restaurant to raise some money. Luciano wrote a letter to them that was intercepted by the police.

Luciano's letter thanked Henry Rubino for sending him letters and photographs and for "what you did at the cemetery." The police suspected this was code for some criminal service. Luciano then asked Rubino to give his best regards to Tony B., Pat R., and Tommy. These were Tony Bender, Pat and Tommy Eboli—who also used the name Ryan—and all lieutenants for Vito Genovese, but in the case of Bender, he had changed sides to help Luciano, Lansky, Costello, and Gambino nail his boss. Rubino later claimed that the service he did for Luciano was to lay a wreath on his mother's grave—a highly plausible explanation—but the FBN weren't satisfied with that.

The FBN linked the Rubinos to three narcotics-smuggling fugitives called Vincent Mauro, Frank Caruso, and Salvatore

Maneri. They had jumped bail in New York to spend their money in various Caribbean islands, before finally ending up in Barcelona, Spain. In the meantime, the Rubinos had returned to Naples in November 1961. After spending a week with Luciano, the Miami couple received a phone call from Spain and hurried to Barcelona, where they supposedly met the three narcotics smugglers. After a few days in Spain, the Rubinos flew back to Naples and carried on their socializing with Luciano and Rizzo.

At Christmas, the two couples went to Taormina, the resort on the east coast of Sicily near Mount Etna. Photographs show Luciano posing on the beach in shorts with both women in two-piece swimwear. After their holiday, Luciano returned to Naples and the Rubinos went back to Spain. They were accompanied by a Sicilian called Francesco Scimone and met the three drug-smuggling fugitives at the Palace Hotel in Madrid. Trailing the Rubinos back and forth across the Mediterranean, the FBN and their Italian police associates were convinced this indicated that some smuggling ring was being formed with Luciano at the center of it. Caruso and Mauro were arrested in Barcelona and Maneri in Majorca.

On the morning of January 26, the Italian police picked up Luciano and questioned him about this sequence of events. Luciano shrugged and smiled wearily, saying there was no conspiracy behind it. It was all merely social, purely coincidence, and his biggest concern was his meeting with Martin Gosch later that day about his movie script. Yes, Gosch was flying in from Spain, but that's where he lived. To prove his innocence, he invited an Italian officer, Cesare Resta, to accompany him to the airport.

On the afternoon of January 26, 1962, Luciano drove his Alfa Romeo car to Capodichino Airport, four miles northeast from the center of Naples. It would be the last meeting he would ever make.

Death in Naples

The aircraft landed at Capodichino Airport in Naples about 4:00 P.M. on January 26, 1962. Luciano was waiting in the terminal for the connecting flight from Rome. He'd had an irritating morning answering pointless questions from the Italian police and had one of them next to him when Martin Gosch stepped off the aircraft and made his way toward the pair. Once Luciano got the script off Gosch, he could finish with the whole damned mess of the movie. He was wearing smartly pressed gray flannel slacks with a navy blue blazer. He introduced Gosch to the police officer and they both walked off toward his car. A few steps outside the terminal, Luciano stumbled, putting an arm around Gosch.

"Charlie, what's wrong with you?" said the producer.

Luciano said nothing and slumped to the floor.

An airport doctor was called and felt his pulse. He shook his head.

"This man is dead."

A green canvas sheet was placed over the body. It was 5:25 P.M. One of the most famous gangsters in the world had suddenly passed away. He was sixty-four years old.

The news flashed around the world. The next day, the London *Times* said "Charles 'Lucky' Luciano, the immigrant boy who became undisputed boss of a multi-million dollar New York vice racket, collapsed and died." The article said Luciano "owned a fashionable apartment in Naples and sold electrical medical appliances" but that Senator Kefauver claimed that he "still directed the American underworld by remote control from Italy."

Lucky's death made the front page of the *New York Times*. He was still big news in his home city. They led on the story that Luciano was about to be arrested for his part in an international narcotics ring. "We were ready to move against him with the Italian authorities," said Henry Giordano, deputy commissioner of the U.S. Narcotics Bureau in Washington. The ring was alleged to have smuggled heroin worth up to $150,000,000 into the country over the previous ten years. Three smugglers had already been taken down in Spain, and Luciano was to be next—the legend lived on.

An FBI memorandum sent to J. Edgar Hoover on March 21, 1962, revealed the truth of the matter. It said that the Federal Bureau of Narcotics was "still following leads in an attempt to prove Luciano's involvement in international narcotics but all indications are that the case will be closed with no startling developments."

As soon as they heard of Luciano's death, his younger brother, Bartolo Lucania, and two nephews, Salvatore and Gino, children of his sister, flew to Naples to arrange the funeral. On January 29, violent scuffles marred the funeral service as crowds of reporters tried to take pictures of the mourners. It started during the requiem mass held at the Holy Trinity Church, where photographers clambered over a statue above the altar to take shots of the service from behind the crucifix.

Some three hundred people were present, including Bart

Lucania, Luciano's girlfriend, Adriana Rizzo, and some minor Mob associates, including the Fischetti brothers, Joe "Cock-Eyed John" Raimondo, Nick di Marzo, and Joe di Giorgio. Joe Adonis was the most senior mobster to attend the funeral, although he turned up late just before the service ended. He had ordered a large floral tribute in the style of the old mobster funerals, inscribed with the farewell "So long, Pal." Lansky also, reputedly, sent flowers, though he had nothing to say in public about the death of his good friend; neither did Costello.

The fact that the majority of the crowd was Italian police, government agents, and journalists underlined the extent to which Luciano had become a creature of law enforcement agencies rather than being a genuine criminal mastermind at the heart of the Cosa Nostra. Among the U.S. agents present were two officers of the U.S. Immigration and Naturalization Service, three agents of the Office of Naval Intelligence from the U.S. Navy headquarters in Naples—Luciano's old wartime allies— and officers from the Federal Bureau of Narcotics, but no one, apparently, from the FBI. Adriana wore a long black veil and sobbed dramatically throughout the service into a white silk handkerchief. As the photographers surged toward the mourners after the church service, some of the mobsters grew angry and swiped at them. "Somebody is going to get hurt," growled one of them.

"A lensman was punched, knocked down and kicked outside the church," said a reporter for the New York *Daily News*, "and his camera was smashed by Luciano henchmen." He had been trying to take a photograph of Adriana. "Two of Adriana's girl friends kicked and slapped the photographer as he lay on the ground."

Eight plumed black horses pulled a silver and polished black wooden funeral carriage carrying Luciano's coffin to a chapel at the English Cemetery in Poggio Reale on the outskirts of Naples. The U.S. consulate said it could stay there for two or three days while a decision was made on whether Luciano's body could be returned to the United States. Bartolo Lucania made the request, saying that his brother had wished to be buried alongside his mother and father in the family tomb he had bought in New York.

Before Bartolo left Naples, he quickly sold Luciano's penthouse apartment for less than half its value. This meant throwing out his grieving girlfriend. Only after the intervention of Pat Eboli did Bartolo relent and give her $3,000, plus allowing her to take her clothes and personal possessions. Some land belonging to Luciano was also sold for a reduced price, while the only bank account that could be located contained the sum of $16,000. Only the Mob knew where the rest of Luciano's money was, and they quietly absorbed that for themselves.

Two weeks after Luciano had dropped dead, his body was returned to America. On February 7, a Pan American World Airways cargo plane delivered the body to Idlewild Airport in Queens, New York, where it was met by his two brothers, Bartolo and Joseph, and a large contingent of FBN agents and city police. The large wooden crate containing the casket was placed in a hearse and driven eight miles to St. John's Cemetery in Middle Village, Queens. It was accompanied by one car containing the mourners and two dozen containing police and reporters. There was no ceremony at the cemetery as the coffin was placed in the family vault.

Luciano had bought the vault, adorned with bronze doors and Greek columns, for $25,000 in 1935—the year before he went to prison. His mother, father, an aunt, and uncle were buried there, with space for sixteen more family members. A small stained-glass window at the rear of the vault bore a representation of a bearded saint leaning on a shepherd's staff. One of the reporters asked Bartolo who the saint was in the window. "I don't know," he said. "I'm not acquainted with saints."

The family tomb of Vito Genovese stood only a hundred feet away from Luciano's vault. Seven years later he would be placed in there.

An obituary published in the *New York Herald Tribune* quoted an interview with Luciano from a couple of years earlier. If he had his life to lead again, would he do it all the same?

"I would do the same things all over again," he said, "only I'd do it legal. I learned too late that you need just as good a brain to make a crooked million as an honest million. These days you apply for a license to steal from the public.

"If I had my time again I'd make sure I got that license first."

♠

It did not take long before rumors of murder and conspiracy arose around Luciano's death. One newspaper story claimed that he had been assassinated at the airport by underworld rivals who gave him potassium cyanide. This seems to have derived from witnesses seeing the dying mobster being given a tablet. An FBI report clarified what they thought happened at the airport.

"A few minutes after meeting Gosch in the Naples airport," said the FBI, "Luciano collapsed and Gosch, who knew that Luciano suffered from a bad heart, frantically searched Luciano's pockets for pills that he knew Luciano took. He did find the pill box, removed one of the pills and placed it in Luciano's mouth. This activity was observed by a number of the people who had witnessed Luciano's collapse and is believed to be the source of the story to the effect that Luciano was poisoned."

A Madrid newspaper quoted Gosch as saying that Luciano was poisoned. "He appeared as though he were drugged," Gosch told the Spanish reporter. Arriving in New York, Gosch then announced that elements from the underworld had asked for the film on Luciano not to be made, but that he planned to go ahead anyway. The FBI were unimpressed by Gosch's comments, saying, "It would appear from this that Gosch might be obtaining a good deal of free publicity for his proposed film."

A later FBI report alleged that Gosch met Pat Eboli on the day after Luciano died to talk to him about the film script. Eboli wanted to know what Luciano had said between his heart attack and his death. Gosch reassured him that he had said nothing. Eboli then asked for the script, but Gosch refused to give it to him.

The most sensational tale accused Luciano of working with federal government agencies to disrupt narcotics smuggling from the Middle East to the United States. The story was based on an interview with Bill Mancuso, a former bodyguard for Luciano, which appeared in an Italian newspaper. It claimed also that Martin Gosch was, in fact, an FBI agent pretending to be a film producer. Mancuso told the Italian journalist that Luciano had long worked for the U.S. government, citing his help to them during the Allied invasion of Sicily in World War II. These claims were undercut somewhat by the article alternating the FBI with the FBN, as though there were no difference between the two organizations. The article ended by saying that Luciano was killed by narcotics gangsters who substituted poison for his heart medicine.

The FBI was scathing in criticisms of these reports. "There is, of course, no substance whatsoever to these claims," said a memorandum addressed to Hoover. "The Italian press will publish stories which have absolutely no basis on fact but which are drawn out by reporters in connection with sensational-type stories."

In the years following his death, newspaper stories linked Luciano to all kinds of crimes. In 1965, the Italian minister of the interior declared war on pinball tables and slot machines. They were leading the nation's youth astray and pushing law-abiding citizens into debt. The importation of slot machines was blamed on exiled American gangsters. A parish priest from near Naples pointed the finger at Lucky Luciano as the man responsible for the business in his city. It was certainly possible, as Frank Costello was the king of slot machines back in America and could have supplied them to Luciano.

At the beginning of the 1960s, gang warfare had piled up bodies on the streets of Palermo. One car bomb had killed seven policemen. When one of these gang leaders, Rosario Mancino, was finally put on trial in 1967, he was said to be a friend of Lucky Luciano. It was his death, it was claimed, that had been the catalyst behind this struggle for power among Sicilian mafiosi. As happened during his life, the power and influence ascribed to Luciano was way beyond his capacity as a largely semiretired American mobster in Naples.

An FBI memorandum of September 1965 put Luciano's role in a more proper perspective. "Over the years," it said, "there have been many allegations that Luciano continued to be the 'Mafia boss' of the United States, directing criminal activities from his place in exile. Information developed during the past several years indicates that these allegations generally have been overstatements."

There was, however, "some indication that an association continued between Luciano and some of this country's top hoodlums who, from time to time, visited Luciano in Italy." That was about the strength of it.

♠

Martin Gosch stayed true to the promise he made the mobster and waited exactly ten years after Luciano's death to publish his memoirs. Gosch hired former *New York Times* writer Richard Hammer to help write the book based on his notes from conversations with Luciano. But Gosch died shortly afterward from a heart attack in 1973, closing down the last direct link between Luciano and the writing project. The resulting book, *The Last Testament of Lucky Luciano*, caused a tremendous publicity stir—not least because its publishers, Little, Brown & Co., falsely declared it was based on long-lost recordings of the gangster.

When the *Washington Post* carried a full-page advertisement on September 25, 1974, heralding the forthcoming publication of *The Last Testament of Lucky Luciano*, the FBI were intrigued, especially as the ad showed a pyramid of politicians and government department heads all linked to Luciano at the top of the picture—and that included Hoover. As the book was being serialized in *Penthouse* magazine before publication, FBI agents got hold of two installments and subjected it to an exhaustive analysis. Their conclusion was that "the book is a complete fraud." The editors at *Penthouse* claimed the book was based on a year of tapes made by Gosch listening to the reminiscences of Luciano.

"Obviously, if such a manuscript was valid," said the FBI reviewer, "it would be of considerable value to law enforcement, but there are many instances of internal evidence to indicate that Gosch probably resurrected a few random quotes gathered during interviews with Luciano and then put them together with an old movie script of his and some recent research to produce a book that capitalized upon the current public interest in the subject of organized crime."

It quoted the FBI's legal attaché in Madrid, who said that Gosch admitted that his movie script about Luciano had been largely "made up out of the whole cloth" and bore little resemblance to anything that actually happened. Apparently, Gosch had already approached the FBI in 1972 for their help in transforming his script into book form. He told them that he was being assisted by Hammer and they already had access to the files of the New York City police department. "As regards Hammer," said the FBI, "Bureau files show only that he is a successful author and reporter who may, or may not, be aware of the fraudulent nature of Gosch's manuscript.

"An in-depth analysis of [the] book," concluded the FBI, "indicates that the material contained therein consists of old information gleaned from the hearings of the McClellan Committee [investigating criminal infiltration of labor unions] and other Congressional groups, plus a number of unverified allegations to the effect that Luciano dabbled in the political campaigns of Al Smith and Franklin D. Roosevelt, paid $90,000 into Tom

Dewey's gubernatorial coffers, and once turned down a $5,000 offer from Director Hoover if he would tell the FBI where Louis Lepke Buchalter was hiding. For these reasons, and the description of how it came to be written in the first place, it is not believed that this book has any value to the FBI, or to anyone else for that matter."

The FBI review was made in secret in October 1974 and had little impact on the publicity for the book, which spiraled upward. Aside from its serialization in *Penthouse,* paperback rights were sold for $800,000 and it was chosen as the main selection by the Book-of-the-Month Club and the *Playboy* Book Club. *New York Times* journalist Nicholas Gage was determined to prick this bubble. He took exception to the publisher's main claim on the book jacket: "Dictated during the final months of his life to film producer Martin G. Gosch, this powerful inside chronicle is literally the 'last testament' of America's most notorious gangster."

In a substantial article published in the *New York Times* on December 17, 1974, Gage declared that the tapes had never existed and most of the information published in the book had appeared elsewhere. He also pointed out that some of the events described would have been impossible for Luciano to witness as he was in prison at the time. The publisher struck back by saying they had two sworn affidavits and three signed letters from close friends and relatives of Luciano testifying to the truth of his interviews with Gosch. One of these was Rosario Vitaliti, then in his seventies, who declared that "everything [Mr. Gosch] says is true." Five percent of the book's royalties were said to be shared among members of Luciano's family, Vitaliti, and former girlfriend Adriana Rizzo.

Richard Hammer was very forthcoming about the faults of the book, telling Gage, "while there are some inaccuracies in it, the work is what it purports to be—the life story of Lucky Luciano as he told it." Gosch's widow said that her husband made tapes for Hammer in which he discussed the notes and subsequently didn't think it was worth keeping the actual notes. Hammer said there would never have been a moment when Luciano would have consented to be recorded. "Luciano would have had to be out of his mind to sit with a tape recorder," he said.

Gage spoke to Peter Maas, the author of *The Canary That Sang: The Valachi Papers*, published in 1969, who said *The Last Testament* was "almost an exact compilation of all the available published material on organized crime in general and Luciano in particular." He said it paralleled much of what Mafia informer Valachi had already said. Luciano's former lawyer, Moses Polakoff, read a selection of the book featuring him and said "not 5 percent of the accounts bear any resemblance to reality."

As a direct result of Gage's article, New American Library suspended its plans to publish the paperback, but Little, Brown was undaunted and proceeded with the publication of the hardcover in January 1975. The publisher was, however, forced to make a public statement in which it clarified its position, saying that the original interviews with Luciano were written down, but these handwritten notes were "not completely legible to anyone" and so Gosch read them out to his collaborator, Hammer. "The whole process was tape recorded," asserted the publisher.

It then explained that the bulk of the original notes was burned after his death—leaving only thirty-seven pages, which were in the possession of the publisher. Neither these nor the supposed dictated tapes have survived. In March, Gage revealed the existence of the FBI's own damning comments on the book, telling its agents not to trust it. Little, Brown made no comment on the FBI memorandum. As one commentator wrote, Luciano must be "enjoying the last laugh from beyond the grave."

A year later came another major book on Lucky Luciano. Written by Tony Scaduto, a former *New York Post* journalist noted more for his show-business biographies, he did his best to puncture any myths about the mobster. Perhaps annoyed at *The Last Testament* stealing attention away from his work, Scaduto furiously denounced the book, devoting a twelve-page appendix to its demolition. Not only was the book a fraud, he declared, but Gosch was a hustler and con man. "[Gosch] did not even make notes of those so-called conversations with Luciano until long after the talks were supposed to have taken place," alleged Scaduto. He said the original film script belonged to Barnett Glassman, who had sued the publishers when Gosch went ahead with the book based on Glassman's conversations with Luciano. Glassman apparently received a substantial sum of money as a result and would have received a large percentage of the receipts of any movie made from the book.

Hammer, in turn, is scathing in his criticism of Scaduto. "When I was approached to collaborate with Gosch," says Hammer, "Glassman went on a search to have a book of his own written, begged several writers to do it, all of whom refused because he told them they would have to do the research because he had nothing. Finally, he found Scaduto and Scaduto was a gun for hire. Almost all of Scaduto's claims and charges were refuted by people close to Luciano who were aware of the mobster's feelings and relationship with Gosch."

A film was eventually made about Luciano, but it had nothing to do with Gosch, his script, or the book. It came from the Naples-born film director Francesco Rosi, who had made a name for himself with realistic portrayals of the Italian underworld, most notably his award-winning movie about the Sicilian bandit, *Salvatore Giuliano*, in 1962.

Rosi's *Lucky Luciano* (1973) was a good attempt at depicting the reality of Luciano's life, concentrating mainly on his period in Italy. It showed vividly how Vito Genovese dominated the black market in stolen American goods at the end of the war and worked closely with corrupt American officers. Its great triumph of veracity was to have FBN agent Charles Siragusa play himself, some twenty years after the event, and some of the dialogue parrots the Narcotic Bureau's view of events. Gian Maria Volonté played the part of Luciano well; his most famous roles before this were a leading villain in Sergio Leone's *A Fistful of Dollars* and *For a Few Dollars More.* But because it was essentially an Italian movie that was dubbed and cut for the English-language market in 1975, Rosi's film had limited impact.

"Unfortunately one can only recommend the picture with reservations," said London film critic Philip French. "I doubt if it ever was as good as Rosi's other work, and *Godfather II* has stolen a lot of its thunder." This was true, the *Godfather* movies have been the most successful versions of Mob activities in recent decades and still set the standard for such depictions. Their fictional characters, first created by Mario Puzo in his 1969 novel *The Godfather,* are based on elements of the most notorious real-life mobsters. The character of Michael Corleone is the closest to Luciano. Scenes are set on the Lower East Side in the 1910s and then in Las Vegas and Havana in the 1950s, all charting the history of the American Mafia as directed by Lansky, Costello, and Luciano.

Luciano has been played by several notable actors over the years, including Telly Savalas in the 1960s TV series *The Witness,* Andy Warhol star Joe Dallesandro in *The Cotton Club* (1984), and Stanley Tucci in *Billy Bathgate* (1991). In 1981, thriller writer Jack Higgins published *Luciano's Luck,* heavily elaborating on the mobster's help during the Allied invasion of Sicily. In 1991, the film *Mobsters* portrayed the rise to power of Luciano and his criminal comrades, Lansky, Siegel, and Costello, in the 1920s. Christian Slater played Luciano, while F. Murray Abraham took on the role of Arnold Rothstein; Anthony Quinn was Joe Masseria, and Michael Gambon played a Maranzano character.

Bugsy (1991) focused on Siegel and the founding of Las Vegas, with Warren Beatty well cast as the handsome hoodlum and Bill Graham playing Luciano. In the same year, a TV movie was made called *White Hot: The Mysterious Murder of Thelma Todd.* In 1997, *Hoodlum* concentrated on the gang rivalry in Harlem between Dutch Schultz, played by Tim Roth, and Ellsworth "Bumpy" Johnson, played by Laurence Fishburne. The story plays loose with history, having Johnson as the main author of Schultz's murder and DA Thomas Dewey on the take from the Mob. Andy Garcia starred as Luciano.

Recently, interest has been sparked in making a film based on *The Last Testament of Lucky Luciano*. Joe Isgro, a music promoter sentenced to several months in jail for extortion and loan-sharking, claimed he had the rights to the book. "Rights to what?" said Richard Hammer. "There are no rights." Since then, film producer Bob DeBrino said he had the movie option and was pressing ahead with the project and looking at George Clooney, Mark Wahlberg, Matt Damon, Brad Pitt, or Johnny Depp for the lead role. It seems the legend of Lucky Luciano is destined to carry on for many more years.

NOTES

INTRODUCTION

My lunch with Richard Hammer on April 3, 2009. Quotes from T. Scaduto, *Lucky Luciano*, London: Sphere Books, 1976, and Lacey, R., *Little Man: Meyer Lansky and the Gangster Life*, London: Century, 1991. For a thorough analysis of *The Last Testament of Lucky Luciano*, see Rick Porello's AmericanMafia .com, Web site article in two parts in issues 8-26-02 and 9-2-02, and the final chapter of this book

CHAPTER 1: LUCKY IN NAZI GERMANY

Diamond's failed trip to Germany is covered extensively in contemporary newspapers. The reference to Lucania accompanying him is in "Ireland Will Refuse Landing to Diamond," *New York Times*, August 30, 1930. The reference to Del Grazio appears in "Seized in Germany on Narcotic Charge," *New York Times*, December 6, 1931. The Kefauver Del Grazio reference comes from E. Kefauver, *Crime in America*, London: Victor Gollancz, 1952. The FBI memorandum that quotes Federal Bureau of Narcotics information on Diamond and Luciano visiting Germany is dated August 28, 1935; and is kept in FBI files 39-2141 section 1.

An early description of the dangers of drug addiction in New York appears in C. B. Towns, *Habits that Handicap*, New York: The Century Company, 1915. Luciano quote about smoking opium is from Scaduto. Brewster testimony is in "Hearings before the Committee on Ways and Means, House of Representatives on HR7079, a Bill Prohibiting the Importation of Crude Opium for the Purpose of Manufacturing Heroin, April 3, 1924," Washington, D.C., Government Printing Office. Russell Pasha's report on the international drug trade appears in "Illicit Drug Trade–Poison Factories," London *Times*, January 23, 1930. For "junkie" derivation see M. Booth, *Opium: A History*, London: Simon & Schuster, 1996. Booth also makes the point that opium was referred to as "junk" at the turn of the twentieth century and "hop," derived from Chinese slang, in the late nineteenth century, hence "hophead." British Ministry of Health report on European meeting on heroin, dated November 21, 1923, London National Archives: HO 45/24817.

CHAPTER 2: HOW TO BECOME A GANGSTER

Dates for Luciano's arrival in New York vary. The FBI files claim both 1905 and 1907 as dates for his entry. Accounts of the Lower East Side and the crime associated with it appear in contemporary newspapers, especially "The Bands of Criminals of New York's East Side" by Frank Marshall White, *New York Times*, November 8, 1908, and "Black Hand Crimes Doubled in Year Just Ended," *New York Times*, December 31, 1911. The Dopey Benny quote comes from H. Asbury, *The Gangs of New York*, New York: Garden City Publishing, 1927. The Jewish quote about living in a tenement block comes from H. Roskolenko, *The Time That Was Then*, New York: The Dial Press, 1971. For an impression of life in a typical tenement block, visit the Lower East Side Tenement Museum at 97 Orchard Street, New York, and see their associated publications.

Luciano quotes from Scaduto; Lansky quotes from D. Eisenberg, U. Dan, and E. Landau, *Meyer Lansky: Mogul of the Mob*, New York and London: Paddington Press, 1979. For failed Masseria shooting, see "Gunmen Who Shot Down 8 Elude Police," *New York Tribune*, August 9, 1922. The shooting of Valenti is reported in "Gang Kills Gunman, 2 Bystanders Hit," *New York Times*, August 12, 1922, and "Mystery in Rum Street Battle Near Solution," *New York Tribune*, August 12, 1922. Several anecdotes relating to Luciano's early life come from Siragusa letter to Anslinger, January 5, 1954, cited in detail in chapter 15.

CHAPTER 3: UPTOWN GAMBLER

L. Katcher's *The Big Bankroll*, New York: Harper & Brothers, 1958, still stands as a good account of Rothstein's life, as he claimed to have spoken to many principals involved with Rothstein, including his widow and Luciano while in prison, although he does not attribute any quotes directly to him. "The Rothstein Case: An Underworld Tale," *New York Times*, October 6, 1929, is an interesting feature-length profile.

Luciano quotes from Scaduto; Lansky quotes from Eisenberg et al. The Bendix jewelry fencing story comes from trial testimony dated June 2, 1936, in the New York City Department of Records, Luciano closed-case files, box 13, file 9; Joseph Corbo hijack case in box 11, file 5. Secret Canadian police reports on narcotics smuggling into Canada and the United States. by Howe and Deleglise in 1923 and 1924 are contained in Metropolitan Police file in British National Archives: MEPO 3/425. "Big Six" informant quote from FBI report on Longy Zwillman, dated June 7, 1950.

CHAPTER 4: SURVIVING THE RIDE

J. Bonanno's *A Man of Honour: The Autobiography of a Godfather*, London: Andre Deutsch, 1983, is a good source for quotes on Maranzano and Castellammarese War; Lansky quotes from Eisenberg et al. Transcript and digest of Luciano's testimony at Richmond County Court on October 29, 1929, police memorandum on the ride, May 27, 1936, and memorandum on pheasant shooting, June 2, 1936, all are in the New York City Department of Records, Luciano closed-case files, box 11, file 5; 1931 police photograph in box 11, file 4. Costello's version of the ride is quoted in G. Wolf, with Dimona, J., *Frank Costello: Prime Minister of the Underworld*, London: Hodder & Stoughton, 1975; Vizzini's account of the ride is in S. Vizzini, *Vizzini: The Secret Lives of America's Most Successful Undercover Agent*, London: Futura, 1974.

It has been claimed that it was in the early 1920s, as Lucania worked for Rothstein, Diamond, and Masseria, that he first acquired his famous nickname: Lucky. Biographer L. Katz quotes Frank Costello as saying it was Lucania himself who adopted it: "He felt that people are attracted to a guy when he's lucky. Everyone wants to be with a winner." It was Lucania who pushed others to use it, he says, and had "Lucky" tattooed on his arm. But this flies in the face of other accounts. People close to him say he hated it, claiming there was no luck in what he did. "I never heard nobody call him Lucky," said Frank Costello to his attorney, "not even behind his back." This directly contradicts Katz's quote. Generally, it is believed the moniker came later after he survived a terrible beating in 1929. In the light of seeing the actual court transcript of Luciano's statement just two weeks after the ride, and the *New York Times* article the day after, this all now seems wrong. Luciano was already known as "Lucky" and was happy to use the name. See " 'Ride' Victim Wakes on Staten Island," *New York Times*, October 18, 1929, and Katz, L., *Uncle Frank: The Biography of Frank Costello*, London: W.H. Allen, 1974.

CHAPTER 5: WAR OF THE SICILIAN BOSSES

Descriptions of the Castellammarese War shootings of Morello, Masseria, and Maranzano are from contemporary newspaper coverage. For the death of Masseria, see "Racket Chief Slain by Gangster Fire" *New York Times*, April 16, 1931, "Rivals Here Kill 'Joe the Boss,' Capone's Agent," *New York Herald Tribune*, April 16, 1931, and "Police Mystified in Slaying of 'Boss,' " *New York Times*, April 17, 1931. One authority claims that Luciano wasn't even at the lunch meeting, but sent his assassins to carry out the hit; see D. Critchley,

The Origin of Organized Crime in America, London: Routledge, 2008, on this and the myth of Luciano's modernizing of the Mafia. Valachi's testimony of events is published in P. Maas, *The Canary That Sang: the Valachi Papers,* London: MacGibbon & Kee, 1969.

Alongside Bonanno and Valachi, the third great witness to the Castellammarese conflict is Nick Gentile. His memoirs were published as *Vita di capomafia,* Rome: Editori Riunti, 1963, but an earlier unpublished translated transcript of this has survived. It is little different from the book and appears to have been produced in Palermo, Sicily, in 1947. Gentile was a senior mafioso in New York in the 1930s and became a major narcotics dealer, but he felt betrayed and ignored by the other chief mobsters of the period, and this may explain why it is alleged that he became a U.S. government agent in the mid-1940s. This typescript—a copy of which was supplied to me by crime historian James Morton—looks like an intelligence report and may well have been typed up by OSS agents in Palermo at the time. In the 1950s, Gentile carried on with his narcotics dealing but was turned by an FBN agent in 1958 and was subsequently ostracized from the Mafia.

For death of Maranzano, see "Alien-Smuggler Suspect Slain in Park Av Office," *New York Herald Tribune,* September 11, 1931; for his people-smuggling business, see "Seek Official Link in Alien Smuggling," *New York Times,* September 12, 1931. For interesting analysis of sources for the Castellammarese War, see Rick Porello's AmericanMafia.com Web site articles beginning 6-10-02, including the suggestion that "Buster from Chicago" was in fact Valachi; for other identification of Buster, see M. Dash, *The First Family,* New York: Random House, 2009.

CHAPTER 6: TOP OF THE PILE

Peter Ross's homecooking Barbizon-Plaza anecdote comes from interview memorandum dated April 3, 1936, in the New York City Department of Records, Luciano closed-case files, box 11, file 7; the police memo on Luciano's family home is in box 11, file 5. Description of the May 1933 Park Avenue convention comes from Scaduto, forming the opening chapter of his book and defining Luciano's character as a master criminal. Scaduto credits Nick Gentile and Joe Valachi as sources for it, but I have not been able to corroborate this. For Broadway gunfight, see "2 Women Wounded as Gangs Open Fire," *New York Times,* May 25, 1933.

Dewey quotes from R. Hughes, *Thomas E. Dewey: Attorney for the People,* London: Constable, 1940; Dewey and Schultz story in B. B. Turkus, and S. Feder, *Murder, Inc.: The Story of the Syndicate,* London: Victor Gollancz, 1952. Fabrizzo/Waxey Gordon assassination attempt on Lansky and Siegel described in FBI profile of Siegel dated July 22, 1946; its details vary from those related in *Mogul of the Mob.* Gang warfare between Waxey Gordon and Luciano reported in "Held in Shooting of 3 Pedestrians," *New York Times,* September 11, 1933.

CHAPTER 7: LUCKY IN HOLLYWOOD

Numerous reports on Thelma Todd's death from the *Los Angeles Times*, including "Body of Thelma Todd Found in Death Riddle," December 17, 1935, "Miss Todd Reported Seen Long After 'Death Hour,'" December 19, 1935, and "Hotel Left by Di Cicco," December 20, 1935. See also Associated Press reports from Los Angeles in the *New York Times*, December 17, 18, 25, and 26, 1935. The definitive study of the case is A. Edmonds, *Hot Toddy: The True Story of Hollywood's Most Shocking Crime—the Murder of Thelma Todd*, London: Macdonald, 1989; see also T. Adler, *Hollywood and the Mob*, London: Bloomsbury, 2007. California drug problem articles published in *Los Angeles Times*, November 6 and 8, 1926.

CHAPTER 8: CITY OF SEX

All accounts in this chapter taken from primary evidence held within the sixty-six Luciano closed-case file document boxes in the New York City Department of Records: July 3, 1931, informant's letter to Sixty-seventh Precinct and related telephone conversation of September 1, 1931, contained in box 2, files 2 and 1; July 7, 1935, letter about homosexual prostitutes in box 3, file 19; Balsam & Co. brokers protection racket case, box 11, file 5; Danny Brooks and Flo Brown record of Fredericks, Davie, and Luciano conversations, summary of all pretrial testimonies in box 13, file 3; further Flo Brown testimony in box 14, file 13; Al Weiner complaint of extortion, box 12, file 7; statement of Mildred Curtis, box 5, file 36; testimony of Thelma Jordan in box 15, file 5; story of Pauline Burr in box 4, file 2. FBI memorandum on Luciano dated August 28, 1935. See also E. Poulsen, *The Case Against Lucky Luciano*, New York: Clinton Cook, 2007, for a good summary of the vice context of the trial. Gentile quotes from previously cited source.

CHAPTER 9: LUCKY ON TRIAL

All primary evidence for trial taken from Luciano closed-case files in the New York City Department of Records: setting of bail court transcript in box 12, file 4; trial summary of examination and cross-examination of Luciano, box 13, file 2; Dewey's copy of transcript of trial minutes, June 3, 1936, box 56. Testimony on Luciano's tax returns in box 20, file 32; letter about Madges brothel in box 3, file 19. Dewey quotes from R. Hughes, *Thomas E. Dewey: Attorney for the People*, and numerous contemporary newspaper accounts, including "Lucania Convicted with 8 in Vice Ring on 62 Counts Each," *New York Times*, June 8, 1936.

CHAPTER 10: NAZIS IN NEW YORK

All primary sources for trial appeals in this chapter taken from Luciano closed-case files in the New York City Department of Records: recantation of Flo Brown in box 16, files 9 and 13; Thelma Jordan's testimony, March 1939, box 15, file 5; Dewey's testimony about retrial, box 15, file 12; 1938 judge's report on trial, box 20, file 24. Lansky quotes from Eisenberg et al; Zwillman quote from FBI memorandum dated November 30, 1938; Costello quoted from Wolf. Katcher quotes from *New York Post* article, 1938; Resko quotes from *Reprieve*, London: MacGibbon & Kee, 1959.

Accounts of Fascist activity in New York appear in: "27 Hurt as NY Fascisti Invade Socialist Hall," *New York Herald Tribune*, August 17, 1925; "Six Men Stabbed in a Fascist Riot," *New York Times*, August 17, 1925; "Green Warns Labor of Fascist Menace," *New York Times*, December 23, 1925; Tucker, M., "Carlo Tresca," *Greenwich Villager*, April 22, 1922; link between Tresca and Mob mentioned in "Carlo Tresca Assassinated on Fifth Avenue," *New York Herald Tribune*, January 12, 1943; "Mussolini Foes Kill 2 in Bronx Fascist Feud," *New York Herald Tribune*, May 31, 1927, and "Kill Two Fascisti in Bronx Street," *The World*, May 31, 1927. See P. V. Cannistraro, *Blackshirts in Little Italy*, Bordighera, 1999, for an excellent short account of the Fascist politics in New York. On Nazis in America see A. Stein, "More Fond Memories of Menahan Street," *Times Newsweekly*, Ridgewood, N.Y., July 29, 2004, and Max Hinkes's story in R. Rockaway, *But He Was Good to His Mother: The Life and Crimes of Jewish Gangsters*, Jerusalem, 2000.

CHAPTER 11: TALKING TO THE DEVIL HIMSELF

For the burning of the *Normandie*, see "12-Hour Fight Vain," *New York Times*, February 10, 1942, and "Giant Vessel Afire at Pier, Is Kept Afloat," *New York Herald Tribune*, February 10, 1942. The primary source for the deal between Lucky Luciano and U.S. Naval Intelligence is the Herlands Report of 1954 in the Thomas E. Dewey archive, University of Rochester Library, New York. Produced as a secret report, it was never published. New York State Commissioner of Investigation William B. Herlands was one of Dewey's original racket-busting legal team in the 1930s and headed the inquiry at the request of Dewey to scotch rumors of duplicity following the early release of Luciano. Some fifty-seven major witnesses were interviewed—including Haffenden, MacFall, Marsloe, Hogan, Gurfein, McCook, Polakoff, Lanza, and Lansky—giving sworn testimony of their involvement and producing a total of 2,883 pages of evidence, which was edited down to a 101-page report with appendices. Lansky's recollection of conversations with Haffenden and the whole World War II project come from the Herlands investigation interview conducted on April 13, 1954. FBI report on Luciano in Great Meadow prison, June 25, 1942. For more detail and extensive documentation, see T. Newark, *Mafia Allies*, St. Paul: Zenith Press, 2007. Haffenden's son, Charles Radcliffe Haffenden Jr., says of the whole affair: "I was but a young lad of fourteen when all of this occurred. U.S. Naval Intelligence would not support my father in this effort, and basically turned their back on what he was doing."

CHAPTER 12: LUCKY GOES TO WAR

Naval Intelligence gathering of information about Sicily is based on the findings of the 1954 Herlands Report, including quotes from Haffenden, MacFall,

Wharton, Marsloe, Polakoff, and Lansky. For Marsloe's testimony regarding Sicily and working with underworld contacts, see Herlands investigation interview with him on June 3, 1954. For Wharton's claim that Luciano was prepared to go to Sicily to help the war effort, see Herlands investigation written statement by Captain Wallace S. Wharton, June 23, 1954. Del Grazio story comes from Kefauver, E., *Crime in America*, London, 1952, based on testimony taken during the Kefauver Senate Committee inquiry into organized crime in 1950.

A copy of the *Special Military Plan for Psychological Warfare in Sicily*, a report prepared by the Joint Staff Planners for the U.S. Joint Chiefs of Staff, April 9, 1943, is in the British National Archives: WO 204/3701. The British SIS *Handbook on Politics and Intelligence Services* for Sicily in 1943 is in WO 220/403.

The Don Calo Vizzini/Luciano handkerchief story originates with M. Pantaleone, *The Mafia and Politics*, London, 1966; N. Lewis repeats it in *The Honoured Society*, London: Collins, 1964. "The Daily Journal" of the Forty-fifth Cavalry Reconnaissance Troop, the Operations Report of the Third Cavalry Reconnaissance Troop, and the narrative of the Operations of the Third Cavalry Reconnaissance Troop Mechanized are all in Modern Military Records, NARA, College Park, Maryland. Luigi Lumia's memory of Don Calo interrogated by U.S. troops at Villalba appears in L. Lumia, *Villalba, storia e memoria*, Caltanissetta, 1990, a copy held in Biblioteca Centrale della Regione Siciliana. For more detail and extensive documentation, see Newark, *Mafia Allies.*

For Dewey's statement on Luciano's deportation see Herlands Report, and "Dewey Commutes Luciano Sentence," *New York Times*, January 4, 1946, also M. Berger, "Deportation Set for Luciano Today" *New York Times*, February 9, 1946, "Luciano Taken on Ship," *New York Times*, February 10, 1946, "Luciano Departs for Italy with 3,500 Tons of Flour," *New York Herald Tribune*, February 11, 1946, "Pardoned Luciano on His Way to Italy," *New York Times*, February 11, 1946. FBI teletype memorandum dated February 25–27, 1946, gives a detailed report of an anonymous FBI agent visiting Luciano on board the *Laura Keene*. All FBI Rosen memoranda, as dated in main text, addressed to E. A. Tamm, also an assistant director of FBI, who passed them on to Hoover.

In January 1953, New York radio station broadcaster Michael Stern claimed that Governor Dewey had been paid large sums of money to give Luciano his parole. When Dewey set a lawyer on Stern, the broadcaster implied that Hoover had given him the information while dining with him at the Stork Club. Hoover was furious to be caught up in the allegations, denied knowing Stern or meeting him at the Stork Club, and called him a "name dropper who should be told to put up or shut up" (FBI memorandum from director, March 10, 1953). Memorandum of January 5, 1953, says that Haffenden was helping his associates get a cut from their half-million-dollar corporation known as the Sightseeing Yachts Incorporated, which had a monopoly over mooring rights in New York City.

CHAPTER 13: CUBA FIASCO

The majority of this chapter is based on memoranda held in the FBI files on Luciano. FBI Rosen report on Luciano in Mexico dated July 10, 1946; see also *Excelsior* newspaper article, March 26, 1946, "Vice Czar Intends to Return to Mexico," and *New York Journal American* story on Luciano on September 5, 1946. "Italy's dead" quote is from "City Boy," *Time*, July 25, 1949.

February 10, 1947, memorandum from Rosen to Tamm recording Luciano observed by two SIS FBI agents on February 8 in Havana. Feature on crooked gambling in Cuba, *Tiempo en Cuba*, February 9, 1947. " 'Lucky's' Luck Runs Out Again," by Henry Wallace, *Havana Post*, February 23, 1947. Letter of February 25 from U.S. embassy in Havana to FBI director, says Luciano arrived in Cuba on October 29, 1946. Special agent James P. McMahon and another unnamed agent are credited with spotting Luciano on February 8 and were recommended for letters of commendation. Undated FBI radiogram received late February stated that U.S. Federal Bureau of Narcotics was taking action to get Luciano out of Cuba. "Wrong Friends," syndicated column by Robert C. Ruark about Sinatra, February 20, 1947. "Linked to Luciano— Three Name Suspect in Ragen Death," *Washington Post*, March 14, 1947; Mob interest in Ragen explained in FBI profile of Bugsy Siegel dated July 22, 1946. Second Luciano interview with FBI dated March 19. See also FBI report on whole affair sent from Havana, March 22, 1947. Stacher quotes from Eisenberg et al.

CHAPTER 14: COLD WAR WARRIOR

Luciano in Palermo and his possible Cold War involvement is noted by A. E. Watkins of the British Consulate, Palermo, in a report dated July 5, 1947, now in the British National Archives: FO 371/67786. For Luciano's arrival in Italy, see "Luciano Reaches Naples," *New York Times*, March 1, 1946. For Tresca murder see "Carlo Tresca Assassinated on Fifth Avenue," *New York Herald Tribune*, January 12, 1943; for claim that Luciano knew the identities of Tresca's murderers and was willing to trade this information, see Herlands investigation interview with Anthony J. Marsloe, July 20, 1954.

For an account of Genovese's black market activities in Italy, see FBI File No: 58-7146. For British criticism of Poletti, see telegram from "Resident Minister, Algiers, to Foreign Office," January 16, 1944, and Lord Rennell's comments on Macmillan's telegram, both in British National Archives: FO 371/43918. An August 27, 1944, report from Captain J. Kane, Allied provincial public safety officer in Viterbo, trying to identify Vito Genovese with another bad character comes from the collection of Poletti's papers and letters lodged at the Herbert H. Lehman Suite and Papers, Columbia University Rare Book and Manuscript Library (AMG file, S9).

Not everyone, however, has bad words to say about Poletti. Lawrence L. Miller, a major in the U.S. Fifth Army AMG from 1943–47, worked directly for Poletti and said, "Charlie Poletti was a very good lawyer and a very smart man. He did have great connections and political friends in New York State and they gave him positions of great responsibility. I can't believe he would ever do anything illegal." Thanks to his son, Robert Miller, for this quote.

References to Nick Gentile and an American colonel occur in memorandum on "Sicilian Separatist Disturbances" by special agents Gabriel B. Celetta and Saverio Forte for U.S. Army Counterintelligence Corps (CIC) Naples Detachment, January 29, 1946, British NA: WO 204/12619. CIA Cold War strategy comments come from *The Current Situation in Italy*, Central Intelligence Agency, October 10, 1947. Link between CIA and Corsican Mob mentioned in Scheim, D. E., *The Mafia Killed President Kennedy*, London: W. H. Allen, 1988. Death of Giuliano reported in "Sicilian Bandit Shot Dead" London *Times*, July 6, 1950. See also April 1949 issue of *Esquire* magazine that links Luciano with Giuliano, "Lucky and the Angel." For more detail and extensive documentation on all the subjects covered in this chapter, see Newark, *Mafia Allies*.

Chapter 15: Narcotics Overlord

For a good overview of the world situation in illicit drug trafficking, see "Traffic in Narcotics," London *Times*, November 15, 1947, and "World Traffic in Drugs," London *Times*, September 19, 1951. For British embassy comments on illicit traffic in narcotics, January 15, 1954, and "Remarks of the Honorable Harry J. Anslinger, United States Representative on the United Nations Commission on Narcotic Drugs, Eighth Session," April 15, 1953, see British National Archives: FO 371/112506. See New York *Daily Mirror* "Link Luciano to $300,000 Dope Seizure," January 1948. Luciano "banana" quote from "City Boy" *Time*, July 25, 1949. Newark-Luciano heroin connection appears in FBI report on Zwillman dated June 7, 1950. Collace reference in FBI monograph on the Mafia, July 1958, Section II. Gentile quotes from previously citied source. Lansky account of meeting Luciano in Rome, Kefauver Committee hearings, February 14, 1951 (part 7-K609).

International Criminal Police Commission Reports from 1952 and 1956 listing major narcotics arrests in Italy contained in British National Archives: MEPO 3/2954. Correspondence and reports regarding alleged drug smuggling based in Allied administered Trieste, including criticisms from Venezia Giulia Police Force, in British National Archives: FO/371/112506. For a short profile of Charlie Siragusa, see "One-man Narcotics Squad" by Andrew Tully in J. D. Lewis, (editor), *Crusade Against Crime II*, London: T. V. Boardman, 1965. Giuseppe Dosi memorandum to Anslinger quoted in K. Meyer, and T. Parssinen, *Webs of Smoke*, Lanham: Rowman & Littlefield, 1998. Many anecdotes relating to Luciano in Naples come from a five-page letter written by Siragusa to Anslinger in January 5, 1954, reporting information coming from two undercover FBN agents who had befriended Luciano in Naples, see NARA, RG 170, DEA Files, entry 71A-3555. Quotes from Giannini letters to FBN come from F. Sondern, *Brotherhood of Evil: The Mafia*, London: Victor Gollancz, 1959.

See also H. J. Anslinger, and W. Oursler, *The Murderers*, London: Arthur Barker, Ltd., 1962.

Rago/Scibilia story and related anecdotes come from an FBI summary of a three-part article appearing in *L'Europeo*, January 11, January 18, and January 25, 1959, entitled "The Secret Life of Lucky Luciano"; this article is probably the source for the similar stories later told in *The Last Testament of Lucky Luciano*. The Antonio Calderone slap anecdote is told in P. Arlacchi, *Gli uomini del disonore—vita del grande pentito Antonio Calderone*, Milan: Arnoldo Mondadori, 1992; see also S. Lupo, *Storia della mafia*, Rome: Donzelli Editore, 1993; although it is a little suspicious that this incident is recalled twenty years after it appears in the Francesco Rosi movie. Valachi, Lansky, and Bonanno quotes from previously cited sources. Monzelli quotes from D. Hanna, *Vito Genovese*, New York: Belmont Tower Books, 1974.

Bonanno's Palermo Mafia conference is described in Sterling, C., *Octopus: The Long Reach of the International Sicilian Mafia*, New York: WW Norton & Co., 1990; see also P. Arlacchi, *Addio Cosa Nostra: La vita di Tommaso Buscetta*, Milan: Rizzoli, 1994. But Sterling gives too much weight to Buscetta's claim that Luciano set up the conference and quotes too frequently from Hammer and Gosch.

CHAPTER 16: GENOVESE'S GAME

Kefauver quotes come from E. Kefauver, *Crime in America*, London: Victor Gollancz, 1952. Costello quotes from Wolf. Torriani quotes from Hanna. Bugsy Siegel hit on Goering and Goebbels story comes from D. Jennings, *We Only Kill Each Other*, New York, 1968, but the ultimate source is the Countess di Frasso talking to Hollywood mogul Jack Warner. Valachi, Bonanno, Stacher, and Lansky quotes from previously cited sources. See "Anastasia Slain in a Hotel Here," *New York Times*, October 26, 1957, and "Apalachin Story Still Unsolved Mystery," *New York Times*, December 22, 1957.

CHAPTER 17: LUCKY IN LOVE

Lissoni quotes from Scaduto and *Time* article, cited previously. Dorothy Kilgallen's Broadway column and Seattle office memorandum both in FBI files on Luciano, along with Times Union clipping, "White Slavery Foe in Italy names Luciano," March 19, 1956. Naples court ruling reported in "Lucky Luciano Wins Freedom Ruling in Court," *Washington Post*, March 21, 1958. On December 14, 1952, the *American Weekly* carried an interview with Luciano by Llewellyn Miller in which she talked to the mobster in the Turistico Hotel in Naples. WMCA radio series on Luciano broadcast on March 23 and 30, 1959. For Vizzini meetings with Luciano and quotes, see S. Vizzini, O. Fraley, and M. Smith, *Vizzini: The Secret Lives of America's Most Successful Undercover Agent*, London: Futura, 1974. Several anecdotes relating to Luciano and Lissoni in Naples come from Siragusa letter to Anslinger, January 5, 1954, cited elsewhere.

For Colleen Lanza anecdote see R. Strait, *Star Babies*, New York: St. Martin's Press, 1979; see also G. C. Kohn, *Encyclopedia of American Scandal*, New York: Facts on File, 1989. *Scarface* quote from B. Hecht, *A Child of the Century*, New York: New American Library, 1955. FBI analysis of *The Luciano Story* dated March 7, 1955. Glassman quotes come from Scaduto and it should be noted that he is very anti-Gosch. For Gosch version see introduction to *The Last Testament of Lucky Luciano*. Jack Anderson's *Washington Post* article "The Last Days of Lucky Luciano" seems to be very much the source for the final conspiracy described by Gosch and Hammer in *The Last Testament of Lucky Luciano*; they merely give it a twist by saying that it is all part of Genovese's vendetta against him.

CHAPTER 18: DEATH IN NAPLES

Numerous contemporary newspaper reports on the death of Luciano include "Luciano Dies at 65; was facing arrest," *New York Times*, January 27, 1962, "'Lucky' Luciano Drops Dead," London *Times*, January 27, 1962, "Luciano Dies as Police Close In," *New York Herald Tribune*, January 27, 1962, "Luciano's Violent Life Spills Over into Rites" New York *Daily News*, January 30, 1962, "Luciano Is Buried in Queens Vault," *New York Times*, February 8, 1962.

There are different versions as to what Luciano's last words were. In the *New York Times* report of January 28, Gosch said Luciano said nothing, but in *The Last Testament of Lucky Luciano*, he has him gasping, "Marty . . ." Scaduto has Gosch asking him "Do you feel ill?" and Luciano says, "Yeah" before collapsing. Jack Anderson has him saying, "Martin, Martin, Martin."

FBI memorandum addressed to Hoover denying veracity of more sensational Italian stories after Luciano's death, dated February 12, 1962; "Lucky Luciano worked for the FBI," *Telesera*, February 5, 1962. FBI memorandum about death of Luciano dated February 19, 1962. FBI memorandum on Gosch's Spanish article, dated March 8, 1962. "War Against One-Armed Bandits in Italy," London *Times*, January 22, 1965; "113 Mafia Suspects Stand Trial" London *Times*, October 24, 1966. Conclusion that Luciano as master criminal was overstated occurs in FBI memorandum dated September 17, 1965. FBI review of *The Last Testament of Lucky Luciano* dated October 2, 1974. See also N. Gage, "Questions Are Raised on Lucky Luciano Book," *New York Times*, December 17, 1974. "Film Bio of Lucky Luciano in the Works," mafia-news.com, July 6, 2007, and "Hollywood Eyes Luciano Tale," *New York Post*, August 12, 2007.

BIBLIOGRAPHY

UNPUBLISHED SOURCES
For precise archival references see Notes.

NEW YORK, NY
New York City Department of Records
Luciano closed-case files

Thomas E. Dewey Archive in the University of Rochester Library
Herlands Report of 1954

Herbert H. Lehman Suite and Papers, Columbia University Rare Book and
     Manuscript Library
Polelli papers and letters from World War II

WASHINGTON, D.C.
U.S. Department of Justice, Federal Bureau of Investigation
FBI files on Lucky Luciano, Vito Genovese, Meyer Lansky, Bugsy Siegel, and
     Longy Zwillman

COLLEGE PARK, MD
U.S. National Archives and Records Administration (NARA)
RG 38 Records of Office of Chief of Naval Operations

RG 59—Records of the Department of State
RG 165—Records of the War Department
RG 170—Records of the Drug Enforcement Administration
RG 226—Records of the Office of Strategic Services
Modern Military Records

LONDON, UK

British National Archives, Kew
MEPO—Records of the Metropolitan Police Office
HO—Records of the Home Office
WO—Records of War Office and Armed Forces
FO—Records of the Foreign Office
CAB—Records of the Cabinet Office
PREM—Records of the Prime Minister's Office

PALERMO, SICILY

Biblioteca Centrale della Regione Siciliana

PUBLISHED SOURCES

Adler, T. *Hollywood and the Mob*, London: Bloomsbury, 2007.
Anslinger, H. J., and W. Oursler, *The Murderers*. London: Arthur Barker, Ltd., 1962.
Arlacchi, P. *Addio Cosa Nostra: La vita di Tommaso Buscetta*. Milan: Rizzoli, 1994.
———. *Gli uomini del disonore—vita del grande pentito Antonio Calderone*. Milan: Arnoldo Mondadori, 1992.
Ashbury, H. *The Gangs of New York*, New York: Garden City Publishing, 1927.
Block, A. A. "A Modern Marriage of Convenience: A Collaboration Between Organized Crime and US Intelligence," *Organized Crime: A Global Perspective*, edited by R. J. Kelly, Totowa: Rowman & Allanheld, 1986.
Bonanno, J. with S. Lalli. *A Man of Honour: The Autobiography of a Godfather*. London: Unwin, 1984.
Booth, M. *Opium: A History*. London: Simon & Schuster, 1996.
Cameron, I. *A Pictorial History of Crime*. London: Hamlyn, 1975.
Campbell, R. *The Luciano Project*. New York: McGraw-Hill, 1977.
Cannistraro, P. V. *Blackshirts in Little Italy*. New York: Bordighera, 1999.
Carpozi Jr., G. *Bugsy: The Godfather of Las Vegas*. New York: Pinnacle, 1973.
Caruso, A. *Arrivano i nostri*. Milan: Longanesi, 2004.
Central Intelligence Agency. *The Current Situation in Italy*, Washington, 1947.
Chandler, D. L. *The Criminal Brotherhoods*, London: Constable, 1976.
Corvo, M. *OSS Italy 1942–1945*, New York: Enigma Books, 2005.
Critchley, D. *The Origin of Organized Crime in America*, London: Routledge, 2008.
Curzon, S. *Legs Diamond*, Derby: Monarch, 1962.
Dash, M. *The First Family*, New York: Random House, 2009.

De Leeuw, H. *Underworld Story*. London: Neville Spearman, 1955.

Dickie, J. *Cosa Nostra*. London: Hodder Headline, 2004.

Edmonds, A. *Hot Toddy: The True Story of Hollywood's Most Shocking Crime—the Murder of Thelma Todd*. London: Macdonald, 1989.

Eisenberg, D., U. Dan, and E. Landau. *Meyer Lansky: Mogul of the Mob*. New York and London: Paddington Press, 1979.

Faenza, R. and M. Fini. *Gli americani in Italia*. Milan: Feltrinelli, 1976.

Feder, S. and J. Joesten. *The Luciano Story*. New York: Popular Library, 1956.

Finkelstein, M. S. *Separatism, the Allies, and the Mafia: The Struggle for Sicilian Independence. 1943–1948*, Bethlehem, Pa: Lehigh University Press, 1998.

Frasca, D. *King of Crime: The Story of Vito Genovese, Mafia Czar*. New York: Crown Publishers, 1959.

Fried, A. *The Rise and Fall of the Jewish Gangster*. New York: Holt, Rinehart and Winston, 1980.

Gallagher, D. *All the Right Enemies: The Life and Murder of Carlo Tresca*. New Brunswick, N. J.: Rutgers University Press, 1988.

Gentile, N. *Vita di capomafia*. Rome: Editori Riunti, 1963.

Gosch, M. and R. Hammer. *The Last Testament of Lucky Luciano*. London: Macmillan, 1975.

Grennan, S. and others. *Gangs*. New Jersey: Prentice Hall, 1998.

Hammer, R. *Playboy's Illustrated History of Organized Crime*. Chicago: Playboy Press, 1975.

Hanna, D. *Vito Genovese*. New York: Belmont Tower Books, 1974.

Harris, C.R.S. *Allied Military Administration in Italy 1943–1945*. London, 1957.

Harvey, C. *Normandie: Liner of Legend*. Stroud: Tempus, 2001.

Hecht, B. *A Child of the Century*. New York: New American Library, 1955.

Heym, S. *Nazis in the USA*. New York: American Committee for Anti-Nazi Literature, 1938.

Higham, C. *American Swastika*. Garden City, New York: Doubleday, 1985.

Hughes, R. *Thomas E. Dewey: Attorney for the People*. London: Constable, 1940.

Jennings, D. *We Only Kill Each Other*. London: John Long, 1968.

Katcher, L. *The Big Bankroll—Life and Times of Arnold Rothstein*. New York: Harper & Brothers, 1958.

Katz, L. *Uncle Frank—The Biography of Frank Costello*. London: WH Allen, 1974.

Kefauver, E. *Crime in America*. London: Victor Gollancz, 1952.

Klerks, C. *Lucky Luciano: The Father of Organized Crime*. Canmore: Altitude Publishing, 2005.

Kohn, G. C. *Encyclopedia of American Scandal*. New York: Facts on File, 1989.

Lacey, R. *Little Man: Meyer Lansky and the Gangster Life*. London: Century, 1991.

Lewis, J. D. (editor). *Crusade Against Crime II*. London: T. V. Boardman, 1965.

Lewis, N. *The Honoured Society*. London: Collins, 1964.

———. *Naples '44*. London: Collins, 1978.

Lomartire, C. M. *Il bandito Giuliano*. Milan: Mondadori, 2007.

Lumia, L. *Villalba, storia e memoria*, Caltanisetta, 1990.

Lupo, S. "The Allies and the Mafia", *Journal of Modern Italian Studies*, vol. 2, no. 1 Spring 1997.

———. *Storia della mafia*, Rome: Donzelli Editore, 1993.

Maas, P. *The Canary That Sang: The Valachi Papers*. London: MacGibbon & Kee, 1969.

Mangiameli, R. "La regione in Guerra (1943–50)," La Sicilia, Le Regioni dall'Unita a oggi, Turin: Einaudi, 1987.

Maxwell, G. *God Save Me from My Friends*. London, 1956.

Meyer, K. and T. Parssinen. *Webs of Smoke*. Lanham: Rowman & Littlefield, 1998.

Morton, J. *Gangland International*. London: Little, Brown, 1998.

Nelli, H. S. *The Business of Crime*. New York: Oxford University Press, 1976.

Newark, T. *Mafia Allies*. St Paul, Minn.: Zenith Press, 2007.

Pantaleone, M. *The Mafia and Politics*. London: Chatto & Windus, 1966.

Pernicone, N. *Carlo Tresca: Portrait of a Rebel*. Basingstoke, U.K.: Palgrave Macmillan, 2005.

Poulsen, E. *The Case Against Lucky Luciano*. New York: Clinton Cook, 2007.

Powell, H. *Ninety Times Guilty*. London: Robert Hale, 1939.

Raab, S. *Five Families*. New York: St. Martin's Press, 2005.

Reid, E. *Mafia*. New York: Signet, 1954.

Reid, E. *The Shame of New York*, London: Constable, 1954.

Renda, F. *Storia della Sicilia dal 1860 al 1970*, Vol III, Palermo: Sellerio, 1987.

Rockaway, R. A. *But He Was Good to His Mother: The Lives and Crimes of Jewish Gangsters*. Jerusalem: Gefen Publishing, 2000.

Roskolenko, H. *The Time That Was Then*, New York: The Dial Press, 1971.

Santino, U. *Storia del movimento antimafia; dalla lotta di classes all'impegno*. Rome: Editori Riunti, 2000.

Scaduto, T. *"Lucky" Luciano*. London: Sphere Books, 1976.

Scheim, D. E. *The Mafia Killed President Kennedy*. London: W. H. Allen, 1988.

Schneider, J. C. and P.T. Schneider. *Reversible Destiny: Mafia, Antimafia, and the Struggle for Palermo*. Berkeley: University of California Press, 2003.

Sheinman, M. and others. *A Tenement Story*. New York: The Lower East Side Tenement Museum, 2004.

Short, M. *Crime Inc*. London: Methuen, 1984.

Sifakis, C. *The Mafia File*. New York: Facts of File, 1987.

Smith, R. N. *Thomas E. Dewey and His Times*. New York: Simon & Schuster, 1982.

Sondern, F. *Brotherhood of Evil: The Mafia*. London: Victor Gollancz, 1959.

Sterling, C. *Octopus: The Long Reach of the International Sicilian Mafia*. New York: W.W. Norton, 1990.

Stille, A. *Excellent Cadavers*. London: Jonathan Cape, 1995.

Strait, R. *Star Babies*. New York: St. Martin's Press, 1979.

Talese, G. *Honor Thy Father*. London: Sphere, 1972.

Towns, C. B. *Habits that Handicap*. New York: The Century Company, 1915.

Turkus, B. B. and S. Feder. *Murder, Inc.: The Story of the Syndicate*. London: Victor Gollancz, 1952.

Vizzini S. Fraley, O. and M. Smith. *Vizzini: The Secret Lives of America's Most Successful Undercover Agent*. London: Futura, 1974.

Wolf, G. with J. DiMona. *Frank Costello: Prime Minister of the Underworld*. London: Hodder & Soughton, 1974.

For newspaper articles consulted see Notes.

INDEX

31901050148073